Additional Praise for The Family Office Book

"*The Family Office Book* is a truly unique piece of work. Richard has thoroughly explained the workings of the modern day family office, a world that is highly secretive and little understood, even amongst finance professionals. His status as a trusted adviser is attested by the quality of the interviews with family offices and his incisive views on the future of this powerful investor class. An essential study that is relevant to anyone who is keen to understand the family office, either from a professional perspective or purely out of intrigue."

— Max Kantella, CEO McLaren Global Partners PE Ltd

"Richard's book on family offices is the most complete, organized, and compelling book on an extremely important and growing segment of the wealth management business. I plan to use this book as a gift to our family office clients to prove to them they made a good decision in setting up their own family office!"

— Don F. Wilkinson, Family Office Consulting, LLC

"*The Family Office Book* is a rare and well-documented guide for anyone in the wealth management industry. The interviews cover a wide array of family office professionals and were in-depth, informative, and extremely helpful. There is no better way to learn than hearing the experiences, advice, and insight straight from the experts themselves!"

— Tom Thiel, McAdams Wright Ragen

"As someone who has worked in both a SFO and MFO, Richard and his extremely well qualified lineup of family office professionals have done an excellent job of outlining exactly how the family office industry works. This book is pretty much all you need in order to fully understand how the industry operates."

— Dave Trunzo, Family Office Investment Professional

"The family office industry is a secretive and complex niche of the wealth management industry, and much of how it worked was hidden, until now. Written from the best, this is certainly a book that everybody who works in the finance, fund management, or wealth management industry should hold in their library."

— Alexis Alexiou, Portfolio Manager

"*The Family Office Book* is really great because it explains exactly how the family office industry works, how the ultra-wealthy are investing their money, and how the fund manager selection process works. Interviewing top family office executives about their experience provides a realistic view of the industry picture of how everything is applied in the industry today."
—Michael Skapoullis, Certified Hedge Fund Professional (CHP) designation, Ceo Societe Goldfinger

"*The Family Office Book* is the most comprehensive informational resource, with respect to family offices, that I have read. Although its main audience is family offices and ultra-high net worth individuals, it is a valuable resource for anyone who wants to learn about the operations, perspectives, motivations, and inner workings of family offices. The multiple interviews with seasoned family office representatives provide a keen insight to the world of the family office. Richard Wilson provides a history of the family office, the definition of what constitutes the current day family office, and perspective on where this market is headed. And his use of interactive media, i.e., audio interviews, videos, and external links, lends an added dimension to the comprehensiveness of the material. I highly recommend *The Family Office Book* to anyone who is interested in learning more about family offices and this often underpublicized market."
—Eric Warshal, Fund Associates

"Richard Wilson's family office book is a valuable resource that improved my firms focus and success immediately. The examples from his practice and the leading experts he interviews are to the point and provide subtle insights. We have incorporated several key strategies from this book into our marketing and client retention plans. The book's emphasis on a consistent, well developed approach to your messaging and the creation of an educational tone to your potential investors is unique and effective."
—Stephen Chunias, CPA, Chief Financial Officer, Cazenovia Creek Investment Management

The Family
Office Book

Founded in 1807, John Wiley & Sons is the oldest independent publishing company in the United States. With offices in North America, Europe, Australia and Asia, Wiley is globally committed to developing and marketing print and electronic products and services for our customers' professional and personal knowledge and understanding.

The Wiley Finance series contains books written specifically for finance and investment professionals as well as sophisticated individual investors and their financial advisors. Book topics range from portfolio management to e-commerce, risk management, financial engineering, valuation and financial instrument analysis, as well as much more.

For a list of available titles, visit our web site at www.WileyFinance.com.

The Family Office Book

Investing Capital for the
Ultra-Affluent

RICHARD C. WILSON

John Wiley & Sons, Inc.

Published by John Wiley & Sons, Inc., Hoboken, New Jersey.
Published simultaneously in Canada.

For general information on our other products and services or for technical support, please contact our
Customer Care Department within the United States at (800) 762-2974, outside the United States at (317)
572-3993 or fax (317) 572-4002.

Wiley also publishes its books in a variety of electronic formats. Some content that appears in print may
not be available in electronic books. For more information about Wiley products, visit our web site at
www.wiley.com.

Disclaimer: Please review the following: Every individual has different risks and needs for wealth
management. Before joining a family office or wealth management firm of any type, you should seek
professional legal counsel and conduct your own thorough due diligence. The words you read directly from
heads of family offices in this book do not replace speaking with an expert one-on-one about your unique
situation. No investment, fund manager selection, or wealth management decisions should be made based
solely on the information provided in this book.

Your specific city, state, and country may regulate capital raising or marketing of family office, wealth
management, or RIA services. Please speak with legal counsel before taking action on the information
provided within this book if you are a wealth advisor of any type.

Nothing presented in this book should be construed as a solicitation, offering of securities or sale of
investment products, wealth management solutions or private placement vehicles or any other legally
binding statement.

Library of Congress Cataloging-in-Publication Data:

Wilson, Richard C.
  The family office book : investing capital for the ultra-affluent / Richard C. Wilson.
     p.   cm. – (Wiley finance series)
  Includes index.
  ISBN 978-1-118-18536-0 (cloth);   ISBN 978-1-118-22743-5 (ebk);
  ISBN 978-1-118-26516-1 (ebk);   ISBN 978-1-118-23326-9 (ebk)
  1. Investment advisors.   2. Financial planners.   3. Financial services industry.
4. Families–Finance, Personal.   5. Rich people–Finance, Personal.
6. Wealth–Management.   I. Title.
  HG4621.W47   2012
  332.6–dc23

                                                                            2012009221

Since the 1700s the Wilson name has stood for taking action and focusing on something instead of simply talking about ideas. This book is dedicated to the entire Wilson family for creating an environment for our generation of the family that fosters creativity, a strong work ethic, entrepreneurship, and tenacity.

Contents

Introduction

I am writing this book for single and multi-family office professionals and ultra-high net worth individuals who want to further explore how family offices operate and deploy capital.

 See the video "Welcome Message," at www.FamilyOfficesGroup.com/Video1.

My current role involves providing the best-of-breed fund managers to family offices. Years ago, when I first started working with family offices, I wanted to learn more about this industry. Much to my surprise, I found there were very few books or web sites dedicated to the subject.

After several years of working with family offices, I started FamilyOfficesGroup.com, the first free-to-access educational web site on the family office industry. Since then, we have been posting new educational resources to the web site each week, and we have seen the association's membership grow from five initial members to its current level of 40,000-plus members from all over the world.

Objective: The objective of this book is to provide you with a $1,000 multimedia training experience for just the small price of this book. In my attempt to create this value, I provide you with insights on the operations, capital deployment best practices, investment processes, portfolio allocations, investment committees, and fund manager selection processes of family offices using instructional videos, audio MP3s, and other unique resources you simply won't find anywhere else.

IS THIS BOOK RIGHT FOR YOU?

While this book was written primarily for family office professionals, ultra-high net worth individuals and fund managers will also gain a better understanding as to why family offices exist, what function they serve, and how they manage capital. Moreover, this book will assist you in making a more-educated decision when selecting a family office to meet your needs.

Understanding how family offices invest their capital is important for the healthy growth of the industry so family office executives and entry-level professionals can see how their peers are investing. It is also important for ultra-high net worth individuals to know what to expect, how a family office may invest their money, and what questions to ask when they sit down to hire a family office.

WHAT THIS BOOK IS NOT

The main purpose of this book is to explore how family offices operate and deploy their capital through fund manager selection, cash management, and portfolio construction. This book is not a quantitative, statistical research study, or set of recommendations that family offices should follow. You will not find PhD-level mathematical models showing how to calculate the true risk of particular asset classes, or in-depth financial models of efficient portfolios, as there are dozens of books already written on these important topics. Instead, this book contains valuable insights from some of the world's top family offices.

WHAT IS UNIQUE ABOUT THIS BOOK?

Most books present only one perspective, opinion, or angle on an issue or industry. Rarely does a single individual's expertise present the complete diverse picture of what is going on regionally or globally within any industry, however, making those books an incomplete resource.

To prepare for this book, I read and reviewed each of the other family office books currently in print. Many of them are valuable and worth reading; they provide valuable quantitative statistics, research, and case studies in a few instances. I know for certain, however, that this book is unique; you get to read the direct thoughts of dozens of global family offices, including several that are frequently listed as being among the largest and most successful top 50 family offices in the world.

To write this book, I leveraged the 40,000-plus member family office association that we manage, the Family Offices Group. To make sure this book presented ideas as diverse as the family office industry itself, we spoke with thousands of family offices and conducted recorded interviews with dozens of single and multi-family offices to create both the *Family Office Monthly Newsletter* and this book. The interviews were conducted with family offices from Australia, Israel, Dubai, Monaco, United States, Switzerland, Singapore, and many other locations. Each of these interviews lasted for 30 to

90 minutes, and, once transcribed, the interviews in total resulted in 225,000 words' worth of family office advice and insights. The average family office executive we interviewed had 22 years of experience, so in total this book and our newsletter constitute 756 years of industry experience.

This is the only family office book that contains family office interview transcripts, MP3 audio interview downloads, dozens of instructional video modules, recorded family office conference presentations, and free PDF templates. I have made every effort to ensure that this is not simply a book, but a high-end multimedia training experience for those who have the time and interest to use it as such.

NAVIGATING THIS BOOK

Throughout this book we have added bonus resources that are actually far more valuable than the text of this book alone. This is part of our commitment to seeing that you get a 20-times return on the time and money that you invest in this book.

 This symbol represents a link providing free access to an MP3 recording of a phone interview.

 This symbol is shown throughout the book whenever one of the 30-plus free video modules on a related topic is available on our web site.

 This PDF symbol represents a free PDF template or tool that our team created for you to download.

I have been completing research on and working with family offices of different types for almost 10 years now, and I think it is important to share what my perspective has been of family offices so that readers can understand where I am coming from in this book. I study family offices because my entire career and business revolves around the family office industry; it seems the more I share in the form of speaking, recording videos, publishing articles, and so on, the more I am rewarded in unexpected ways for this hard work.

 See the video "FOG Overview," at www.FamilyOfficesGroup.com/Video2.

I am motivated to dig as deep as I can into the truth of how this industry operates and invests capital; if I don't know what family offices are looking for, I fail in operating the Family Offices Group association and our

Richard Wilson Capital Partners business. If I don't have strong value-first relationships with family offices, I'm out of work. I care very little about collecting $8 book royalties and I care a lot about making this book so valuable that it is a conversation starter between you and me.

Your friend in the family office space,

RICHARD C. WILSON
Family Offices Group

P.S. Feel free to reach out to me to ask questions about the book's content or what we do at Richard@FamilyOfficeGroups.com and I will get back to you as soon as possible.

Family Office Fundamentals

RES NON VERBA

wilson

CHAPTER 1

The Family Office Industry

We often tell our ultra-wealthy clients that they have been in the get-rich business and we are in the stay-rich business.
—Paul Tramontano (CEO of Constellation Wealth Advisors, a top 50 multi-family office who we recently interviewed)

Chapter Preview: The family office industry can be challenging to learn about. This chapter will provide you with a high-level, 10,000-foot view of the family office industry. It will cover the basics of how the industry operates and serve as a foundation upon which the rest of the book will build upon.

The family office industry is secretive. While speaking at the Latin American Family Office Summit recently, I was reminded by Thomas Handler (interviewed later in this book) of an adage I hear used often in the industry: "A submerged whale does not get harpooned." This quote sums up why so many family offices are so secretive and difficult to learn more about. Many family offices and ultra-high net worth individuals see that media attention and press often attracts sales professionals, possibly compliance headaches, and others looking only to harvest ideas or competitive angles on the family's operating business.

The goal of this book and chapter is to show you exactly how family offices operate, provide their services, and invest their capital.

WHAT IS A FAMILY OFFICE?

 See the video "What Is a Family Office?" at www.FamilyOfficesGroup.com/Video3.

A family office is a 360-degree financial management firm and personal chief financial officer for the ultra-affluent, often providing investment, charitable giving, budgeting, insurance, taxation, and multigenerational guidance to an individual or family. The most direct way of understanding the purpose of a family office is to think of a very robust and comprehensive wealth management solution that looks at every financial aspect of an ultra-wealthy person's or family's life.

Single Family Office Definition: A single family office is a full-balance-sheet 360-degree ultra-affluent wealth management and CFO solution for a single individual or family.

The Security and Exchange Commission (SEC) recently defined single family offices as "entities established by wealthy families to manage their wealth, plan for their families' financial future, and provide other services to family members. Single family offices generally serve families with at least $100 million or more of investable assets. Industry observers have estimated that there are 2,500 to 3,000 single family offices managing more than $1.2 trillion in assets."

John Gryzmala, a single family office executive we recently interviewed, states: "The definition of the single family office for me is: an entity or an individual that helps relieve the family members of certain, if not all, mundane tasks that they would prefer not dealing with, be it investments, be it household staff, be it insurance, be it handling legal issues, trusts and estates issues, and tax planning. That's it. So however you want to structure it to handle and help you, the family member, with those issues is my definition of the single family office."

Multi-Family Office Definition: A multi-family office is a full-balance-sheet, 360-degree ultra-affluent wealth management and CFO solution for multiple individuals and families.

Multi-family offices can serve anywhere from two clients to 500-plus ultra-wealthy individuals and families. In both the single family and multi-family office, what is really being offered is a full balance sheet financial management solution to ultra-high net worth individuals. The implementation of the family office model is diverse. In both single and multi-family offices, a very narrow set of services could be offered so that one family office has just one or two functions, while others can provide a fully comprehensive solution. Every family's model is unique as a result of its budget, needs, and wants also being unique.

It is important to note that many hybrid models are very much closed-door single family offices, yet they serve just two to three families and never accept outside money. This is an exception to the rule, but important to fully understanding how the industry operates.

Traditional wealth management firms advise on your investments and sometimes help you make insurance-related or budget-related decisions. Most wealth management firms are not specialists in taxation, charitable giving, or even in multigenerational wealth management. Family offices can provide those solutions and more with a single team, allowing several diverse experts to speak with one another in order to create a cohesive plan for preserving and/or growing the wealth of the ultra-high net worth client.

There is a constant debate over the definition of a "true" family office. Some professionals believe single family offices are the only authentic family offices, and multi-family offices are simply wealth management firms in disguise. Others believe that you must have $250 million to launch a single family office, though there are many successful single family offices with as little as $50 million. I believe that a family office is defined by how it operates and what solution it provides to the family, not by its asset size. A hedge fund is a hedge fund and a venture capital firm is a venture capital firm, based on the structure of their investments, fees, and purpose, not by their asset size; the same goes for family offices.

This will be covered in more detail later in this book, but it is important to note that some multi-family offices start out as single family offices and gradually add more clients. The recent rising costs of talent and compliance has driven up interest in converting single family offices into multi-family offices.

THE FAMILY OFFICE UNIVERSE

It is helpful to look at the family office industry and think about how closely aligned different parties are to the central needs of ultra-wealthy clients. The diagram in Figure 1.1 depicts how closely aligned the goals of various parties are to the needs and goals of ultra-wealthy clients.

You can see that there is a symmetrical ring around the ultra-wealthy. That first ring represents single family offices that focus solely on the needs of an ultra-wealthy individual or single family.

The second ring represents multi-family offices that are almost completely aligned with the ultra-wealthy client; at the same time they need to please several or even hundreds of other ultra-wealthy clients as well, so they are not 100 percent aligned with the goals of a single ultra-wealthy client, but close.

The third and fourth rings represent service providers and regulators. The service provider grouping includes consultants, placement agents, traditional wealth management firms, and general accountants or tax attorneys.

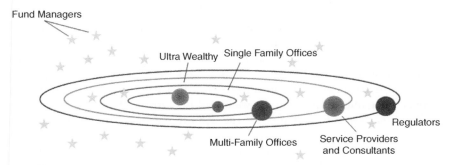

FIGURE 1.1 The Family Office Universe

While a tax attorney is surely more focused on ultra-wealthy client needs than is a regulator (as depicted later in this chapter), all of these groups are, for the most part, not focused on and built around the needs of ultra-wealthy clients or family offices.

The stars within the Family Office Universe diagram represent the tens of thousands of fund managers and investment professionals who are constantly trying to seek capital from family offices. They are sometimes connected to multi-family offices or service providers, or they are disconnected from the industry to the extent that they don't really understand what a family office is or how most of the ultra-wealthy are having their capital managed.

THE HISTORY OF FAMILY OFFICES

Single family offices have existed in different forms for thousands of years. In the article "Family Offices in Europe and the United States" by Dr. Steen Ehlern, the managing director of the Ferguson Partners Family Office, noted that the merchants of ancient Japan and the Shang dynasty in China (1600 B.C.) both used multigenerational wealth management strategies. There are also several accounts of "trusts" being set up for the first time during the Crusades (A.D. 1100). Later, many wealthy banking families of Europe, including the Medicis Bardis and Rothschilds, were said to have used a family office–like structure. These organizations often offered their services to other wealthy families, and in the late 1800s and 1900s they started to look more like modern day multi-family office operations. These operations grew out of single family offices that were asked to serve connected business families and out of private banks and early trust company establishments that were looking to serve more affluent clientele.

Even now the family office industry is relatively obscure and not very well understood. While everyone in the financial industry has a rough idea of what a hedge fund is (or at least knows that they exist), many finance professionals don't know what a family office is or what it does. When it comes to the general public, knowledge of a family office or its operations is close to nonexistent.

Looking at the growth of the hedge fund industry, I believe the model really started to take off between 1970 and 2000. The family office industry is on a parallel growth track, and our market research and interviews have uncovered that we are just 10 years into a 30-year surge of growth in the family office space. For example, I recently spoke on stage at an event with a wealth management professional who has 17 years of experience; while he was very successful and bright and did know what a hedge fund was, he did not know what a family office was. If someone who works in wealth management is not aware of the family office industry, many of the ultra-wealthy are not either. There are more than 10,000 family offices in the industry; I predict that the industry will double in size by 2020.

The wealthy will continue to expand their wealth, and family offices will continue to grow in numbers. That growth is accompanied by an increasing need and desire among the wealthy for wealth management services. Around the globe, more and more wealthy families are looking for something similar to the family offices seen in the United States and Western Europe.

I was fortunate to recently record an interview with one of the founding fathers of the modern-day family office industry, Charles Grace. Charles is a director at the Threshold Group. He is known for founding Ashbridge Investment Management and for building the first open-architecture platform for family office investment management. Charles not only knows the history of the family office industry but also has helped shape it as well. Here is a short excerpt from that interview:

Richard Wilson: Charles, you have been in the family office industry for over 50 years, which is longer than anybody else we are interviewing for this book and our monthly newsletter. So how have you seen the industry evolve?

Charles Grace: It used to be that family offices were based in the financial office of the operating company. There was perhaps a dedicated accountant in there that took care of the operating company. So that was the beginning, and then some of the wealthier families set up distinct offices that were not necessarily housed in the operating company, but which were a part of it, and they provided services to the family. Not too long ago, maybe, say, I don't know, 20 years ago, some of these larger family offices started to provide services to other families and the founding family. And a couple of names that come to mind are us, the Rockefellers, and there were a couple of others that built a multi-family office business on a family office, and so that was the first level of development.

Next came the trust companies. The trust companies were always in this business too, not as family offices, but as a part of the trust work—trust and investment work—and they were always there as competitors in this business and still are. Then along came the brokers; while the brokers were very transaction-oriented in the early days, they found out that they wanted to provide more advice than transactions because transactions were very cyclical. They became involved in the family office's business and they started selling the family office business model. They provide other services, too, primarily outsourced I think, but some of them are housed in-house. I mean I think Goldman Sachs and some of those guys provide other services to their wealthy clients rather than just a dozen products. So that is a third level of development.

Now then out of that came people that spun out of the investment banks, the trust companies, and the family offices and started their own multi-family offices. So you can see there is sort of a tree growing here and you see that the branches have now gone out to sort of third, fourth generation, where you have people spinning out of the family offices, the brokerage houses, the banks in order to start multi-family offices.

Richard Wilson: I think that's a great, brief overview of how the industry has evolved. It was back in the early 1980s that your firm was one of the pioneering family offices that came up with an open-architecture investing platform. Can you talk about that in a little bit more detail since you became well known for offering that early on in the family office space?

Charles Grace: Well that's another revolution, Richard. We started out by—this was in the old days 25 years ago whereby hedge funds were less developed than they are now. Private equity was there, but less developed. So the investment question was sort of a simple one: a set of asset allocation and manager selection. It was based upon rather simple strategies, I mean various types of stocks—big and small stocks, international stocks—weren't regularly considered until later on in the industry's development. Hedge funds came along, I don't know, not at the very beginning. The investment program developed from, it used to be an asset allocation model, just an efficient frontier which was by definition backward looking.

 See the video "History of Family Offices," at www.FamilyOfficesGroup.com/Video4.

Then it grew into an emphasis on manager selection and identifying "the best managers," who generally reverted to the mean, but nonetheless were very good, and so there was lot of work done on the organization and the people themselves, investment managers. Then, [it grew] to a form of a tactical asset allocation rather than just strategic. Strategic asset allocation, manager selection, and now it's moved into much more emphasis on tactical asset allocation across a very, very broad spectrum of investment strategies. So there has been a lot of change in the way investment advice has been offered and utilized by the family offices.

Stay tuned for more of our interview with Charles Grace in Part Two of this book.

STATE OF THE FAMILY OFFICE INDUSTRY

 See the video "State of the Family Office Industry," at www.FamilyOfficesGroup.com/Video5.

The family office wealth management industry is larger and faster-growing than ever before. Family offices are thriving. Ultra-high net worth families shape our economy and communities; that can be seen all around us through their operation of franchises, apartment buildings, operating businesses, and capital infusions. Family offices are an important source of capital for small and medium-sized businesses and investments, which fuel much of the global economy.

Family offices are often global in their presence and investing. To date, I have spoken in more than 20 countries around the world, and every region shows evidence of a thriving industry that is only just beginning to become more widely understood and defined. Throughout this book, you will have the chance to learn more about these industry hot spots, recent trends, operations, investments, and the future of both single and multi-family offices.

WHO USES A SINGLE OR MULTI-FAMILY OFFICE?

While some family office clients inherit their wealth and others earn their wealth as an athlete or movie star, a high percentage of family office clients have recently taken a company public or sold a business. As a result, their net worth is now $20 million, $300 million, or more, assets they did not have to manage in the past. Family offices try to help manage and preserve that wealth, and the goal of this book is to explore how they attempt to do that on a consistent basis.

Examples of well-known individuals who use family offices are Michael Jordan, Paul Allen, Oprah Winfrey, Bill Gates, and Donald Trump. Almost everyone who runs a single family office has between $100 million and $1 billion in assets, with a smaller percentage having over $1 billion and an even smaller percentage having under $100 million under management.

Most multi-family offices require $20 million to $30 million in investable assets to join their platform, but due to economic conditions and hunger for business growth, some family offices are allowing $5 million and $10 million clients in the door. At the other end of the spectrum, some high-end family offices, including several we interviewed for this book, require $100 million to $250 million in investable assets to participate in their multi-family office. For the purposes of this book, we will be referring to ultra-affluent clients as individuals or families with more than $20 million in investable assets.

 See the video "Ultra-Affluent Clients," at
www.FamilyOfficesGroup.com/Video6.

While we don't have room in this book to detail the line item costs or requirements of running a family office, I want to dispel one myth: Many industry studies will tell you that you need $100 million to $250 million or more to set up your own single family office solution. Experts will tell you that running a family office will cost at least $1 million a year. I don't believe that is true. Due to technology and the ability to leverage taxation and risk management experts and consultants, I have found some successful single family offices with "only" $30 million to $50 million in assets.

I asked one successful single family office executive, Louis Hanna of Corigin Holdings, when it makes sense to consider forming a single family office instead of working with a multi-family office. "I think it's kind of on a case-by-case basis, but arguably and it's a large subset, but I would say beginning at 50 approaching 100 million, again depending upon the situation. And also obviously it is not based upon just asset level but also investment management experience, level of financial sophistication, and goals of family members." The amount of assets needed to set up a single family office depends on the type of risk the family has to manage, what they invest in, what global taxation issues they face, and what goals they have for the family and family office, but, as Louis notes, other factors besides assets should be considered before forming a single family office.

I had the opportunity to interview Angelo Robles, head of the Family Office Association, an exclusive association for single family offices. You can hear exactly how he responded to my question on this topic during the recorded audio interview.

Richard Wilson:	How much in assets do you think that someone needs to have before it makes sense to form a single family office?
Angelo Robles:	I often think those numbers are thrown about, and sometimes I am guilty of that as well. So, why not $67.2 million, how come $50 million or a $100 million? My views on this issue have also changed in the three years since I launched FOA. A part of the reason for my change was about a year ago, I had a chance to come across a significant wealth owner who noted to me, "You know, Angelo, I'm liquid in the ballpark of about $45 million." And I said, "$45 million, I mean congratulations, you are successful. But I think you may be a little bit small for creating your own entity, your single family office. And it's expensive relative to your assets."

And he leans forward and says, "Let's get a couple of things straight, Angelo. First of all, don't tell me what's expensive. If I have, whatever, $45 million, and I want to create for a couple of thousand dollars a private operating company and hire someone who may be paid a couple of hundred thousand dollars, I have got $45 million. I think I have the resources to do that. And by doing that, I am taking control of my assets and my money. I have talent; it may be one person, but talent that's going to be exclusive for me. Why do I have to have a billion dollars? Isn't that a little different than a traditional definition but still a definition of a single family office?" And that really caused me to rethink.

Now, I think, to be optimized to have a multiple of talent inside the single family office, sure, it's going to be superior to have $200 million, if not even more. But I have come around to the gentleman's point of view that there really is no clear-cut definition on how much assets someone has to have to find it worthwhile because a lot of people that want to create an single family office, they are *entrepreneurial* in nature; they are type A personalities; they are successful on some level; and they believe in the opportunity for control, customization, and privacy. And if they are able to build the governance and the philosophy around that and hire even one person to help them in their initiative, doesn't that qualify to be a single family office? Just because they are not worth $300 million, $400 million, or $500 million yet, doesn't mean that they don't have the opportunity to build something that we would broadly still describe as an single family office.

There is probably a sweet spot or a medium, $500 million to $1 billion, and we have some families that are Forbes 100, a couple of Forbes 10. Those families have tens of billions of dollars. But we also have some that are "only"—and again I use that word loosely—$50 million or $100 million or $150 million. So I think the opportunity here is to not define an single family office by too restrictive of a definition. If someone sees value in the benefit of control, privacy, and customization, then I don't think we could contain their desire to create one or maintain one just because we perceive they don't have the classic $100 million in assets.

 To download the full 40-minute audio interview with Angelo Robles, please visit www.FamilyOfficesGroup.com/audio1.

WHY FAMILY OFFICES?

There are many reasons why the ultra-high-net-worth are forming and joining family offices faster than ever before. We will explore the four drivers of growth in the industry within Chapter 10, "The Future of the Family Office Industry," because you may be wondering, "*What are the core motivations of these ultra-wealthy individuals looking to start or join a family office?*"

Once you begin dealing with $10 million, $100 million, or $500 million or more in assets, many issues that may sound small become very important to manage closely. These issues include global taxation, risk management, and even things like cash management. A section of this book in Chapter 6 will focus exclusively on cash management best practices; well-managed cash can often pay for most (if not all) of the expenses of using a family office.

MORE MONEY, MORE PROBLEMS

It really is true: The more money you have, the more problems and challenges you face, no matter how "high quality" the problem may be seen by some. A good analogy for understanding how small details become more important as wealth grows is the managing of currency risk exposure for Procter & Gamble versus managing that same risk within a $1 million-a-year small business with global clients. Surely the small business does not have a full-time currency risk expert on its team, while Procter & Gamble most likely employs several full-time professionals who do nothing but hedge global currency risks. The same goes for the importance of tax matters for someone with $80 million to invest versus $800,000.

Here is a list of the top benefits of working with a family office instead of a single CPA or traditional wealth management professional:

- Central financial management center for the wealth so more holistic decision making can be made.
- Higher chance of an efficient and successful transfer of family assets, heritage, values, and relationships.
- Access to institutional quality talent, fund managers, and resources that would be difficult or impossible to obtain as an individual.
- Reduced costs in achieving a full balance sheet financial management and investment solution.

 See the video "More Money, More Problems," at www.FamilyOfficesGroup.com/Video7.

FAMILY OFFICE INDUSTRY CONFERENCES

Around the world, there is a growing awareness and interest in family office wealth management. Fund managers want to raise capital from family offices, wealth management firms want to convert into family offices, and ultra-wealthy individuals want to learn more about the industry before start-ing their own single family office or joining a family office. One way to reach family offices is to attend a conference. Like other types of conferences, some are more valuable than others. Some family office conferences are invitation only, some are free to attend if you operate a family office, and most of them are held annually.

These conferences are most useful for family offices that are looking to connect with fund managers, service providers, and fellow family offices to explore partnerships and trends. While it may add to your credibility in the industry to speak at such an event, you will most likely not directly get any new clients for your family office business by attending such a conference. I attend family office conferences every quarter and I've spoken at more than 50 conferences now. Please do come up and introduce yourself if you see me at one of these events; it would be great to meet you in person.

CONCLUSION

Family offices have been around for a long time in different forms, but for only a very short amount of time in their current state. The industry is quickly evolving and provides a critical solution to the ultra-affluent who are willing to pay for more holistic management of their finances. In the following chapter, we will expand on the actual services that many family offices are providing.

CHAPTER 2

Family Office Services

The secret of success lies not in doing your own work, but in recognizing the right man to do it.
— Andrew Carnegie (second-richest man to have ever lived)

Chapter Preview: This chapter will list and review the services that family offices are known for providing to their affluent clients. Every family office is different, but this chapter should help ensure that you are aware of the breadth of services that family offices are capable of providing.

As described in Chapter 1, family offices offer a 360-degree full-balance-sheet wealth management solution to ultra-wealthy clients and families. This entire book could be written solely on describing the types of services that family offices often offer, but our focus is on how they deploy capital, so this chapter will just briefly review the suite of services often offered at family offices.

ULTRA-AFFLUENT CLIENTS HAVE DIFFERENT NEEDS

The ultra-affluent demand highly specialized financial services. While there are no set rules on what services a family office can or cannot offer, as was shown in the first chapter, there are common investment and finance-related services that most of them provide for their clients.

Many of these advanced services are not available within a private banking or traditional wealth-management setting, because they are affordable and for the most part, necessary only for the most affluent clientele.

Family offices also offer superior expertise on constructing or selecting alternative investment portfolios and products. Many have invested heavily in systems, reporting, and institutional consultants to help select the most ap-propriate alternative investment managers and products for their high-net-worth clients. Almost everything done within a family office is done with long-term planning in mind. While recently speaking in Vaduz, Liechten-stein, I heard someone describe the royal family office there as managing portfolios with a multigenerational time horizon in mind, and I think that is a good way to describe the focus of many family offices.

While writing this chapter of the book, our team completed an interview with Tal Speilman of Shekal Group, one of the leading multi-family offices in Israel. In the following quote, Tal summarizes his long-term dedication and approach to the client, even to go so far as to eventually know the needs of the client better than the client does:

> *I think that if you really want to give your clients the best product for him and not for another one, only for him, I think you should know him very intimately. I think you should know your clients from all aspects, and this is the only way that I think for the long run, first of all to have the relationship between you and the client, and secondly to improve for your client that you know his real needs. Sometimes you will be the only one that will know his needs, and when I said the only one I could say that it's the only one including him, because sometimes they don't really have the time or the ability to know exactly what they need, and because they need somebody from the outside to look and see what they really need, and I'm talking for the long run aspect. And if you will ask an advisor as I mentioned you will have the trust for many, many years with the client.*

We also recently had the chance to interview Todd Spearin of Waxwing Advisors, who formerly worked inside of a 100-plus client multi-family as a managing director of wealth transfer. Here is what he had to say about the focus of service in the family office that he worked for:

> *What I really valued about the true family office environment is that you really are stewards for the family. Every employee at the firm I worked at had a deep sense of ethics and service and a real strong sense of putting other people's needs before their own. I really cherish that environment where the fiduciary level of responsibility for the clients' affairs are placed first, all daily activities are focused clearly on the client first. There was no pressure from an organi-zation, from superiors, from stockholders to put the profit before the client's needs. And so it's a real service organization serving the client's needs, and that is a real refreshing environment for me to be in after some of the past experiences that I have had.*

FAMILY OFFICE SERVICES

To understand why the family office industry exists and is thriving, it is important to understand what types of services are provided to clients of family offices. Table 2.1 presents the most common of family office services that I have come across while working with family office clients, interviewing family offices, and being advised by family offices.

 See the video "Multi-Generational Wealth Management," at www.FamilyOfficesGroup.com/Video8.

ADDITIONAL BENEFITS AND LIFE MANAGEMENT SERVICES AS A COMPETITIVE ADVANTAGE

While many single family offices structure services to provide many life management services on top of financial management solutions, this is not always the case with multi-family offices. Many times when multi-family offices offer these types of additional services, they are at far reduced prices or for free. As a line item they lose the firm money but are offered to create a marketplace advantage over other offices. Benefits that are nonfinancial and could be used for strategic advantage include life coaching, golf or private club memberships, or use of vacation properties, luxury vehicles, or yachts. As competition among family offices grows, it is expected that these types of additional benefits of becoming part of a multi-family office will steadily increase in popularity.

While some family offices are adding new services to be more competitive, others are "sticking to their knitting" so they don't start reaching beyond their core competencies. The following is a short excerpt from our interview with family office executive Brian Hughes from the Threshold Group, a top multi-family office. Here he shares a quick best practice for family offices that are looking to improve their service delivery.

"I think based on my experience that family offices have to really know what they are good at and be able to provide those services, whether it's pure investment advisory, pure family office services, or a combination of investment advisory and family office services. Knowing what you are good at, having the scale and efficiencies within the organization to deliver those services, and then doing it in a way that's profitable for the firm is key to a successful family office. Certainly one of the biggest challenges in our industry is just making sure that you are sticking to your knitting and not trying to do things that you may have done as a one-off for your clients."

TABLE 2.1 Family Office Services Breakdown

Services	Explanation
Portfolio Management & Investments	Portfolio and investment management services are core to what a family office typically offers clients; it often includes selection of fund managers, implementing the investment plan and policy of clients, and managing investment risks and cash requirements.
Tax Advisory	Ultra-wealthy individuals have many types of assets, global assets, and enough income and potential tax liability that a small improvement in their tax efficiency could quickly help pay for the extra fees involved in working with a family office.
Reporting & Record Keeping	This service involves the organization of financial paperwork including compliance documents, investment documentation, or insurance details. This helps simplify the lives of the ultra-wealthy, who may hold over a dozen insurance policies alone. Reporting and record keeping is being offered more as competition within the family office industry increases.
Philanthropic Management	Charitable giving and philanthropic management can involve the formation of foundations, help with maintaining or running a foundation, or advisory and assistance with making effective charitable donations.
Multigenerational Wealth Management	Ultra-wealthy need assistance in setting up trusts and managing how they will pass on wealth to their children and grandchildren in a way that is responsible, tax efficient, and appropriate for the type of culture the family is trying to foster long-term.
Compliance & Regulatory Assistance	State and country regulations can affect the investments, assets, and business operations of the ultra-wealthy. Family offices can help ensure the consistent compliance with the laws that govern the activities of clients.
Risk Management & Insurance	Separate from investment management and portfolio management, some family offices recruit top risk-management experts and insurance specialists to their team. Sometimes this type of professional is brought in as a service provider, but the larger the family office is in terms of assets the more likely it is to have such a professional in-house.
Life Management & Budgeting	The lives of the ultra-wealthy are often chaotic; many run operational businesses on top of taking care of a family. The ultra-wealthy typically hold many assets, which take up even more of their time. Family offices offer life management and budgeting services to help simplify the lives of the ultra-wealthy and ensure that the monthly budget is in line with their long-term wealth preservation goals.

TABLE 2.1 *(Continued)*

Definition	Explanation
Fleet Management & Shared Asset Perks	Many family offices own real estate, luxury cars, partial shares of private jets, private shares of yachts, and other assets that clients of a family office can access. A single family office may help maintain or purchase such an asset directly for a single family, while a multi-family office leverages its large client base for use by those clients who qualify based on assets or through paying extra dues each month.
Training & Education	Everyone needs continuing education to keep up with changing economic conditions, financial tools, and global investment opportunities. Many times, family offices can help educate younger family members on the basics of wealth management and financial literacy.

SINGLE VERSUS MULTI-FAMILY OFFICE SERVICES

The most important thing to remember about comparing single and multi-family office services is that single family offices are built around the needs and goals of a single family. Everything is catered directly to those needs. In a multi-family office, there will be some chances for greater efficiency, in theory, but less of a 100 percent focus on serving the goals of any one family. That is not to say that multi-family office clients do not receive custom solutions; they do, but they do not have the full attention of a whole office. Many times, though, this results in multi-family offices' offering some perks and miscellaneous services that would just not be feasible unless the costs were spread out among many families.

While multi-family offices can bring to the table lessons learned from working with multiple clients, a single family office will, over time, become more and more specialized in managing the types of investments and services that one family needs. Single family offices, by their nature, provide more privacy and confidentiality; for some ultra-wealthy individuals who are consistently in the public eye, this may be an important point to consider.

Oftentimes, hedge fund managers and finance professionals ask me why they can't set up a family office for themselves with just $1 million or $2 million under management. The short answer is that you can; nothing is stopping you from doing this, though the costs are high. If you truly want to hire professionals to manage your wealth full-time, you will want to make sure they know what they are doing; that talent costs money. If you are not careful, you will quickly spend your $1 million just setting up your family office.

The solution for most with less than $20 million in assets under management is to join a multi-family office that accepts smaller clients, join a wealth management firm that is trying to climb up to family office levels of service, or form your own network of a CPA, wealth manager, life insurance professional, and so on and be a manager of sorts of your own virtual family office. You can attempt to run your virtual family office, though most highly successful professionals already have more than a full-time job's worth of responsibilities.

DIFFERENCES IN GLOBAL FAMILY OFFICE SERVICE OFFERINGS

Family offices offer different types of services in different regions of the world. The family office model is more developed and mature in the United States and Western Europe and is still fairly rare in countries in Africa, some countries in Latin America, and some areas in Asia. In many non-Western countries, family offices are simply a more sophisticated wealth management firm that has access to alternative investments and trust services. These offices normally do not offer services in areas such as insurance and risk management, budgeting, life planning, charitable giving, or tax compliance.

Family office services also differ based on whether an individual or wealthy family is a first-generation wealth creator or a second-, third-, or fourth-generation wealth inheritor. Typically, the closer individuals are tied to wealth creation instead of inheritance, the more of an appetite they have for risk to further grow their wealth instead of strictly preserving it. In other words, the entrepreneurs responsible for creating the great amount of wealth in the first place often make what looks like risky investment decisions when compared to those who inherit wealth.

An Australian family office I just interviewed for this book serves first-generation ultra-high net worth individuals who are often still operating a business. This means that they are very busy, have operational business risk exposures, have very little free time, and may be involved in merger and acquisition activity, and often are in great need of more communication between their family office accountant and their business accountant. Compare this to a family office that services mostly third- and fourth-generation wealth inheritors of $100 million to $1 billion. Families grow over time, so after four generations, just as a function of statistics, most families are going to be made up of mostly nonsignificant wealth creators and entrepreneurs who do not find great success. This means if they lose the money, it is gone forever; for these offices and families, protecting the wealth is their number one objective.

During my interviews with family offices, I also learned a number of other things about global family office services deliver, including:

- Typically, Canadians are slightly more conservative in their investing than Americans and Europeans.
- Many Asian family office clients have a higher tolerance for volatility and risk in exchange for growth.
- Related to Asia, I found by speaking at conferences in the region that Hong Kong has been the location of choice in Asia for many family offices and that Singapore is now growing at a faster rate due to its business-friendly regulations and tax regime.
- I also learned that in places such as Israel, Indonesia, and Brazil the competition and business model is still young; more education is needed to identify and work with new clients in those marketplaces.
- In Australia and many other countries, there are typically more first-generational wealth individuals than third or fourth generation, and that changes the appetite for risk and expectations for family office services.
- In many locations around the world, the trend of the ultra-wealthy using family offices is just starting to catch on. The global trends affecting where family offices are based, and why they are based there, directly affects what types of services they provide.

If you want to learn more about global family office trends, our team at the Family Offices Group has created more than 30 regional profiles on the family office industry, one for each major family office hub that we have connected with through the operation of our association. To get free access to these regional profiles, which include Monaco, Singapore, Argentina, Lichtenstein, Switzerland, and many other regions, please visit www.FamilyOfficesGroup.com/2008/07/family-office-regional-profiles.

CONCLUSION

The goal of almost all family offices is to first protect the capital of the client and then provide necessary or requested ancillary services that help the ultra-wealthy individuals more effectively manage their wealth, investments, and sometimes their life. The main difference to remember between single and multi-family offices is that single family offices are customized solutions for a single individual or family, and multi-family offices are set up as platform solutions that aim to customize their solutions, but really help leverage centralized resources across many ultra-affluent clients. The next chapter, on family office operations, will help you further understand how these services are typically delivered by top family offices.

Family Office Operations

If you can't describe something as a process, you don't know what you are doing.
—Edward Deming (famed operational improvement guru)

Chapter Preview: In this chapter, we explore how family offices operate their businesses. This chapter discusses team structure, service providers, corporate governance, the centrality of certified public accountants (CPAs) in the industry, three common models of family office operations, and how the best family offices are run like well-oiled machines.

The family office industry can be broken into three types of family offices: the Outsourced Model, Expert Generalist Model, and Institutional Offering.

 See the video, "Family Office Operations," at www.FamilyOfficesGroup.com/Video9.

OUTSOURCED MODEL

In this model of operation, one person is put in charge of the family office while 80 to 90 percent of the value-added services are outsourced. This core person may have the ability to help manage a portfolio, select fund managers, or investigate tax consequences of decisions, but primarily acts as a manager of external service providers. The one or few people who do work full-time for the family office in this model play the important role of coordinating conversations and ensuring that information flows smoothly between parties. Their aim is to offer the benefits of running a full-fledged family office model without all the costs.

Typically, those without significant enough wealth to form their own single family office, or those who want to remain very private select this option. Many times it later evolves into the Expert Generalist Model, which is described next. This model is fairly common for small family offices, which makes family office industry statistics difficult to calculate. This operating model usually requires one or two full-time professionals.

Expert Generalist Model

The multidisciplinary nature of running a family office calls for someone to have deep experience in many financial and life management areas that most people don't possess. Oftentimes these professionals are referred to as "expert generalists," meaning that they have a great breadth of experience that is just deep enough in each area to know when to hire someone or outsource a decision or function, but also enough experience in a few core areas to really provide a lot of value there as well. In this model the expert generalist runs the entire operation while less experienced professionals with five to seven or more years of experience or a few outside experts are used as needed to provide the complete solution. This is different from the outsourced model because in this case most services and value added solutions are completed and managed in-house.

The term "expert generalist" is relatively new and Linda Mack of Mack International is credited with first making it popular in the industry. I recently spoke at a family office summit in South America alongside Linda, who you will probably also see speak in the future if you frequent industry conferences.

It is expensive to retain an expert generalist and many times that is why single family offices convert to multi-family offices; the costs are just too great for all but the wealthiest individual families to burden. That being said, this is the most popular operating model that I have seen; I would estimate 70 percent of all single and multi-family offices operate under this model.

Institutional Offering Model

In this model, the family office moves from having just one expert generalist to also hiring four to seven in-house experts, all with 15 to 20 or more years of experience in areas such as global taxation, trust and multigenerational wealth transfers, life insurance, portfolio management, risk management, cash management, and so forth. The costs of finding and retaining this much talent is an indigestible level of expense for everyone but those with $3 billion or more in total assets under management.

Family office executive talent is in fact so rare that many family offices I know could grow their business much faster if it weren't for a lack of experienced talent in the marketplace. In my most recent set of industry interviews, this lack of industry talent came up several times as the number one thing restricting the growth of many family office businesses. This institutional model is just now taking hold in the industry.

I would estimate that only 1 to 2 percent of all family offices actually use this operating model, but it is important to know about because it is where the industry is headed for the largest of multi-family offices. As family offices grow in number, they will become more competitive with each other and after more mergers and acquisitions there will be more and more family offices large enough to actually pull this off.

FAMILY OFFICE TEAM MEMBERS

 See the video "Family Office Executive Directors," at www.FamilyOfficesGroup.com/Video10.

Family office executives generally need to have 10 to 15 or more years of experience in many areas, whereas seven-plus years is often enough in other areas of the investment industry. This experience and expertise is needed to handle the complex, multidisciplinary challenges that come with managing large amounts of wealth. Expert generalists are highly compensated professionals who have a great breadth of experience and can reach out to niche experts as needed to effectively run the family office. To be best in class, as noted in the preceding section, you have to outsource unless you can afford a series of three to five very-high-end experts as well as assistants underneath that expert generalist. This can quickly become a 20- to 50-person operation and be very expensive.

Compensation ranges from $100,000 at the low end to $1 million plus a bonus of 20 to 200 percent. Most professionals get paid a base salary of $200,000 to $450,000 plus a bonus of 50 to 100 percent. Multiple long-term factors, such as portfolio protection or returns, rolling multiyear coinvestment, and carried interests motivators are also put in place to attract top talent.

 See the video "Family Office Jobs," at www.FamilyOfficesGroup.com/Jobs.

The hierarchy of employees within a family office represents that of a normal business, though is a bit more flat. Oftentimes, the executive director or CEO has only one or two levels underneath him, as most family offices are just 10 to 30 professionals large. As mentioned previously, the most critical members of the team will be the people with portfolio management and investment expertise, those with risk management and insurance expertise, and those who can help the family meet multigenerational wealth transfer and trust-related planning.

There are many other types of expertise needed to run a family office, such as accounting, auditing, record keeping, compliance, project management, business management, internal budgeting, and so on. These are more common skills to have in the job marketplace, and therefore there is less of a bottleneck in the industry. Many family offices are growing at 10 percent a year instead of 30 percent as a direct result of scarce talent in the industry with deep experience in working inside of a family office.

One may wonder if the top family offices have every type of expert needed on their staff once they reach a certain size, but I have found this not to be the case. One person we interviewed for our Family Office Veteran Interview Series was Paul Tramontano, co-chief executive officer and founding member of a top-50 family office, Constellation Wealth Advisors. Here is what he had to say about this issue:

> *In our opinion, it is not advisable to have everything in-house. It is one of the mistakes that bigger investment firms consistently make as it is impossible to assemble the extensive/broad expertise needed for wealthy families under one roof. When we require legal and accounting assistance/participation, we work with the best firms in the country, and when we are seeking investment ideas, we search for best in class managers across every discipline. At Constellation, we have a very methodical way of approaching outside investments and are extremely careful in how we incorporate them into our investors' asset allocations. In addition, we regularly invite outside managers and economists to our investment committee to help us gain a different perspective. It is important to have checks and balances in any process, but it is crucial, as allocators, to hold your clients' best interests at the forefront and to stay away from group think.*

There are some strategies that family offices can use to attract more talent to their team. These strategies include: speaking at master's degree programs, speaking at national CPA conferences or association meetings, or writing a blog or column. One strategy used by a single family office I interviewed, Kinnear Financial, is to hire very bright, well-educated, and relatively young professionals. Kinnear compensates for that lack of experience by putting the new hires through a thorough training program and cross-training rotation of responsibilities within the family office. Many times this can be a more cost-effective option when the only other option is to get in a bidding war for talent.

Training options for family office employees can include attending conferences, earning a hedge fund designation or private equity designation, completing a master's degree in the evenings, or attending finance industry workshops or seminars. Another option is to complete a family office training or certificate, such as the Qualified Family Office Professional (QFOP) program.

FAMILY OFFICE INVESTMENT COMMITTEES

The family office investment committee is a critical part of a family office operation. Though it is used by both types of family offices, an investment committee is more often employed formally in a multi-family office setting. In Chapter 8, "Family Office Investments," we discuss investment committees in great detail and hear directly from many top family offices on how they approach this area of their business.

BOARD OF ADVISORS

 See the video "Family Office Board of Advisor," at www.FamilyOfficesGroup.com/Video11.

A board of advisors is something that many family offices do not formally have in place. A board is much different from an investment committee in that it should be made up of very senior or well-connected executives from outside the family office. The goal of the advisory board is to hear unique perspectives and strategies on preserving capital, running a family office, or growing the business of the family office. Most operating businesses, including family office organizations, have a sounding board of trusted advisors in related industries. The more intention a family office puts into building a diversified and robust board of advisors, though, the more it will benefit from having such a resource in place. If you need help building out a board of advisory team for your family office please contact us for assistance.

FAMILY OFFICE GOVERNANCE

 See the video "Family Office Governance," at www.FamilyOfficesGroup.com/Video12.

The governance of family offices is growing in importance in parallel with fund manager governance. Every year, many clients in the wealth management and fund management industries are tricked or misled by someone with greedy intentions. Even more subtle are the hundreds if not thousands of firms that make decisions that, though not illegal, are borderline unethical and not in line with their promises made to clients when they are brought on board. The core role of governance is to establish an internal watchdog for the client so that the office takes no actions that are not in the best interest of the client and so that the office at least strongly considers the interests of the client base. Governance procedures can also improve the operations of a family office by putting in place rules on how an executive is hired, how someone may be fired, how the investment committee is formed, and what exactly must be done before a new fund manager can be selected. These types of policies can prevent conflicts, such as a chief investment officer allocating capital to a hedge fund run by his cousin. Family office governance is not discussed enough in our industry, but its importance will continue to grow. Family offices that follow strong corporate governance frameworks will reap operational, reputational, and business development benefits from doing so.

INDIVIDUAL FAMILY GOVERNANCE

The governance procedures for an individual family could include family values, vision, mission, strategic plan, succession plan or next-generation plan, family council, written policies and procedures, clear roles and responsibilities or committee structure, annual board assessment process, outside director and board rotations, and written conflict of interest and ethics policies. Governance overall is critical when deciding who makes decisions, who needs to sign what, who controls the money, who has authority to know balances or investments, how allocations are made, how the board is formed, who can be fired when and by whom, and how to set the rules and procedures for running the family office. Policies related to this are set by the family, such as outsourcing versus in-sourcing, software selection, succession planning, and defining roles.

Here is how Lukas Doerig of Marcuard Family Office, a top-50 multifamily office, describes family governance:

> In a nutshell, it's basically how the family and its members are linked to each other, how their fortune is passed on and as I always like to say, "The thing is, people care less about a few basis points of performance than they care about what will happen once they are no longer there." What will happen with the son? What will happen

with the daughter? Can they deal with the amount of money they are going to inherit? Are philanthropic issues taken care of?

There is an advantage for a multi-family office because the first thing you have is experience and the second thing is that you are really independent. You might also be in a position to bring up an inconvenient truth about the family and be open and communicate about problems you are just seeing, which need to be addressed, while maybe in a single family office the people in charge there might not be there to bring up the sort of thorny and difficult issues a family might have.

FROM CPA TO FAMILY OFFICE CEO

Many business owners trust experienced CPAs as a source of sound advice on how to reinvest profits in a way that is relatively tax efficient while using their own knowledge on what may produce financial returns.

I spoke with Harvey Abrams, a CPA with over 25 years running a single family office, on how his accounting background has been an asset in managing a family office. He pointed to one area, investing, in which his nonfinance background came in handy. "Well, before I joined the Principal, I didn't know very much about the stock market. And I found that to be an asset as you look back, because what happened when I was asked, 'Gee, should we buy this company or should we invest in that company?' I was doing the research and coming up with things that the Principal, who had been an analyst, didn't see from an accounting point of view." Harvey found that his background as an accountant gave him a good sense of how a business should operate and thus helped guide his family office's investment decisions in a way that might not have occurred without his accounting knowledge.

Naturally, when business owners experience a liquidity event and suddenly their wealth increases many fold, entrepreneurs turn to their CPAs to help them form a family office solution. This is why there are so many family office executives with accounting backgrounds.

Following are a few examples of how CPAs often get pulled into this business:

> **Eric Bennett,** CEO of Tolleson Wealth Management, a 100-plus-client multi-family office, told me:
>
> > *I spent 11 years with the Big Four accounting firms and from day one I did the predecessor to the term wealth management and family office that was, you know, financial planning. So I worked for Coopers and Lybrand and Ernst*

& Young and they all had groups specialized in doing personal financial planning for high-net-worth business owners and senior executives of public companies, and that's how I met the Tolleson family with John Tolleson, who was a CEO of the public company, and he was assigned to me as a client in the early '90s. He sold his business in 1997 and asked for me to join him full-time to start the family office. So we started off and it was just me, him, and his assistant back in 1997.

Thomas Handler, partner of Handler Thayer, LLP, remembers:

I started my career in accounting and public accounting primarily on the tax side and had the occasion to work with ultra-high-net-worth families and entrepreneurs while in that space. And then from there, I went on to doing similar work as an attorney, and fairly early in my career I was fortunate to work with some highly successful entrepreneurs who had exit events and became single family offices. I was also fortunate to be hired by a large multinational, multibillionaire family that contributed greatly to my education in this space. So in some regards it was happenstance, and in the case of the international family, it was literally a beauty pageant of 15 law firms. We were fortunate and won and worked with them over time on some very complicated and large transactions, and that got us into the space.

Bret Magpiong, a family office consultant with over 20 years of experience in the industry, said:

I often have people ask me, 'How did you get in here? Did you go to school for this?' The answer is no. I started with a large accounting firm, and a component of my job was to provide personal financial services to many of the executives of some of the large corporations that were clients of the firm. And ultimately I serviced some very senior executives, mostly in the entertainment industry, and we handled everything from soup to nuts for them, from paying their bills all the way up through estate planning, tax work, investment planning and analysis, and everything in between. So, it really started from a discipline around, I would say,

> *the CPA world and the tax world, but extended to asset al-location and investments and just taking care of very complex situations for some very wealthy people.*
>
> *It is difficult to find someone with experience in running a successful family office. While there is no one skill needed to run a family office, there are some core skills and sets of experience more critical than others, such as accounting, business management, trust and multigenerational wealth management, global taxation, or portfolio management experience. The reality is that nobody is great at all of those things, and there are not any family offices that truly have every single required expert and piece of talent completely in-house on salary with the firm on a full-time basis.*

FAMILY OFFICE SERVICE PROVIDERS

Family offices of every size rely on service providers. These service providers can include auditors, accountants, attorneys, risk consultants, insurance consultants, private jet brokers, investment bankers, fund managers, and institutional consultants. The type of business model a family office employs will change, whether it depends on a few or dozens of services providers.

While many of these service providers are large organizations, such as global accounting firms, others are highly specialized and provide solutions exclusively to family offices and no other type of client. The benefits of a global brand, such as a global accounting firm, include client recognition, potentially thousands of employees worth of support, and a seemingly unlimited supply of resources to meet the family office's needs. The advantage of working with a service provider that focuses only on family offices is that the family office can be more certain that their needs and immediate challenges can be directly addressed and heard, and that a custom solution will be provided.

The world of family office–focused service providers is growing, and it will continue to grow as the industry as a whole continues to thrive. We recently interviewed several family office executives who now own industry service providers that cater exclusively to the industry. Two include Tim Calveley from FORS Limited, which provides reporting solutions to family offices, and Thomas Handler of Handler Thayer, LLP, which provides taxation, estate planning, and asset protection to family offices. Richard Wilson Capital Partners, LLC, our own business of bringing best-of-breed fund managers to family offices, is another example of how the family office space is large enough to support these types of custom solutions for the industry.

DEVELOPING A WELL-OILED FAMILY OFFICE MACHINE

One thing that has made a big difference in the stability and growth of the Family Offices Group association and my own operating businesses is having a detailed set of processes and procedures that document every action someone in the company needs to take more than just once. If there is some repeating action, like bringing on a new client, managing risk, or selecting a service provider, then the process of doing so should be written out so that it can be optimized and so best practices can be documented.

We began this chapter with an Edward Deming quote, which emphasizes the importance of understanding what you're doing and why. He said, "If you can't describe something as a process, you don't know what you are doing." Drawing or writing out how a process works forces you to understand it at a deeper level, and it makes for an easier transfer of knowledge between those on your team with different levels of experience or years of history within the family office.

While many large corporations are run smoothly based on set processes and procedures, very few family offices are run this same way. Most have policies and procedures in place, but they are high-level and not used day to day in carrying out the value delivered to family office clients.

IMPLEMENTING PROCESSES, PROCEDURES, AND SYSTEMS IN YOUR FAMILY OFFICE

I recently had the honor of interviewing author Sam Carpenter, an expert on implementing practical systems, procedures, and checklists within a fast-growing small to medium-sized business such as a family office. He provided some great insights within the interview, which you can download in MP3 form at www.FamilyOfficesGroup.com/Audio2.

CONCLUSION

The family office business model is challenging to deliver. Client demands are high, talent is scarce, and the solution often needs to be comprehensive and relatively seamless. Our hope is that this chapter has provided you with a high-level overview of family office services and the challenges that family offices face day to day.

CHAPTER 4

The Ultra-Affluent's Guide to Selecting a Family Office

*You have to be careful. If you don't know where you are going,
you will wind up somewhere else.*

—Yogi Berra (baseball legend)

Chapter Preview: This chapter has been written primarily for ultra-affluent individuals who are reading this book to learn more about family offices, how to evaluate them, and what the real benefits are of hiring one to help them manage their wealth.

This short chapter is unique from the rest in this book as it is directed toward ultra-affluent individuals exclusively.

STARTING A SINGLE FAMILY OFFICE VERSUS JOINING A MULTI-FAMILY OFFICE

For most ultra-affluent clients, starting a single family office is not a realistic option. Doing so requires being comfortable with running a financial firm, or at least with hiring the right talent to make sure the operation is worth the high costs of operating the firm. Most single family offices require a relatively large investment of time, compliance monitoring, and at least $50 million to $100 million in capital to provide an efficient solution for the ultra-affluent client. These combined factors lead most ultra-affluent clients, even those with $100 million to $300 million or more in wealth, to turn to a multi-family office solution.

Coming into a lot of wealth can be a lonely place. You may feel distanced from some otherwise close friends; talking to them about what you should do with your capital can create an awkward situation, resentment, or worse. Even though I have found successful family office executives to be of the highest level of integrity and character, many times the professionals who are knowledgeable and want to speak with you about your challenges are on some level sales professionals, experienced in acquiring new clients, and compensated on how well and efficiently they can get your capital placed inside their product or family office offering.

Disclosure: This chapter is not a complete guide to the specific analysis that you will need to complete to make sure a family office is a good fit for you. To select a family office right for you, seek the counsel of your current business advisors, CPA, and legal counsel. Many times, completing a background check on the key executives and asking for references is wise as well. Please treat the following information as a high-level overview and a helpful resource in navigating this process, but always seek the counsel of a professional expert who understands your specific situation and needs.

OBJECTIVE FAMILY OFFICE SELECTION ADVICE

I do not run a family office at the time of publication, and I am not compensated for persuading you to join a certain family office or even a certain type of family office. I hope this perspective, combined with my knowledge and connections in the family office space, will allow me to provide you with some objective guidance on how to select a family office. In addition to my experience in the industry, my conversations and interviews with family office executives also gave me the opportunity to hear directly from top family office experts on exactly what you should look for and ask, while selecting a family office for your own wealth management needs.

WHAT DO YOU WANT?

This chapter opens with a quote by Yogi Berra: "You have to be careful. If you don't know where you are going, you will wind up somewhere else." Before you go out and meet with several family offices, you should review this book carefully and decide exactly what type of family office you are looking for. Do you want a hands-off solution, or do you want to control the direct investments of some of your capital in an industry that you are familiar with? Do you want to take advantage of life management services, budget and record keeping help, and fractional jet ownership, or do you want to keep things focused exclusively on the management of a portfolio of alternative investment fund managers? Do you want to work with someone in your city, or could the family office be based anywhere in the world?

If you spend just a few hours of speaking with your spouse, planning, reflecting on what you really want and what will serve you and your family's needs most, you will be rewarded handsomely over the long term.

CHARACTER JUDGMENTS

Knowing who you are working with on a personal level is very important. Are they impatient, stretched thin, and edgy? Are they going to provide you with sound objective advice during volatile market environments or a national debt crisis?

One of the advantages of Richard Wilson Capital Partners is our additional focus and dedication to work only with fund managers who have a high degree of character and world-class institutional experience. You can apply this same advantage for yourself while selecting a family office to manage your wealth. There are a few very specific methods of quickly judging the strength of one's character.

The best way I have found for quickly evaluating someone's character is to gauge their time horizon or outlook on life. Most people, by default, have a bias for short-term actions, rewards, and planning. This focus on short-term results and costs conflicts with the very nature and planned benefits of working with a family office, which should have a bias toward long-term planning.

While evaluating a family office, ask yourself a few questions regarding this issue. Does the family office executive look to do things the quick and easy way, or the right way? I learned many years ago from studying with business management author Brian Tracy and master's-level psychology at Harvard University that those with a low degree of character and integrity will do things for a quick profit regardless of the consequences; those with the highest quality of character will always take the higher road, no matter how painful or slow the progress. Look for signs of taking the lower or higher road in the family office professionals you meet with. Who have they hired to build their team? How long have they been around in the industry? Are they truly committed to the service of clients and fulfilling their role as a 360-degree financial management solution for you? Or are they looking to gather assets above all else?

The topic of character judgment came up within our interview with David Thomas, the CEO of Equitas Consulting. Here is what he had to say on this topic when I asked him about how to evaluate another party while hiring an investment consultant or fund manager:

> *I will say the first thing that you do is you sit down with someone like me and have a lunch or have a dinner away from everybody's office, and you get to know the people outside of the business. Everyone in the family office, they have had their whole lifetimes of experience with people skills. You need to be able to just get eyeball to eyeball without numbers or charts—I wouldn't even talk about investing—and just get to know the person; character matters, honesty, integrity all of those type of things. And if you have a good feeling there, then you can go on to question number two, but if you don't there are a number of other questions—and I think the family offices are very big on loyalty, integrity, confidentiality. Just the people skills that they use now in their own business translates into the investment management business very nicely I think.*
>
> *So I would have a dinner. I might get a couple of beers with the guy and see if anything changes. You just want to get to know them as people, and after that, then you can go forward and see what kind of value-added services, what kind of industry background that they have, check references with some investors that use them, you can even talk to investors that no longer use them. You can just find out if there is a quantitatively calculable value-added that they have for the investors, how many investors they have, what is the background. They can start going through that whole series of questions.*

For more on character analysis, please see Chapter 9, "Fund Manager Selection and Deal Flow," where I present the 6 Cs of Character Analysis model in detail.

SEVEN CRITICAL FAMILY OFFICE QUESTIONS TO ASK

To make your on-site visits to family offices more effective, I would suggest creating a custom set of questions based on your unique wealth needs. For example, if you want to make direct investments in commercial real estate or as an angel investor, your questions will be unique from someone who wants a low-risk, hands-off, diversified investment solution. As a starting point, however, the following seven questions are fundamental and should probably be asked by everyone who goes in to meet with a family office they may hire:

1. What types of ultra-affluent clients does the family office serve?
2. May you speak with a few of those clients as references?
3. How thorough and objective is the fund manager selection process?
4. What is the portfolio construction methodology used by the family office?
5. What family office governance best practices are in place today?
6. Does the family office show a long-term commitment to each piece of its business?
7. What are the top three strengths and top three genuine weaknesses of the family office service offering compared to the competition?

 See the video "Family Office Due Diligence," at www.FamilyOfficesGroup.com/Video13.

FAMILY OFFICE VETERAN QUOTES ON HOW TO SELECT A FAMILY OFFICE

As mentioned earlier, the typical problem with asking family office executives for advice on selecting a family office is that they often are trying to sell you at that same meeting. I recently had the chance to ask industry-leading risk consultants, chief investment officers, and executive directors from leading family offices what questions they would ask if they were giving someone advice on how to choose a family office. Their answers were diverse and insightful. Here are six of the responses:

1. **Graham Harrison:** The following is a quote from a top single family office expert, Graham Harrison of Asset Risk Consultants, based in Guernsey. He explains common mistakes made while seeking a solution to manage family wealth:

   > *The first big question that a family should ask themselves before starting this process is, "What's the money for?" That might seem a fairly obvious question, but it's surprising when you're dealing with families, there're very often opposing views as to what a pool of assets is actually for, and of course there are only really three things you can do with money. Firstly, you can bury it if you like aiming to preserve capital. Secondly, you can try to make more of it—you know, invest it—and thirdly you can spend it. Trying to get that balance right is actually quite difficult for families and they quite often appreciate having an*

independent person kind of acting as chairman with the discussions and trying to put that down on paper.

Actually, too few families have done this and often we find that they have jumped into an investment solution that was offered by somebody they trusted, very often an investment bank for example who helped them with the transaction and ended up saying, "Well, what about this or that investment solution?" And they've gone for it, but then they're not entirely sure why they've done it because they started, you know, not with the first principles but actually almost with the end game. And it's only after a little bit of time has elapsed that they realize that perhaps that wasn't quite what they wanted to do.

Essentially, once a family has worked out what the money they've got locked in investment balance is for, it might be called an investment policy statement. And from that then, we think the next step really is to risk profile the family, but also some of the individuals involved. And this is a second really interesting area of debate because you always have risk takers within a family and those who're very risk averse and it doesn't necessarily go with age, although clearly, older people do tend to be more risk averse. And that risk-profiling process is actually crucial if you're going to avoid future disappointment with the result of either not enough return being generated or too much risk being taken.

2. **Andrew Hector:** Following is advice on selecting a family office from Andrew Hector of Candor Financial Management, a multi-family office based in Australia:

> *I think the question for families to ask is "How are you going to look after my best interest?" A very broad, wide-open question, but really what you're trying to extract there is to understand the alignment of interest between the family and the multi-family office and make sure that there is no conflict of interest or if there are, they're acceptable.*
>
> *The next question that we would suggest they ask is to explain their business's core values and the advisor's personal core values. Obviously that's important because the advisor's values need to be replicated at the business level.*
>
> *If the families can't gain trust with the advisor or has any doubt that they should trust the advisor, that's the next point. After that it gets down to the normal things, such as experience, explain to me their experience and their education. And*

then from that point onwards it's try it and see if the results are basically going to be forthcoming.

3. **Charles Grace,** with more than 50 years of experience in the industry and currently serving as a director at the Threshold Group, a top 50 multi-family office, had the following advice on how to select a family office:

> *Actually select a family office that has a history and that has all of the resources required. Once you get past that, you will find there are a bunch of them that can do this. Once you get past that, it's a question of the relationship that you are able to develop and accomplishment you feel in your communication with an individual, primarily with an individual in the organization, typically with a very senior individual in the multi-family office. That level of communication is the most important. So many people can provide excellent investment advice, but the most important thing is, is he going to communicate it to you in a way that you can understand it? So you need to be sure that you can understand what he is saying to you and that he is giving you all the information that you need in order to approve his decisions or to hire him to represent you.*

4. **Tim Voorhees,** from the multi-family office Virtual Family Office Services, Inc., provides the following advice on selecting a family office:

> *Effective planning leads to deeper discussions about vision and values. The more we work with high-net-worth clients, the more we see that families universally accumulate wealth when there is clarity of vision. Members of a successful family have a deep understanding of the family's vision and ranked priorities. Even if family leaders do not actively articulate the family's vision and values, the leaders often achieve success because the people around them, when interviewed, can communicate the vision and values effectively.*
>
> *The multi-family office, above all else, needs to have staff members who can understand and support the vision of each client's family. Too often staff members may say that they understand the vision but, if the client follows up a few months after first meeting the staff, the client may be surprised to see that very often family office staffers will struggle to state the*

vision in a way that the client readily affirms. Even if the family office employees can articulate the vision and values of the family, staff members may struggle to explain how those ideals guide the portfolio management and the estate management process. There is often a huge disconnect between the vision statement and the practical planning. Within this disconnect is the starting point for true planning.

Almost every multi-family office will tell clients that they care about their values. It is common to see advertisements about family offices being values-centric or values-driven. These ideals must be translated into statements of goals that unite family members and advisers. The family office team needs to spend time with the client in order to rank and quantify the client's goals that can guide effective planning.

At VFOS, we meet with the patriarch and/or matriarch for four to six hours in a "retreat." Throughout that meeting, we refine the statement of the client's vision and then rank and quantify goals in response to the client's feedback. Our process is similar to what the optometrist uses when finding the pair of lens that helps the client see most clearly. As we develop a more concrete list of goals, we are often able to refine language in the vision statement to inspire more unified action.

Once we help the client define vision and values, we then illustrate how we can change or update a vision-focused and values-driven plan as tax laws change, family members change, or cash flow needs change. We use flowcharts, numbers, and legal document summaries to show how our planning results in the best after-tax lifetime income as well as ample funding of for-profit and not-for-profit entities that fulfill the family's vision. As the multi-family office develops and executes plans to reflect ranked and quantified goals, each client family can have confidence that the family office knows how to implement plans based on a clear vision and unifying values.

5. **Arnold Bon,** based in Luxembourg with more than 12 years of multi-family office and single family office industry experience, provides the following advice on selecting a family office:

   The family itself should really first ask questions to themselves: "What do I want the family office for or do I simply need to do wealth management or do I want somebody who picks fund managers?" If they want to go a step further and say, "Okay, we also want them to take care of the personal administration, the house, etc.," then I think they should definitely ask for references, and they should ask for the experience of the team, the turnover, and who are their clients because the world of the rich and wealthy is sometimes a very small world and also there are people who like each other and who don't like each other. And heaven forbid they work with somebody who is also doing work for one of the people they don't like.

So therefore, what I found out was that as soon as some people can afford it, they would rather have somebody exclusively working for themselves, which acts as some sort of trusted officer. In many cases, that is let's say the former accountant of the company they had, somebody who is working for them for a long time, rather than that they go to a family office where they say okay you can do the administration of my plane or my boat, whatever, except if it's a trust company and it needs to be based in a certain jurisdiction, that's different.

But first of all, I think the most important question, and that's for the family themselves, is what do I want, do I want simply administration services, do I want investment management advice because if you ask administration services to a wealth manager, it's a recipe for disaster and vice versa, or do you want tax advice? So you really have to find out what you want.

6. **Paul Tramontano:** Here is some further advice on selecting a family office from a top-50 family office co-chief executive officer and founder, Paul Tramontano:

If I had a family member who was evaluating family offices, I would advise them to start with each firm's ability to ask questions. Most people know what they want from their investments and family office services, but many people have a more difficult time distilling and prioritizing their specific goals. It is our job, as a family office, to ask pertinent questions to clearly identify and work toward achieving those goals. I would also encourage potential clients to do several solid reference checks with both existing clients and professional firms, such as reputable law and accounting firms. Some examples of helpful questions for professional firms are listed here:

What has your experience been working with this family office? Are they good on the service side?

Do they provide tax information accurately and in a timely manner?

Are they helpful on the planning side, particularly estate planning?

Have your clients been pleased with the recommended asset allocation and the way in which accounts have been invested and monitored?

Has the review process been helpful to the families with whom you work?

Have they been able to build relationships with the next generations of your family clients?

The last point above is a very important aspect because you do not want a patriarch to put an advisory/investment relationship in place that everybody else in the family resents. With this in mind, it is important that a family office have touch points with the other members of the family in addition to the patriarch.

FAMILY OFFICE ONE-PAGER EVALUATION FORM

I have seen some industry resources for the ultra-affluent that include 50-question questionnaires or due diligence forms for family offices to complete. They look painful. I agree with David Thomas of Equitas, who you read about earlier in this chapter, when he said that much of the decision has to be based on trust and the type of individuals you are going to be hiring to work for you over the long-term.

It is good to be thorough, but many times a single lunch meeting can tell you more than 20 pages worth of details.

 For more resources and help in selecting a family office, please see our page dedicated to this topic:
www.FamilyOfficesGroup.com/Advisory.

CONCLUSION

Selecting a family office is an important decision for those who require the services of a family office. As you have learned from this chapter's insights, choosing the right family office for you and your family involves more than weighing the costs associated with one multi-family office versus another; the decision often comes down to factors such as how well you trust the family office team, the character of the manager and other qualities that can only be gleaned through a thorough due diligence process. Whether you are establishing a single family office or placing your trust with a multi-family office, the decision should not be taken lightly, and it should be appreciated as a long-term relationship built on trust and a mutual commitment to preserving and increasing your wealth.

If you need additional resources on selecting a family office or solution for your unique situation our team is here to help; e-mail me directly at Richard@FamilyOfficesGroup.com.

CHAPTER 5

Family Office Marketing

*Talent is cheaper than table salt. What separates the talented
individual from the successful one is a lot of hard work.*
        —Stephen King (best-selling author of more than 50 books)

Chapter Preview: This chapter provides a framework for executing a marketing or business development strategy for a multi-family
office. Most family office executives have deep expertise in taxation,
fund manager selection, or risk management, but not marketing,
sales, public relations, or business development. This chapter aims
to provide some best practices, models, and tools for those multi-
family offices looking to consistently build their client base.

This chapter came to life by accident while recording dozens of interviews
with family offices for our newsletter and this book. Many times, after
asking the questions I had planned for the interview, many of the family
offices wanted to speak off the record about how they could build their
practice, expand their client base, and in short improve their marketing and
sales efforts.

I have advised a few family offices on how they could grow their assets under management by changing their marketing, and this chapter will
share some of the models I provide them with. There are some best practices
that every family office should implement in their marketing, yet only 3 to
5 percent of all multi-family offices today are doing these things.

 See the video "Family Office Marketing," at
www.FamilyOfficesGroup.com/Video14.

The goal of this chapter is to focus in on the big pieces of a family office marketing campaign that should be in place regardless of your family office's size or geographical location.

Warning: Please do not take any action on these strategies or any others found within this book before first getting counsel from your compliance and legal counsel to make sure that you can take these actions without violating any rules or laws in your state, country, and organization.

YOUR CLIENT AVATAR

The very first thing that you need to do to begin improving your marketing is to narrow your focus. To do this you need to define your client avatar. A client avatar is a 360-degree picture of exactly who you are marketing to. To figure this out, you need to first see where the bulk of your most common clients or most profitable clients have come from. What do they have in common? Are they dentists? Surgeons? Professional sports players? Do they all own boats? Are they golfers or heavy travelers? Are they all connected to a few charity organizations in your community?

The goal here is to identify one single client avatar that you can direct all of your marketing toward. It will be easy for you or your team to say, "Our clients are all different," but that is the lazy way. If you want to improve all of your marketing, you need to complete this step. If you think about it long enough, you will find that 50 to 80 percent of your clients have many things in common and can be boiled down to a common set of traits, interests, past investments, careers, or desires and fears.

I have heard several marketers talk about creating your client avatar, but one strategy that I picked up from trainer Eben Pagan was actually naming your avatar. By providing a real name to the avatar, you further humanize your marketing and by directing all of your advertisements and marketing messages toward that imaginary person, so people will feel like you are speaking with them one on one instead of mass marketing toward them.

Some of you may now be thinking, "If I only target one type of client, I will alienate everyone else." If you are thinking that, you are mostly right: You will be alienating some other types of clients. That is planned; you don't want to be the average, gray-colored, try-to-please-all family office. You want to be the premier, most talked about family office within the very-well-defined niche space that you stake out as your own. Aim to be the Bentley or Ferrari of family offices, not the Honda.

 See the video, "What Is a Client Avatar?" at www.FamilyOfficesGroup.com/Video15.

Make sure you mark this page so you remember to create your client avatar, or, better yet, write out what it looks like now so that you can use the rest of the advice within this book to the fullest extent possible.

 If you would like to complete our Client Avatar Worksheet to help you with this exercise, you can find that online at www.FamilyOfficesGroup.com/Avatar.

 See the video, "The Engagement Factor" at www.FamilyOfficesGroup.com/Engagement.

I recently spoke at a family office summit in Singapore on family office investments, and on the way to the event rented a Ferrari so I could record a few training videos next to it. One of these videos is called the "Engagement Factor" and I recorded it to show you immediately now why having your client avatar defined is critical to getting the attention and engagement of your targeted ultra-wealthy clients.

CRYSTAL CLEAR EDGE

The second thing you need to do to improve your marketing of family office services is to come up with what I like to call your "crystal clear edge," also sometimes referred to as a Unique Selling Proposition (USP). This absolutely has to be just one sentence long, and every word should be carefully chosen and there for a reason. When your target clients hear your edge, they should, quite literally, appear physically more engaged in learning how they can gain access to your services. The goal is to come up with something that gives your firm a competitive edge that is five times greater than that of your closest competition.

Most family offices do not have a clear edge over other family offices. Sure, their business model gives them an edge over commission-hungry advisors or those who are fee-based yet only help manage the investment portfolios, but that is not enough if you want to become a top multi-family office operation. You must identify your top five local competitors and top five national competitors and figure out why they have been able to attract clients. Which of their best practices can you emulate? What seems to be their edge?

Now that you have done this research, rethink what exactly your edge really is. It cannot be a copy of what someone else is claiming; it has to be based on the skills, insights, and abilities of your team, and it must be powerful and meaningful to your targeted client base.

For example, your unique edge could be that clients get access to a fleet of local luxury cars, yachts, and private jets without having to worry about the pains of ownership such as insurance, maintenance, and secure storage. This makes them feel important without sucking away their valuable time and attention. If nobody else in your city offers this, then in your market that is a crystal clear advantage.

Perhaps your clients are typically first-generation wealth creators and need a very institutional, diversified approach to managing their assets. Your competitive edge could include recruiting a top-10, most-well-known expert, consultant, or professor who is an industry icon and combine that with over-staffing with institutional consultant-quality fund manager selection experts. Overinvest in the area that your clients genuinely need and care about, in this case diversification of their invested assets. The trick is to overinvest in an area that matters to the client, as you will never have enough resources to be the best of the best in every area of the business.

 See the video "What Is a Crystal Clear Edge?"at www.FamilyOfficesGroup.com/Video16.

Note: If you are having trouble coming up with your crystal clear edge, think back over the history of the firm, your best clients, or why the family office was launched in the first place. Those foundational reasons for the existence or success of your family offices may provide some clues.

Now write out your crystal clear edge:

_____

_____

_____

BRIAN TRACY INTERVIEW EXCERPT ON CAPITAL RAISING

 Brian Tracy is one of the most well-recognized sales experts and speakers of all time; he has written more than 70 books, spoken to 5 million people in more than 50 countries, and helped thousands of groups raise more capital and make more sales over his long career. I had the honor of recently being on the *Brian Tracy Show* and I also interviewed Brian Tracy. In the interview, we covered how his experience, knowledge, and sales best practices could be applied to capital raising and family office marketing, and I want to share this full audio interview with you. We don't have room in this book to publish the 20-page transcript, but you can get it through this page on our web site: www.FamilyOfficesGroup .com/Audio3.

FIGURE 5.1   Capital Raising Trifecta

CAPITAL RAISING TRIFECTA

In my experience, to really raise a lot of capital you have to combine the power of proactive selling with writing and public speaking or video content. Yes, you can raise capital by only having a proactive sales professional, but why not use all of the tools if they are available? Why make the process harder than it needs to be?

I call this combination of writing, speaking/video, and proactive selling *The Capital Raising Trifecta*. It is diagrammed in Figure 5.1.

Oftentimes, I present this concept at a full-day training workshop or a conference and I can see by the look on people's faces that this idea alone is not very exciting to think about. In short, it looks like hard work and something that is not very fun to do. I think that out of all the pieces of capital raising advice I provide, the Capital Raising Trifecta may be the most powerful concept that almost everyone in this industry ignores. That is why I started the chapter with this quote by Stephen King: "Talent is cheaper than salt. What separates the talented individual from the successful one is a lot of hard work."

 See the video "Capital Raising Trifecta," at www.FamilyOfficesGroup.com/Video17.

I want to explain how the Trifecta works in detail so that you see the full value of completing this strategy, and to do so I need to explain in this next section the Capital Raising Funnel that will naturally be created if you pursue the Capital Raising Trifecta Strategy.

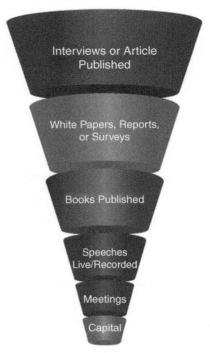

FIGURE 5.2   The Capital Raising
Funnel

CAPITAL RAISING FUNNEL

One tool that I have developed to help explain while adding value first is called the Capital Raising Funnel and is shown in Figure 5.2. The idea is that the more potential clients are exposed to your expertise and knowledge, the more likely it is that some of them will filter up through the funnel to the next level and eventually hire your firm.

I learned this strategy from my mentor, Jeffrey Gitomer. Jeffrey was a relatively average salesman until he started sharing his sales knowledge in a local newspaper. His articles there got syndicated to a couple of other local papers, and then a few more and now his weekly sales article appears in more than 150 newspapers around the world. He went from making $50,000 a year to earning millions per year, and most importantly he moved from being an unknown cold caller to having people call his office every single day wanting to hire him. He now turns away more business every day than he used to get in a month from cold calling.

Why? Because the marketplace views him as a top expert on sales, and they want to work with the expert who has added value to them through his articles. Jeffrey explains this as his number one "secret" to success that nobody will follow because it takes so much hard work. I was determined to prove the "nobody will follow" part, so in college I wrote my first book, *Rainmaker*. I learned a lot from that experience, and I saw how it raised the eyebrows of just about everyone I showed it to. Since then, I have been writing, on average, at least one book a year on different topics related to alternative investments, hedge funds, family offices, sales, and marketing. This hard work is what has led to my web sites and articles being viewed 10 million times and more than 200,000 professionals joining my family office and alternative investment associations. It is not because I am a nice guy (well, that may be part of it); it is because I try to give away consulting-quality advice that others charge $300 an hour for. I give it away at conferences, in YouTube videos, through books, and daily on my blog to grow relationships in the investment industry.

That story illustrates the power of giving value first. The funnel shown in Figure 5.2 provides you with a model to constructing a structure around that giving, so that it will serve you well over many years.

Level 1—Interviews or Articles Published

Start by looking at the wide end of the funnel. This part is the widest because it represents the high number of individuals consuming the material. In this case, marketing the services of a multi-family office, your articles, blog posts, and interviews with the media may be read by more than 100,000 people a year. Many of these people will read the content and forget you exist. Others will be college students or job seekers, and a small percentage of them will be potential clients with needs that you can meet. A few of those who read these articles will contact you to learn more about your family office services.

Level 2—White Papers, Reports, or Surveys

The next level up is the writing of white papers, reports, or surveys that are very niche industry specific. A slightly higher percentage of this smaller group of prospects will contact you about hiring your family office, but again most people who do contact you will never work with you. A few people who read your articles though will look for more work by you, and they may find—or you may lead—them to these more sophisticated reports or white papers. Some people may search for white papers and not want to waste their time with reading any articles that they may see as lower quality information.

Level 3—Books Published

After reading some of your articles or white papers or possibly after just searching on Google for a book on your niche skill or focus, someone may buy a book you have written. Again, since we are higher up in the funnel, this is a more trusted form of communication; it positions you as an author, a top expert, an achiever, and a leader. In a meeting, holding up a book you have written to address a top challenge, need, or client fear is a proven method to help gain clients. Writing a genuinely valuable book on a subject, in a way positions you as an automatic expert who seeks to add value to others first. In other words, if you put an honest effort into researching an area, drawing from your experience, interviewing others, and then writing the best book you can on a niche topic you will become an expert on that niche topic.

Level 4—Speeches (Live or Recorded)

I believe speaking at a conference is more valuable than getting a $10,000 booth. If you give a great speech, you can camp out at a high top table and relax with a cup of coffee as a stream of people approach you with questions or ideas on working together. This is how business gets done more often, I believe, than with a corporate salesy–feeling booth, though I'm sure that using both in tandem would not hurt.

Once you have written a book, you will probably be asked to speak at an industry conference; this is almost guaranteed if, along with the book, you have a few articles and white papers out in the industry. The conference organizers live on Google and hunt around for new speakers constantly, so it is relatively easy to get booked for many conferences as long as you don't try to charge a speaking fee. In fact, for your first few years of speaking, don't expect a speaking fee or your expenses to be paid; you are doing this to attract clients, not start a side business. Consider this a marketing expense.

A few tips about speaking: Have a one- to four-page brochure that includes your story, bio, publications, and topics that you can speak on; this will help you get booked more often. Make a video of every speech you ever give to show to potential clients who could not come to a particular conference. Lots of business gets done via conferences and speaking, and a high percentage of people who hear you speak will want to explore ways of working together. If you think about it, if everything else below Level 4 in the Capital Raising Funnel opens the door to Level 4 success because of your now expanded knowledge, content, and exposure in the industry to conference organizers who book speakers, that time spent would be well worth it. If you need public speaking resources please contact us and we can point you in the right direction.

Level 5—Face-to-Face Meetings

This is the part of the Capital Raising Funnel that is one to one. This is where you follow up with someone 2 to 14 times until they convert into a client. Again, not all of those you meet with one to one will convert into placing their capital with your family office, but the percentage is relatively high, and certainly much higher than all of the levels below this point.

Your capital raising progress can get worse, stay the same, or improve. This Capital Raising Funnel can make the difference in improving your ability to gather many new clients or few clients. The Capital Raising Funnel works if you work the Capital Raising Funnel. If you take lots of shortcuts, if you don't create genuinely valuable content, or you try to hard-sell potential clients in your content, you will waste your time and ruin the good karma intentions of this process. The more you give away, the more you will get in return. I know this because my entire business is based on it, it is not a theory or an idea, it is a proven process that has brought in millions of dollars in revenue for business and capital raised for clients.

Level 6—Capital

This final stage is where you actually land the client, bring them into your firm, and grow your assets under management (AUM) as a firm. The more support structures, processes, knowledge assets, and potential client pathways you create underneath this point in the funnel, the more warm leads will come to your door step every single day. This is not theory, or a nice-sounding idea; I know this works because my entire business is based on this model. For example, this book you are reading right now is part of my 50-point resource platform to add value to family offices so that I can further grow my knowledge and relationships with them by delivering value first.

 See the video "Capital Raising Funnel,"at www.FamilyOfficesGroup.com/Video18.

Implementation Suggestion

It is recommended that you start building your funnel from the ground up. Start with articles, interviews, and blog posts. After that, combine your best articles into two to five short reports and white papers. From there, move up the funnel to a book, speeches, and video content. This way, you always have a library of past produced content to draw from to produce more than enough ideas to write an excellent book or give a great speech.

 See the video "Traits & Habits of Highly Successful Family Office Marketers," at www.FamilyOfficesGroup.com/Marketers.

STORYTELLING

Storytelling is the most important communication skill that a family office business development professional can learn. If you master storytelling, others will listen to you more closely and take your advice more often. Storytelling allows you to build yourself up as an authority in the mind of the listener without sounding like you are a used-car salesman or someone who is trying to hard-sell their way through a conversation using force to make a sale. In the multi-family office industry, you can use storytelling to:

- Explain the crystal-clear advantage your firm has that is based on the story of how your family office was formed.
- Easily come up with an hour of speaking content for a conference.
- Discuss with a client your experience in solving problems of wealthy families.

Most of us already know how important storytelling is, yet I don't know a single person who has ever gone to a conference or training workshop on storytelling, or even read a book on how to tell stories more effectively. That is to your advantage if you take the time to study the art of storytelling.

The best strategy I have found for telling stories is a format called the Hero's Journey. This form of storytelling is popular in Hollywood as well as just about every book of fiction ever written. If you ever are unsure how to structure a story, just fall back on the Hero's Journey structure. In fact, right now I'm writing this chapter while sitting in a coffee shop in Zurich and I was asked by a reporter to write out the story of how I learned how to raise capital. I used the Hero's Journey format to do so. Before I show an example of this approach, here is how it works:

Step 1: You are introduced to a character who is roughly average, has no special abilities or powers, and is an overall normal person. Early in the story, this person is called upon, asked to do something or asked to take on some sort of a challenge. The person ignores the request or dismisses it, however.

Step 2: Something happens that pulls the character into the story. This could a lawsuit, economic recession, being fired from a job, or even a family member in trouble. The character now has to face a problem, go on a quest, or face a significant challenge, perhaps the one they previously ignored.

Step 3: The challenge turns out to be harder than imagined, and the challenge grows ever harder. An evil character is introduced, if he hasn't already been, and the villain personifies the difficult challenge. The villain becomes more and more evil, building up pressure for some sort of resolution.

Step 4: The hero battles and battles and almost loses, but finally overcomes the villain and emerges victorious.

There are different ways to explain the Hero's Journey, but this is the one that has always worked for me, and it is simple enough to understand and use immediately to help you build your multi-family office practice.

Here is an example story of how I got started in capital raising and learned how to attract new clients to me consistently over time:

I was born in Chicago but grew up in Portland, Oregon, always trying to start businesses. Before graduating from high school, I had printed up seven different business cards for ventures I had tried to launch, including selling long-distance phone service to the parents of my school friends and a car-magnet advertising business. A few produced revenue, but in the end they all failed. I then worked for years as an intern for my father's capital raising business, which raised well over $1 billion for their clients. I learned about the importance of listening, the importance of the 80/20 rule while raising capital, the six phases of soliciting capital, how to interview prospects, what a pitch book was, and how to structure a capital raising campaign.

At Oregon State University I studied business and earned a bachelor's degree while working for my father's capital raising business and interning for a few hedge funds in Europe and the United States. During my MBA program, I studied marketing and sales closely. I ended up reading every book ever written by Jeffrey Gitomer, a top global speaker and trainer on sales. He insists that his secret to success was adding value to others first and providing genuine value through writing articles and books on your subject.

I followed his advice and wrote my first book during my MBA program on marketing and capital raising. After completing my MBA, I started thinking long and hard about what I could raise capital for or sell where my income would not be limited by my age or number of years of experience. Although I almost went to work in commercial real estate instead, capital raising for hedge fund managers kept on coming up in conversations and research and I decided to get into the space again.

I started lining up independent contracts to raise capital for alternative investment managers, but I was having a hard time actually raising the capital. I was new to the process, and I didn't

*really know what I was doing yet. At the same time, I started study-
ing influence and the psychology of persuasive communication and
I found that I qualified to take a series of master's-level courses in
psychology at Harvard.*

*Once in Boston, I started working for a successful third-party
marketer, cutting my teeth at his firm and learning his best practices
from 20 years of capital raising experience. The work was brutal; my
first job was to call every single institutional investment consulting
firm in the United States and pitch our fund managers. I was later
taught to cold call 30 to 60 potential investor firms a day, explain the
story of the fund, position it, and follow up enough times to raise
the capital. I started by using Excel spreadsheets and then moved
to using a customer relationship management (CRM) system called
Salesforce.com.*

*For 13 months, I was charging a client $10,000/month, and I
had not raised any capital yet, even though I was making progress.
As you can imagine, the pressure from the client kept building. I
started reading two hours a day about sales and marketing with a
big focus on Jeffrey Gitomer and Brian Tracy.*

*Finally, something clicked—I needed to be a source of value to
these clients, I needed to be someone they respected, and I needed
to use sales and marketing best practices to raise more capital. Unfortunately, my boss at the third-party marketing firm didn't follow
my line of thinking about how I wanted to add value first to clients.*

*Eventually, I did it my way anyway and I started raising
$200,000 to $400,000 a week and eventually averaged $2 million to
$4 million a week. I learned a lot about cold calling, using CRM sys-
tems, and how to raise capital from that position, but in the end my
approach clashed with the owner's more "old school" cold-calling
only approach to sales and it was time I left.*

*I quit my job, got out of directly raising capital, and with noth-
ing to live on financially I tried to grow my hedge fund and family office web site resources and association at www.HedgeFundBlogger
.com and www.FamilyOfficesGroup.com. As those two web sites
became the most-visited web sites in both the hedge fund and family
office spaces, I launched associated networking associations for
each called the Hedge Fund Group (www.HedgeFundGroup.org)
and Family Offices Group (www.FamilyOfficesGroup.com). I
wrote a free-to-download e-book on hedge funds, and after
100,000 downloads it became the most popular book ever written
on hedge funds. This led to a book deal with Wiley & Sons,
and it helped my alternative investment and family office related
associations grow beyond 200,000 total members.*

It turns out that when you write an article every day on hedge funds and/or family offices, you become very knowledgeable very quickly and you get asked to speak around the world at conferences and events. I have now spoken and recorded video content around the world in 20-plus countries and dozens of cities such as Tokyo, Moscow, Singapore, Nice, Chicago, Sao Paulo, Boston, Monaco, and Brussels at the European Business Summit. These speaking opportunities have led to further knowledge on how the family office industry operates globally as well as some unexpected experiences including sharing the stage with two prime ministers of European Union countries, participating in wedding ceremonies, and dinner parties with two ruling princes of European royal families.

While I was speaking at and acting as the opening-day chairman at the largest and oldest hedge fund and family office conference, GAIM International in Monaco, multiple family offices and hedge fund managers approached me and suggested that I should raise capital for them. Their collective urging convinced me on the spot that it was time to get back to raising capital full-time again, and Richard Wilson Capital Partners was born.

Now at Richard Wilson Capital Partners, LLC, I provide single and multi-family offices with access to my stable of best-of-breed fund managers of institutional quality. I only represent high-quality $100 million to $300 million-plus fund managers and $1 billion-plus fund platforms that pass our proprietary Family Office Filter. I also only focus on serving family offices and ultra-wealthy investors and paying very close attention to their needs and preferences alone through the Family Offices Group association web site, and my daily contact with family office executives. By being laser-focused on this area, I can spend time thinking about their needs in fund manager selection every day.

That story may be a bit on the long side, but I wanted to share the full story with you, exactly as I would tell it if we sat down and had a cup of coffee together. This is the story I tell clients. Review this story and compare that to me trying to convince you that you should trust me and work with me because I have written articles for *Forbes*, published a book through Wiley on hedge funds, and I have spoken at the largest and most popular alternative investment and family office conferences in the world. Just writing that last sentence makes me cringe a little because it feels so salesy and attention seeking.

Storytelling lets you "brag" about more points while talking about it in a natural way that gets across to the other person in an under-the-radar type way, which is effective and is more likely to lead to a fruitful long-term relationship. For example, my story sounds genuine because, like most people, I had to overcome setbacks and challenges to achieve some level of success.

 See the video "Hero's Journey Video on Storytelling," at www.FamilyOfficesGroup.com/Video19.

Now, practice writing out the story of how your family office was formed, how you got into the family office space, or how you went above and beyond and solved a common critical problem that wealthy families face. I'm sure you've experienced hardships and challenges, so share your story of overcoming those setbacks with your potential and current clients.

PERSUASIVE WRITING (COPYWRITING)

Persuasive writing in the marketing field is called copywriting. Though you may have heard the term before, this type of copywriting has nothing to do with legal protection. Rather, it is the process of effectively communicating a message and in turn encouraging your readers to take action after reading. Copywriting is one of the highest-paying areas within marketing simply because it is so effective.

Copywriting strategies and tactics can be used to write more effective e-mails, monthly newsletters, book description, personal bios, web site materials, pitch books, speeches, and annual client letters. Literally everything you write can be optimized with copywriting best practices. If, when writing, you keep in mind the client avatar we created earlier in this chapter, everything you do in copywriting will become twice as powerful.

There is a story that explains the value of copywriting that I first heard from trainer Joe Polish, who has been in the industry for decades. Look at a $1 bill and a $100 bill; look at their size, the colors of ink, the paper they are printed on; look at the level of detail on each, and feel the texture of it. You will find that the only difference really between the $1 bill and $100 bill is the message on the paper. In other words, the difference that makes the $100 bill worth 100 times more than the $1 bill is that the $100 bill communicates the $100 value through symbols, patterns of ink, letters, and words.

The same goes for your marketing materials. Your web site, your folder of materials, your one-page description of your family office services is probably printed on the same extra-heavy paper stock that your competitors use. What determines whether your marketing materials are worth $500 million in assets or $20 million in assets is the message on the paper. The quality of your materials is important; it needs to match or beat others in the market-place, but that is just a qualifier.

The best part about copywriting is that it pays dividends because al-most nobody studies it. I have an MBA in marketing and while storytelling may have come up once during my degree studies, copywriting came up ex-actly zero times. Most marketing books don't speak of copywriting, either, as most people have never seriously studied it. By mastering the basics of copywriting you can often increase response rates by 50 to 100 percent in your e-mails, voice mails, and mailed materials. Storytelling is a good exam-ple of a copywriting best practice, but below are some other strategies that you can use to increase the engagement of your potential clients and get them to frequently take action toward becoming a client of your family office.

Copywriting Tactic #1—*Headlines*

Writing a great headline is probably the most powerful copywriting technique you could learn about and employ right now. Headlines are the big font titles of articles, sales messages, or web site pages. One great example of using headlines in family office marketing is the writing of e-mail subject lines. Almost nobody in the family office industry optimizes their e-mails from a copywriting perspective so that they are read more often. Write your headline so that you target a top-3 need, fear, or desire of your prospect. This needs to be done in a way that piques their curiosity, sounds controversial, or comes across as being very urgent and important. This is impossible to do unless you know exactly who your client avatar is. A study by Marketing Sherpa in 2006 showed that people are 35 percent more likely to open e-mails that have their first name in the subject line of the e-mail rather than not. That one simple best practice of optimizing your e-mail subject lines and considering using someone's first name could potentially result in landing an extra client every year. If you want to see some examples of copywriting optimized e-mail message subject lines that we use in our business, please type your first name and e-mail address into the form at www.FamilyOfficeReport.com.

Copywriting Tactic #2—*The Hook*

One fundamental component of a sales letter or page that has been optimized by copywriting is called *the hook*. The hook is the first part of the message after the headline or e-mail subject line; it is the second sentence someone reads once they land on your web site or open your sales page. The mission of the headline is to get someone to open your e-mail or read the next part of the message. The mission of the hook is to get the person engaged enough to keep reading below and consume the next part of your piece of communication, be it an e-mail, book description, or bio. While writing your hook, you want to confirm that they are in the right place by readdressing what the headline promises and starting to deliver on that promise in some way. If you are too formal or boring in doing this, you will lose some readers right from the start. Always write in the most concise and engaging manner possible.

Copywriting Tactic #3—*The Call to Action*

One piece of communication that many marketers miss is the *call to action* part of a message. This is where you share with the reader exactly what you would like them to do. If you would like them to reach out to you, instruct them to write you an e-mail or call you immediately to discuss their situation. If you want them to download your white paper, tell them exactly where to go and how to access that white paper immediately. Don't leave anything up to chance and while much of marketing should be implied, your call to action needs to be overly explicit so nobody is left wondering what to do next. This is the grease that helps them move up the Capital Raising Funnel faster, which will lead to more trust and more new clients for you in a shorter amount of time.

Copywriting Tactic #4—Personalization

 See the video "Copyright Video,"at www.FamilyOfficesGroup.com/Copywriting.

The last copywriting tip is to make sure that you use your real signature, your picture, and your two- to three-sentence professional bio with every communication. To have a "real signature," sign a piece of paper and scan that into the computer, as opposed to using some italic font that is supposed to look like a signature. Use a professionally taken headshot picture of you smiling, and make sure your bio points out your publications, years of experience, and unique crystal-clear advantage that is meaningful to your targeted client avatar. This will make you appear professional, well put together, and detail oriented. Those are all qualifying details that people look for in selecting and hiring a family office to manage their wealth. An example of this is this book's Appendix, where I encourage people to contact me with their questions, join our newsletter, and so forth.

BRIAN HUGHES INTERVIEW ON FAMILY OFFICE BUSINESS DEVELOPMENT

We conducted an interview with Brian Hughes, an expert on family office marketing and business development. Brian is the managing director for

Strategic Relationships at the Threshold Group, a top 50 multi-family office based in Gig Harbor, Washington, in the United States.

Richard Wilson: Can you start out by sharing what your role is at the Threshold Group?

Brian Hughes: Sure. So my role is primarily focused on finding and working with multi-generational families and their private foundations and customizing our own solutions, whether it's investment advisory or family office solutions for those families or foundations. I also provide a network of advisors in all sorts of disciplines to those families and foundations as well.

Richard Wilson: Okay. And earlier we were speaking about your average client and I think you mentioned that it was a little bit north of a $100 million, around $125 million in investable assets. So oftentimes you are working with families that have around maybe $200 million in total net worth. Is that correct?

Brian Hughes: That's correct. Our average client is about $125 million of investable and the majority have a net worth in excess of $200 million.

Richard Wilson: For family offices that are either just getting started or really just haven't seen the type of momentum that you guys have found in the marketplace, what do you think two or three things are that really determine the survival and success of a multi-family office operation?

Brian Hughes: Well, I think based on my experience, it's really A, knowing what you are good at and being able to provide those services, whether it's pure investment advisory, a combination of investment advisory and family office services or just pure family office services. It's also important to know what you are good at, have the scale and efficiencies within the organization to deliver those services, and then do it in a way that's profitable for the firm. So that's kind of number one and that's much easier said than done. Certainly one of the biggest challenges in our industry is just making sure that you are sticking to your knitting and not trying to do things that you may have done as a one-off for your clients.

I think the second, B, is just finding, securing, and keeping talent. Our industry has been really challenged for the last four or five years with finding the type of talent that really can serve the ultra-high-net-worth family, the multi-generational family, and the family that has issues beyond investments. Those could include issues around governance and education; issues around family dynamics, and the complexity around solutions for those types of families. So, finding the talent that really understands all that and can communicate it, build confidence, and build trust with clients is a big challenge.

Until our office opened in Philadelphia, we were kind of geographically hampered by having our main office in Gig Harbor, Washington, which, although a beautiful place, is hard to recruit to. We kind of suffer from that challenge; though not all do, most of our competitors also suffer this challenge in finding the right talent and then keeping that talent. Those are the big things.

Richard Wilson: Sure, that is something I heard a few times during these interviews. Specifically, one of the family offices we interviewed in Australia last week was talking about how the number one bottleneck in their business is finding the right people, and that slows down their growth.

One program we now offer is our family office employee training platform, called the Qualified Family Office Professional (QFOP) program. From your perspective though, does the industry even need more training opportunities in general?

Brian Hughes: Yeah, I wish I knew the answer to that question. Sometimes the technical skills aren't really the issue, it's the personality skills, including being able to communicate, understand, explain, and listen. A friend of mine calls it kind of a Renaissance man or woman, one that has a sense of families and the issues that they are facing and can apply the technical skills to that dynamic. That's a hard person to find. There are not a lot of people out there who know trusts backwards and forwards and understand all sorts of investment structures and solutions in the areas of investments, planning, philanthropy, and tax. Most professionals have a really hard time explaining how they work in a way that our clients need to understand.

Richard Wilson: What advice do you have for those ultra-wealthy looking to hire a multi-family office? How can they avoid just signing up with the first one that sounds "great"?

Brian Hughes: I think it's a great question and it's something that I take a lot of pride in, using a process that I think works. The first thing I do with families that I meet with is to first ask them, "What's your criteria for selecting a multi-family office or a wealth manager?" Most don't have a criteria; most end up I think putting the cart before the horse. They go out and they meet with three, four, five family offices and they end up falling in love with two or three of them and then can't decide which one's a better solution. In fact, what they have done is no different than going and shopping for a car. If you just decide well, we need to go buy a car and then you visit four or five auto dealerships and you find two or three cars that you really like, you end up buying a car that you emotionally fall in love with, but a year later you figure it has none of the features and benefits that you were looking for in a car, it just was the person selling you what you thought you needed at the time.

So the right approach is to sit down and, as a family and as decision makers, really understand what your criteria are. If you don't know what your criteria are, there is a simple list of questions you can ask yourself about what's important, what do you need, what's not working well, what's working well, what are the must-haves in this relationship, what are the nice-to-haves and what are the things that you don't really need. Then, prioritize that list of criteria.

If you feel competent in your ability to go out and interview and identify those firms who could best meet that list of criteria, then do it yourself. Actually, if a family comes to me and says, "We would like to make you part of our interview process," and they haven't built their criteria, I would tell them to stop and to find a consultant that can help them refine their criteria and further prioritize it. Then, they can identify the firms that they know, based on their net worth, that are likely to be the best fit. From there, evaluate them on that basis and then get to the relationship piece. You've got to like the family, you've got to like the firm that you are going to work with and for us it's all about fit.

We built a process at the very beginning when we started our firm as a commercial family office in 2004.

We built something called a Client Selectivity Overlay, and it's basically 16 questions that we ask about the family that's looking to engage with us, and 15 of those 16 questions are qualitative, not quantitative. We ask the questions, "Is this a family that takes advice? Is this a family that works with existing advisors who are collaborative? Do they have a team of advisors? Are they looking for a long-term relationship? Are there any known disputes within family members?" So we are asking a lot of questions about what would be an ideal fit for us, and then we share that with the family so that they can see what we are evaluating because for them, they need to go through the same evaluation process and if we are not doing that then we are doing a disservice to them. We can sit here and sell Russell, the Russell family, and the relationship with Russell Investments and all of our features, if you will, but they won't understand the benefits unless they really know what it is that they are looking for. Frankly a lot of families don't know what they are looking for so we think that we can be helpful.

Richard Wilson: When you work with $100 million and $200 million potential clients, do you have to sell the multi-family office concept against them setting up their own single family office operation? Is that a common challenge?

Brian Hughes: Certainly; when you get north of $250 or $300 million, you can make an argument for building your own family office and building your own infrastructure. Even at that amount of wealth, though, it's pretty hard to leverage real talent and keep that talent and have the assistance and processes in place to mitigate all the risks or most of the risks. So that's why families, even at that level, decide to go to a firm that's built in those resources. That can overcome the negative aspect of privacy where there is a perception of giving up some privacy because you are joining a commercial firm.

There is no evidence out there that if you build your own investment team within a single family office you are going to gain any sort of incremental added alpha in your performance. The reason I say that is because access to products and access to best of class managers is fairly available to most families with at least $25 or $30 million. Where it really makes a difference obviously in private equity where the top 25 percent, the top-quartile managers, are the ones that really have real returns and the rest of them are kind of mediocre. So if you are not in that quartile, then you are not really getting access to good, solid private equity. The rest of them have become more commoditized.

What really makes a difference is tax planning, coordination of assets, location of assets, and then understanding the issues that could make greater impact on the investment returns than the investment products themselves. What I mean by that is premature death, divorce, family disputes—those are the type of things that actually end up having a greater impact on a family's wealth than any sort of incremental investment return. Those are the conversations that we have with families.

Does that mean that one family is going to choose to do a multi-family office as opposed to not? Again, I just go back to what it is that you are really looking for, what are you looking for this family office to do for you? Then, if that ends up being the best solution because you want to keep them all together and you want to get it coordinated, you want the best-of-class expertise in all these different disciplines, maybe a multi-family office is the best solution. If you are looking for an outsourced chief investment officer because you have a family office that can do everything else, an investment consultant is probably the best solution, not the multi-family office. Richard, I can't say that 50 percent of the prospective families I talk to are looking for multi-family office or something else.

Richard Wilson: When you are meeting with ultra-high-net-worth families, you just explained many of the most important things that should be considered, but out of 50 calls or 100 calls you may receive from interested families who might want to have Threshold manage their wealth, what is the burning desire or fear that's driving those phone calls to you? Is it a fear of losing their money, capital preservation, fear of taxation that they just weren't aware of; or is it something else, like multi-generational concerns that really drive the need?

Brian Hughes: Great question. My experience is it's something other than the investment piece. I don't see a good number of families leaving their investment advisor because of investment performance. It was either a transition and maybe the moving of wealth from one generation to the next, there is a succession issue within the family office that they are trying to face, they just had an event and they have either outgrown their existing advisor or their existing advisor hasn't demonstrated that they can now step up to the plate and be more of a holistic wealth manager.

Maybe they are with a stockbroker or maybe they are with a product firm or maybe they are with a bank that has had a lot of turnover or something like that. Those tend to be the reasons why we get phone calls; families are unhappy because of turnover or transition if they are facing some transition issues that are forcing them to look at a totally different kind of solution. That seems to be what's creating the demand for families to move.

I don't see a lot of families moving because their investment return is not what they wanted them to be, so therefore they are going to go and start looking at another firm to have better investment returns. It needs to be part of their criteria; you need to be able to demonstrate that you can add value on that side and you have a sound sophisticated process and you can get access to best-of-class managers and all that, and then you can communicate that. You build confidence that becomes part of the criteria, but it's not really a top reason for families to move that I have seen.

Richard Wilson: Okay. So how is your organization attracting more ultra-wealthy clients to your platform right now?

Brian Hughes: Well, coming from somebody who is thinking about business development every hour it feels like, our process is kind of built on the belief that families have a real trust issue with advisors and you have to be able to overcome that trust issue. There are only a few ways to overcome that trust issue. One way is to get referred by a client; referral is a powerful way to earn trust. That can come from another family or a trusted advisor, be it an attorney or a family business consultant.

Rather than do a more traditional approach of going out and calling trust and estate lawyers and family business consultants, we spend a lot of time developing those relationships by introducing them to our existing clients, getting a real understanding of how they work and what their strengths are. Then we can sit down with the types of families, like our own client families, who would be a potentially good fit for us. In that way they already have a relationship with us and worked with some of our clients and they really know and understand who we are.

That's advanced since we do a lot of programs and a lot of events. They are all educational; none of them are commercials for Threshold. We bring in subject-matter experts in areas like investing, bringing on the next generation in your family foundation, behavioral finance, a number of different areas where we will invite those advisors (intermediaries, if you will) and then I ask them to invite their clients. We have had a lot of success getting in front of the types of families and private foundations who could potentially be a good fit for us and us for them. So it's a strategy that seems to work. Client referrals are pretty tough in our space, too, because frankly a lot of them are extremely private and they don't want to talk about money. You have to handle them a certain way and use an approach that really ensures that we are only talking to those client families who want to help us grow, and that are willing to go out there and talk about the work and the value that we provide for them. That's the way we do it, and we know those families who have no interest in doing that, and we never ask them.

Richard Wilson: Do you have a single best practice or costly mistake that you have seen in the family office industry that you could leave us with here in this interview?

Brian Hughes: I think that the best practice and the costly mistake are one and the same; it's taking the time on a regular basis to sit down with your existing clients and to ask them what's working well, what's not working well, where can we improve, where do you want to see us do better, what are our strengths, and what are the areas that we need to improve on?

It's really just surveying your clients and understanding what's working for them and understanding the value in asking that question. So, what does Threshold do for you; how has Threshold's assistance in solving your problems helped you as a family to get to where you are?

You need to be asking those questions. Doing a client survey is, to me, a best practice that firms just don't take the time to do. You learn so much; you can learn exactly what they are saying about what you need to change and what you can do better.

It also gives you a sense of which clients are potentially at risk. During this process, you can ask questions about referrals and if they would be willing to make referrals and introductions. It's a great way to get real feedback about the work you are doing.

Richard Wilson: Yeah that's interesting. So you basically meet in a room with maybe 12 to 15 people and just kind of openly discuss what's going on and what's working and what needs to be worked on; is that how it would work?

Brian Hughes: It's actually more formal than that. We have an outside facilitator who will sit down with 8 to 10 existing clients from different families and different geographies that have some very different, specific services than others that they are getting from us. In general, our services are all the same for the client. They come from a multigenerational family and they have a certain amount of wealth. They may be from different generations within that family and we start to talk to them about the type of services that they are getting and the areas that need to improve. We even have some workshops and work together on new ideas to create new solutions and determine whether we should get rid of some services we offer now, or how we price our services so we can have great feedback. They have a vested interest in our success.

Richard Wilson: I think that's an excellent piece to end on there; it's a great piece of advice. Thanks so much for all your time.

Brian Hughes: Great. Thanks, Richard. Let me know if I can help any other way.

CONCLUSION

The unique needs and increasingly competitive environment in the family office industry is demanding more institutional marketing processes and models. As the competition intensifies, those who can combine high-pedigree teams and comprehensive platforms with consistent marketing execution will rise to the top in terms of client retention and acquisition. Some of the tools you can employ in growing the business of a family office include the *Capital Raising Trifecta,* the *Capital Raising Funnel,* storytelling, copywriting tactics, referral networks, and client feedback processes that we discussed in this chapter. I hope you have found it insightful and helpful in growing your own family office business. As always, you can find more information on this subject at by visiting www.FamilyOfficeMarketing.com or www.FamilyOfficesGroup.com.

Family Office
Veteran Interviews

RES NON VERBA

wilson

CHAPTER 6

Single Family Office Interviews

If people knew how hard I had to work to gain my mastery,
it wouldn't seem wonderful at all.
  —Michelangelo (Renaissance sculptor, painter, and inventor)

Chapter Preview: In this chapter, we provide the full transcripts from interviews that we conducted with single family offices. The goal of providing you with the raw transcripts of these interviews is to show you several perspectives on how the industry is operating, investing, and evolving without being filtered or synthesized with my own experience in the industry. Through these interviews you can learn about single family office management and capital deployment best practices directly from the executives who run these secretive organizations.

T he single family offices we interviewed ranged from $50 million to several running over $1 billion in assets under management. We were fortunate to interview a few of the largest single family offices that manage the wealth of some of the most well-known and wealthy entrepreneurs in the United States, Canada, Europe, Latin America, the Middle East, and Australia.

We will begin the series of interviews with Michael Connor. He built a career working with $1 billion single family offices and currently works for the Consolidated Investment Group, which manages over $1 billion in assets. Michael provides some advice and insights on cash management, portfolio construction, and how fund managers are selected at his family office. Next, we will share our interview with Elizabeth Hammack of CM Capital Corporation, located in San Francisco. CM Capital Corporation has deep roots in commercial real estate and manages more than $1 billion in assets.

The third interview in this chapter is with Frank Casey, who has 37 years of experience. You may recognize him as being part of the team that blew the whistle on convicted fraudster Bernie Madoff. Next, we interviewed John Grzymala, who has 20 years of experience as a single family office chief financial officer in New York City. We also interviewed Matthew Andrade from Canada, who runs a very niche, focused single family office with an emphasis on commodities. We finally wrap up this chapter with our interview with Angelo Robles, who runs an association of single family offices and works with them daily.

FAMILY OFFICE INTERVIEW WITH MICHAEL CONNOR OF CONSOLIDATED INVESTMENT GROUP

Our first interview is with Michael Connor, who helps run a $1 billion single family office based in Denver, Colorado called Consolidated Investment Group. Michael's background includes more than seven years of experience running another large single family office in the Pacific Northwest. I was honored to conduct this interview with someone who has run multiple single family offices through a wide variety of economic environments. The interview starts with Michael sharing a bit more about his background.

Richard Wilson: Can you share a little bit about where family offices allocate their capital?

Michael Connor: I'd be happy to share the high-level capital allocation of the larger family office I was previously associated with. A large portion of that individual's wealth was still concentrated in the publicly traded stock of the company he co-founded, which was approximately 18 percent. There was also a high level of cash, 18 percent. We held a significant amount of cash due to the illiquid nature of the investments we made. Most of those investments were made directly, were more illiquid and some had significant funding requirements as the businesses grew over time. Nine percent of the assets were in sports-related businesses, 12 percent in real estate assets, 20 percent in private equity, and 9 percent was managed by outside managers. There was also a significant art exposure in the portfolio, approximately 6 percent of total assets. The remaining 8 percent was in personal assets, like residences, aircraft, yachts and other unique assets that were of interest to the Principal.

The unique aspect of this family office was that all of the assets mentioned, other than the 9 percent that was managed by outside managers, were managed in-house with our own investment or operational professionals. This required significant time and a large team of professionals with diverse backgrounds to manage a varied portfolio that held professional sports franchises, a large movie studio, a significant real estate portfolio, a large U.S. cable operator, and a large gas pipeline operator. This family office was very unique and different from other family offices you would typically encounter.

Richard Wilson: When you get to the high enough level single family office, the time horizons seem to be so long that short-term cash and income needs are so negligible that some family offices concentrate in the areas that they are confident in and have some sort of strategic edge, and then invest for the long-term. Is that correct?

Michael Connor: That is correct. Having a strategic edge or operational expertise in a specific line of business does give you a significant advantage in the long term but you still need to pay attention to asset liability matching to avoid a liquidity crunch at an inopportune time. For example, when I first arrived at the Pacific Northwest family office, asset liability matching was not occurring, creating the need to maintain a higher cash level than needed because of the uncertainty of future capital requirements given the illiquid nature of the portfolio.

Other than the concentrated single stock equity position which, quite frankly, was used as the bank, the portfolio had no other sources of instant liquidity to pull from other than cash. If there were missteps in operational execution of the businesses we managed then you could run into a liquidity squeeze if you did not match specific liquidity events with the forecasted capital needs of the entire portfolio and also the family's personal and philanthropic needs. What we tried to do was forecast future cash needs for large liabilities, such as maturing debt, and then try to manage our liquidity events around those occurrences.

Richard Wilson: Cash management is an important subject and a surprisingly dynamic area of family office capital management. Could you share with us a little bit on some of the cash management best practices that you have discovered while running single family offices?

Michael Connor: You bring up an interesting point. A few years ago, I don't think there was a big focus on cash management. People thought it was mundane, boring, and had no risk. The thought was I have cash, I'll put it in some sort of enhanced cash portfolio or money market account and chase yield without having a clear understanding of the risk of that investment and what it really meant. Then, 2007–2008 arrives and people unfortunately discovered that there was some risk to that approach. During that time period, I encountered a lot of bankers pushing products like auction rate securities and the data point that always struck me as being odd was that you'd sit down with the banker, they would discuss the product as an alternative to enhance your yield, but when you started digging into the details, they really didn't understand the product.

One fund that I am familiar with offered a strategic cash reserve fund. Again, that fund was yielding more than other funds in the marketplace, but the securities they held were riskier credits and the other risk that investors did not focus on was the investor concentration in the fund. That fund was one of the first to break the buck because of the type of securities it held and its investor concentration. All it took was the redemption of one very, very large investor and they ran into trouble quickly because of the illiquid nature of the securities it held at that time.

Fast-forward to today: What's changed and what best practices should you put in place? For a lot of family offices today the mandate is preserving capital. An analogy I make on the yield side is if you had an equity portfolio and you decided to enhance the return on that equity portfolio by 5 to 10 basis points, would you increase the risk on that portfolio 20, 30, or 40 percent? The answer is absolutely "no." Why, then, would you do that with your cash? For family offices and the founders or patriarchs of those offices, cash is their "sleep at night" money.

When managing cash today, preservation comes first. Yield comes second, but you must also take into account the purchasing power of the U.S. dollar. While inflation is not a big threat today, down the road it will be and along those lines, what's the future global purchasing power of the dollar? Over the long term the dollar will continue to decline in value, so although you may feel pretty comfortable that you're preserving your capital, at the end of the day it's very possible that your cash is losing purchasing power. For family offices, who travel and acquire assets around the globe, this can be a longer-term issue. When making decisions around cash management, purchasing power and maintaining parity with other currencies is another consideration you need to take into account when designing your cash management program.

Cash management investment policy in this environment should be revisited frequently; you don't need to look at it every month, but it is something that should be revisited on a quarterly or semi-annual basis, just to make sure it's relevant to developments in the current marketplace. For example, the definition of a Triple A Muni-credit six months ago may not be the same now. How you select securities in that portfolio may change. Always make sure your investment policy is up-to-date and relevant to what's going on in the market today.

Going back to the auction rate security debacle, understand what it is you're investing in; dig into the details and ask lots of questions. For most family offices, these types of investments are outsourced, so when looking into your alternatives try to understand what it is you're buying and why you might be getting an enhanced yield. If the person you're speaking with cannot clearly articulate that, then think twice before investing because there is going to be some risk that you may not be aware of and, as in 2007–2008, you don't want to be in a position of having to explain why some of the cash portfolio is losing principal value.

Counterparty risk is another area I believe is very important and needs to be monitored on an on-going basis Again, prior to 2007–2008, I think it was an afterthought and people didn't truly understand or anticipate what counterparty risk entailed and how it could hurt you. I think investors that had relationships with Lehman Brothers have learned that lesson because, in some instances, they still have not gotten their assets back. Lehman's still going through the liquidation process and it's going to take many years to wind down.

This falls outside of the cash realm, but when you consider where assets are going to be held, whether that's cash, equities, bonds, etc., consider using a custodial bank versus a commercial bank or broker dealer because a custodial bank has a higher level of fiduciary responsibility and the structure of those accounts is slightly different from a commercial bank or broker dealer. Your assets will have an additional layer of protection if the broker dealer or bank goes into receivership. MF Global is a recent example where client cash was commingled with the firm's accounts. Had those customers elected to have their cash held at a third party custodian, that whole ordeal would never have happened. That extra layer of protection is a precaution I highly recommend family offices look into and fully understand before moving forward on having their assets held at a broker dealer or commercial bank.

If, for some reason, your Principal is still on the yield-enhancement-bandwagon of cash management, I suggest that you approach the topic as if it is an entirely different asset class with different risk characteristics. Here at my office, we can enhance yield if that is truly what the Principal wants but we understand that entails greater risk. My approach to the issue is we can enhance current income in the portfolio but I'm going to reclassify it into a different asset class, because, in essence, it is. By discussing it with your Principal in that type of framework you can better manage their expectations and also give them a better understanding of the risk involved.

The issue with cash is that everybody thought it was risk-free; the lessons of the last few years have absolutely shown that risk exists everywhere; it's spread across the asset class spectrum and it even exists in what you would have considered a risk-free cash investment two years ago. Those are some of the thoughts around what you should focus on as you're trying to put together a best practices framework around your cash management.

Richard Wilson:	To summarize, those wanting to more effectively manage cash for a family office should watch liquidity closely to make sure it meets their needs, to educate yourself about all of the different types of cash management solutions in the marketplace, and be careful not to be too aggressive so you don't end up losing some of your principal investment while allocating to cash. Is that right?
Michael Connor:	That's correct.
Richard Wilson:	You also brought up the custodial bank versus the commercial bank and the relative dilution of money because of inflation. If you don't watch that risk and manage cash as a separate asset class you could get into trouble.
	Many family offices manage their portfolios in such a way that 60 percent or 80 percent of the investments are in market tracking beta exposure investments or core investments, and then a smaller percentage, say 5 percent, 15 percent, or 30 percent might be in a bit more risky investments, and you get a better extra alpha out of that. Would you recommend something similar within the cash management sandbox? Should you break it up and have 85 percent or 95 percent in something a little bit safer while a part of it might be in something that's a little bit more risky, or how would you go about managing the cash management portfolio itself?
Michael Connor:	I think that is a correct approach if part of the mandate is to increase yield and manage cash within separate buckets. You have your as-close-to-risk-free-bucket and that's where you're preserving capital. Then, maybe a small percentage of the portfolio goes into riskier type investments within the cash realm to boost yield, but with the understanding that there is going to be risk around that. Again, it goes back to what I had said in other portions of the interview it is a good way to manage expectations.
Richard Wilson:	How should family offices approach cash management if they don't already have that expertise in-house?
Michael Connor:	It would depend on the family office and how much time was available. I think training should be on everybody's list, so you have a solid understanding of the asset class. Number one, I would recommend outside training through the various programs in the marketplace. There are many to choose from, and that would be a good first

step. I think speaking with other sophisticated family offices and asking them about their experiences and how they manage their cash would be another avenue you can pursue. In conjunction with that, it would be wise to ask them who they've consulted with, someone who doesn't have a proprietary product, but acts as an advisor or consultant to help work your way through the complexities that actually exist within cash management.

Richard Wilson: Do you have any portfolio risk management best practices to suggest to others who are managing family office investments?

Michael Connor: The most important thing to get your arms around when you step into this role is to fully understand what the portfolio is comprised of, where the risks are, and how you need to manage those risks in times of "chaos" that can come from any direction. It can come from the markets, and can even come from the Principal's reaction to what's going on in the markets. With that in mind it is important to sit down with the Principal and go through the portfolio. It's really sitting down with them and going through the holdings, asset by asset, and making sure they truly understand what it is they own, setting their performance expectations and building a road map around those expectations. That conversation will start to lower the level of chaos because you're no longer shooting from the hip and can now be proactive rather than reactive.

When setting expectations, you're going to be right sometimes and you're going to be wrong sometimes, but if you have the game plan laid out, expectations set, a solid understanding of the various assets, the risks and how they might react in certain environments, then you'll find that the level of chaos starts coming down and as things shift and the tide changes you can move with that flow rather than try to swim against it.

Richard Wilson: Later in Chapter 8 of this book on Family Office Investments I lay out three family office investment models, the Operating Business Sandbox Model, the Diversified Institutional Model, and the Hybrid Model. Which do you think is best?

Michael Connor: I'm not sure there is one best approach. I think there is an approach that the founder or Principal is most experienced in, and that should be a larger piece of the portfolio, but not all Principals feel that way. It's interesting you mentioned that; in my current family office we are now starting to do some direct investing within various sectors of the market. When the Principal and I have discussions on strategy I frequently ask why we don't focus on his previous industry; he built a great franchise, created enormous wealth, and can add most value to that type of investment. You are not just bringing capital to the table; you are bringing experience and knowledge, which creates more value over time.

So, if you're willing to invest in businesses, where are you going to create the most value? You'll create the most value by bringing prior experiences of success and failure to new investments in a way that can help the business navigate potholes; that brings real value. I think it's a great approach but some, like my Principal, do not want to focus solely on that approach. Growing and preserving capital are very important to him but he enjoys other areas as well, such as real estate and philanthropy for example. Is that a wrong approach? No, it's just a different approach and to your point, it runs the gamut among family offices.

At the Seattle office, a small piece of the portfolio was invested in technologies that matched the Principal's vision. He would invest in ideas that were really unique where he could bring his vision or technological expertise to the table and add value. He is a very unique individual and brings a different view to certain investments. I don't know of many individuals who have that type of vision. I hadn't experienced it before then and I haven't since. It was one of those unique situations. That was a long-winded way of saying that for most family offices where they invest is where the Principal has a passion or is most comfortable.

Richard Wilson: One area I am focusing on in this book is *investment committee best practices* so everyone learns from each other's best practices and processes. At the single family offices where you have worked, is there a formal investment committee? Or is it more that the chief investment officer (CIO), CFO, and treasurer types meet with the Principal or patriarch on a weekly, monthly, quarterly basis and it's more of a reporting function than an investment committee that meets regularly?

Michael Connor: I'll first talk about my current single family office. It's not a committee per se; we meet on a weekly basis with the Principal. We give him updates on the existing portfolio; latest developments, etc. We'll also provide him with any new investment prospects, strategy shifts, or tactical adjustments that I want to make. Although we are not a voting committee, because at the end of the day the final decision does rest with him, he relies on us as a committee and wants to hear what we like and do not like about investment ideas. In fact, he expects us to play devil's advocate when he comes up with an investment idea; it's a push back on him as well.

        Again, though we are not a voting committee he does rely on my team and then ultimately the recommendation I make before making a final decision. In my prior office, it was much more of an investment committee where everybody meets with the Principal, usually on a monthly basis. We would discuss the portfolio, discuss what's happening in the portfolio, changes we need to make, and make recommendations on new investments. We would each have a vote, but this is where the family office is different from working for an institution: in an institutional investment committee the majority usually wins. In a family office, even though we have a formal investment committee and they each have a vote, the majority would not always win the day if the Principal was not comfortable or totally disagreed with the investment thesis. It's the comfort factor issue; he could always override the vote and, at times, that was not always in his or the family's best interest but it was what he was comfortable doing.

Richard Wilson: Do you have any best practices on how to make an investment committee more effective?

Michael Connor: I think having minutes of committee meetings is very useful because it reminds staff of the decisions that came out of the meeting. A list of action items and execution dates is also very important. Minutes will remind the group of what was discussed in the meetings and the decisions made and why, it's probably one of the more important things that you should make part of the investment process.

| Richard Wilson: | How should very small family offices build their invest-ment committees? Would you advise they bring in an outside global taxation expert or outside risk manager to add another objective opinion to the table? |

Richard Wilson: How should very small family offices build their invest-ment committees? Would you advise they bring in an outside global taxation expert or outside risk manager to add another objective opinion to the table?

Michael Connor: Absolutely; even the larger family offices should rely on outside expertise if it does not exist in-house. We will bring in an outside advisor if needed. For small family offices, that is the route they should go. It gives them the opportunity to bounce ideas off of a conflict-free outsider.

Richard Wilson: How does the fund manager selection process at either family office work, and how is that interrelated to how the investment committee operates?

Michael Connor: When it comes to selecting a fund manager, I'll focus on Consolidated Investment Group. The other office I worked for did not have a lot of outside fund managers. When looking at our managers, we split our fund managers into what we call a "core" which are the larger or institutional-type managers and other smaller managers who are our tactical players. When we are looking for new managers we're looking for those tactical and strategic components. For us, part of the selection process is taking into account our macro-economic view of the world, what do we think is going to happen, what strategies do we think would perform best in a particular market climate. We think about that internally and also speak with outside experts to get additional perspective. Then, we start contacting people we know in the industry either directly or through other channels such as investment bank cap intro or private wealth sections of the commercial banks. We then start looking at manager performance within the strategies where we are interested in adding exposure. That's part one of the process.

Once we have what we consider the top performers, we narrow it down and start doing a little bit more due diligence. Some managers may not make the cut because we think they are too big. From my perspective, I'd rather have a smaller fund, and when I say smaller I'm not talking $10, $20 or $50 million. I'd like to see assets under management (AUM) starting at around $100 million. I don't want to see $5 billion, just because those funds are not as nimble and their returns gravitate toward the mean; we're going to look for someone in that

	$100 to $500 million fund size with a good track record where the PMs of the fund have quality experience such as working for another reputable fund or a Goldman Sachs-type institution that provides great training and pedigree. Prior experience as an investor in that strategy is also a requirement. We then narrow down the field to what we believe are the top 10 to 15 managers and start sending out questionnaires, interviewing, and doing on-site diligence visits, continually interacting with them as we work our way to the top three that we're going to present to the Principal.
Richard Wilson:	When it comes to the core group or the tactical group, I would guess that maybe with the tactical group you need a little bit less of a number of years of track record. Are you generally looking for five to seven years ideally, but sometimes you'll make an exception or what was that like?
Michael Connor:	Sometimes we will make an exception. I won't name any names, but I recently came across a unique strategy. Earlier in the year, we were looking at mergers and acquisitions as a potential strategy and I found a manager who had a totally different twist on it. They are not doing merger arbitrage; they are doing more of a litigious type process that is focused on the difference between the target company's valuation and the price being offered by the acquiring company. This person never ran a hedge fund before, they had a legal background. Because their track record as a trial lawyer was so strong in that discipline, when the opportunity crossed my desk, I thought, "this is a really interesting twist on the strategy." The fund structure appealed to us, and extensive diligence got us comfortable. We ended up investing with them because of the uniqueness and limited downside of the strategy. Is that what we would typically do? No, but in some cases we will, because a family office is usually more entrepreneurial and flexible than a large institution. We will back a smaller player with a strategy that we like and understand, is not crowded with other participants, and provides a structure that is most advantageous to us.
Richard Wilson:	Do you have any hard lessons learned that you could share with other family offices on selecting fund managers and investments?

Michael Connor: For the smaller family office that relies on their cap intro or private banking relationships, the biggest piece of advice I can give is: Do not rely on the diligence performed by those outside sources. It's a great way to start and is a great way to narrow down the field, but go visit these funds, kick the tires, and talk to their auditors. Ask the auditors questions; ask the custodians questions. Make sure accounts actually exist. Perform the diligence that seems not as interesting, quite frankly. You might ask "Why do I want to talk to the accountants about last year's audit on this fund?" but if people had done that in the Bernie Madoff situation and maybe asked for audit papers or weaknesses found during the audit or reviewed custody records, a lot of what happened wouldn't have occurred. It happened because there was a lot of trust put on either friends of friends or feeders into that organization. The investors did not do their homework.

Richard Wilson: We have heard from many family office veterans that the bottleneck in this industry is talent; there just aren't many experienced family office executives out there in the marketplace to pick from while building or expanding a team. How do you deal with that internally at your family office?

Michael Connor: Given the smaller size of a typical family office it is important to cross-train as best you can on the investment side, so if someone leaves other people are familiar with that person's role and areas of coverage. They are able to find information rather than hunting around for it. It helps manage the chaos I referred to previously. It makes for a smoother transition while you are looking for a replacement; you have everything under control, and you don't have to worry about how to contact the various outside managers.

    I think the worst thing you can do is let your team operate in a silo, meaning this person only does the private equity, that person only does hedge funds, and another person only does cash management and they keep all that knowledge to themselves, creating job security. If someone leaves then you now lose the go-to person for that area. I think the other area to focus on is the back office; that's probably most critical. It's important that staff is cross-trained; if the person who handled all the accounting and taxes or various other things left and no one is familiar with that role, it can become a significant issue. This especially becomes an issue if sophisticated systems are not in place to manage that part of the business. Most small family office operations still use spreadsheets. It's an area that can't be overlooked. I know a lot of the focus is on the front office investment side, but the back office for the family office is also very important.

Richard Wilson: Great point. Are there a few skills that you would look for while hiring for a family office? Can you touch on the top few positions which are critical to fill first?

Michael Connor: For the CFO position, find someone that has a solid understanding of risk management; it's a very important role that position should perform. Because of the uniqueness of the family office, I think having a sophisticated tax background makes sense because of the estate planning issues that come up within the various family offices. Getting someone with prior financial institution experience would be a big plus for understanding portfolio valuations, but it is not as important as the previous experience I mentioned since regulatory reporting is not required of family offices. If you can find a CFO with those three core pieces you have found the optimal individual for the position. On the legal side, because of breadth of everything that you get involved in, in-house counsel is important but additional outside representation makes a lot of sense.

Richard Wilson: Global taxation is a high cost, but it is an important aspect of a family office solution for those ultra-wealthy with international businesses and assets. Does your team have internal global taxation counsel on salary or do you reach out to niche global tax attorneys as needed?

Michael Connor: At this office, we don't have in-house counsel. At the prior office there was large team of attorneys. When it came to seeking specific advice on international tax law and how to set up entities overseas, we would deal with professionals that were very, very specific in their skill set and usually from a top tier legal firm within the tax or relevant business practice. Same on the accounting side; when it came to accounting, tax, risk management or any other advice we would always rely on advice from the best possible sources both internally and externally.

| | Here at CIG, there is a paralegal on staff but when it comes to getting advice on international tax, estate planning, and partnership structures, we will rely on outside advisors who have specific experience in the area. |

Richard Wilson: Most family offices are overwhelmed with pitches and incoming marketing messages from marketers and capital raisers seeking investment capital. How do you manage that deal flow overload?

Michael Connor: That's a tough one, believe it or not.

The best way that we try to manage it here is once we identify strategies that we want to invest in, we will reach out to our numerous conduits and have them make introductions. As for the cold calls and e-mails or whatever you get, you can't really turn that off and I'm not sure you want to. Most of it is not going to be interesting, but that 1 percent that is interesting could turn into an investment that makes sense. I haven't figured out a great way of filtering it. I find it is hard to filter and the unfortunate thing is, to your point, there are not enough hours in the day to return everybody's phone call or e-mail. As for deal management, once you decide what you're interested in, manage it as effectively as possible by letting outside sources know the specific strategies and requirements that will result in a meeting.

Richard Wilson: Do you have any last thoughts you really wanted to get in here on the audio recording or did you get to cover them?

Michael Connor: I think we covered a lot of it. The most important topic I discussed and I can't stress enough is when working with these families, setting expectations is the most important thing that we can do because: (A) it builds confidence over time and (B) it provides you a much more planned-out way of defining and executing your strategy which ultimately is to achieve the longer term goals of the family. At the end of the day, we are here to help achieve those goals.

Richard Wilson: I think that's an excellent last point to end on. So many single family offices are closed-door and it's hard to find actual training and information on family office operations, and even much less on best practices, nonetheless by people who are as experienced as yourself. I really appreciate your time and advice.

Michael Connor: My pleasure, I enjoyed the conversation.

FAMILY OFFICE INTERVIEW WITH ELIZABETH
HAMMACK OF CM CAPITAL CORPORATION

Our second interview was conducted with Elizabeth Hammack from the single family office CM Capital Corporation. This single family office manages over a billion dollars in capital. It is now converting into a multi-family office and accepting some outside capital into the firm. This interview begins with some details on Elizabeth's background.

Elizabeth Hammack: I am a lawyer and I have an MBA degree. I started in-house at a private family-owned, large construction firm in San Francisco and then went into finance through Citicorp. I worked at Citicorp for many years and, in particular, toward the end of my career there I was working in helping the private bankers with some of the other high-net-worth clients. I then moved and it was the Internet era, the dot-com boom. I worked in Silicon Valley as a general counsel at a public Internet company for a short while and got recruited into this family office at an interesting time. It was a dot-com boom and bust, and the family was really looking for assistance at that point to help them make sense of what had just happened in the Silicon Valley with the dot-com bust.

They needed someone that had broad-based corporate and investment legal experience that also brought with them business experience as well. So, they brought me in. I came in as a general counsel and gradually moved into the administration and operations area here because the family office was rather informal back then and smaller. That's how I got here, and I have really loved working here ever since. I really loved working for a family with a dedicated family office that was trusted to manage their wealth. It's been very fulfilling family work here.

Richard Wilson: How many people work at the single family office where you work?

Elizabeth Hammack: We have just over 40 people. It was much smaller when I first joined.

Richard Wilson: I have found that most family offices are formed after a company is sold or goes public on a stock

	market exchange. How did CM Capital Corporation start up?
Elizabeth Hammack:	You know, this family office is rather interesting because we have been in existence for over 40 years now.
	This one was started in 1969 in Silicon Valley by a prominent Chinese family whose sons had started coming over here to go to Stanford. They liked the area, and they liked buying real estate, and that's how this firm initially started, purchasing commercial real estate in the California area. The family originally started in the textile industry in China and Hong Kong. They had textile companies that they started, and then moved into real estate in Hong Kong; they made a fortune in both of those industries.
	The family didn't actually sell a business to make its wealth, as it still owns the operating companies to this day. It still owns textile operations worldwide, as well as some real estate development in Hong Kong and one in China, as well. They did not sell, but they expanded and they looked for areas to invest their wealth and they started this firm. They started buying commercial real estate, started looking around and saying "Hey, we are in Silicon Valley; look at all this great venture activity!" and they moved into venture capital in the late '70s–early '80s then gradually as our portfolio grew and the portfolio was allowed to grow without withdrawal. It grew and we expanded into other asset classes over time.
Richard Wilson:	Can you share with me a high level view of what your investment portfolio looks like?
Elizabeth Hammack:	Sure. I can give you some ballpark figures. Now, while we invest for one family right now, the portfolio allocations I discuss are somewhat aggregated because although we have one family, we have different investment entities with different goals but I can give you an overview.
	Let me first preface by saying this is heavily weighted to our real estate because that was the preference for the family early on. I would say we are 38 percent real estate.

	Also, in regard to commercial buildings, not only are we investors, but we own and we actually operate them, too. We have a real estate department here.
Richard Wilson:	That is unique.
Elizabeth Hammack:	Yes, it's very unique. We operate the properties ourselves, although we have on-site property managers that are not our employees that we have contracted out.

Again, that's 38 percent real estate. We do not own any public stocks as a rule, or mutual funds. We are about 55 percent private equity. Private equity entails venture and LBO (leveraged buyout) and other kinds of structured, private equity-type products.

| Richard Wilson: | Do you have a formal investment committee at your family office? |
| Elizabeth Hammack: | We do have a formal investment committee that meets monthly. There is a regular agenda. The fund investment department puts together due diligence packages and recommendations on various fund managers. They also cover any redemption that needs to be put together or if there is a need for changing fund managers in a certain strategy. They put that together for our discussion and decision. |

I have our investments structured in fund-of-funds vehicles. I have a fund that I call an alternative investments fund, which is mainly a fund of private equity funds. I also have a fund of hedge funds and the real estate separate. Each one of those has an investment committee.

Often they meet together because it's the same member's family investment committee. The investment committee is comprised of myself, the chief investment officer, chief executive officer, and usually the chairman of our board. Then, the funds group comes in and gives reports and we have a discussion every month.

| Richard Wilson: | That partially explains how, even though you are serving one family now, you are structured so that you could start accepting outside money because |

	those processes are already managed by employees in many cases. Is that right?
Elizabeth Hammack:	Right, exactly.
Richard Wilson:	Are there certain types of fund managers that you look for or try to stay away from?
Elizabeth Hammack:	You know, I personally like to stay away from extremely large fund managers because I feel like we don't get any kind of personal attention. You have no flexibility in negotiating agreements. You are just a number to them, and that's it. Having said that, though, we do have investments in some very large, wealthier funds; as you know, their performance numbers are worthwhile. In general, I have to say this firm has always placed an extreme value on relationships. We like to have very long-term, deep relationships with our managers. This is especially true in the private equity area because you are committing yourself to long-term investments. We might try to get to know someone for a couple of years before we decide to invest.
Richard Wilson:	Okay.
Elizabeth Hammack:	We want to really see how they are, how they react with us, how they interact with us, and how their team has gelled together. We really want to make sure it is a good fit for the long-term and not just a quick, short-term return. I would say we place an extreme amount of value on relationships. Having said that, we do have a full analysis we go through with everybody. If anyone fails any of our analysis steps, even though we have a great relationship with them, we will not put our money with them or we will remove our money.
Richard Wilson:	So, it's not that the relationship replaces any type of quantitative or in-depth due diligence or an office meeting. It's a lot like that with private equity; you will go around to a private equity raise and meet with family offices and they will say, "It sounds interesting, we like your team, but we will come back during your next raise or during the next fund you open, and maybe at that point it will make more sense; we will get to know each other better," right?

Elizabeth Hammack: Well, that's exactly the case. I mean we have a lot of people come pitch. Occasionally, we do have an allocation in private equity to emerging managers so we often will find a new team and grant it. Most of the ones that we end up investing in have spun out from more established firms. We are somewhat familiar already with their past individual performance and how they are as an investor, but we have a few cases of new emerging managers, first time managers that we will give $2 or $3 million to. Otherwise, we will tell them, "Let's see how you do in your first fund. Come back to us on your second."

Richard Wilson: That's been my experience with private equity. Specifically with hedge funds, is there a certain AUM that you look for? Is there a size that's too big; what is the minimum? Do you allocate to emerging managers there, as well?

Elizabeth Hammack: In hedge funds I would say we don't generally invest in emerging managers unless they are familiar to us from another shop. There are exceptions that are made; our portfolio manager for public securities, who really essentially only looks at hedge funds, has a preference for smaller managers. Our definition of smaller managers is somewhere between 200 million and 500 million; that's her sweet spot, what she likes, though sometimes we go up to a billion dollars.

Sometimes, what we've seen happen is, after we've invested in someone that has 400 million to 500 million, that we're really happy and great, then suddenly they blow up to 2 billion and they leave their strategy behind. You know, they are too big; they can't execute their strategy properly. Their performance starts falling, and we haven't been happy. That's why we are staying away from the 2 billion-type funds. We would rather be somewhere around 500 to a billion and generally we don't look at fund managers with under 200 million.

Richard Wilson: That's really good important information, and good feedback; many family offices say a 100 million, but I have been surprised during these interviews that people are saying, "Oh, we look at anybody." I know from my personal experience and representing institutional hedge fund managers and calling on family offices that oftentimes, that analyst who is the gate keeper will simply ask what your AUM is and if it's not over a 100 million often they may be polite, but excuse themselves from the phone.

When it comes to that standard process that external fund managers use, whether they are PE funds or hedge funds, does your team use a standard due diligence questionnaire (DDQ) or some Web-based portal, or is it a custom due diligence questionnaire that your team has created for these different types of managers?

Elizabeth Hammack: That is a good question. I have actually been an advocate recently to get a standard DDQ. I am also serving right now as a compliance officer and I would really like to have a standard DDQ, but right now we don't have it. We do have one that we tailor to each fund manager, and we have a standard list of issues that we cover for everybody.

We focus on risk. What's the risk involved in this fund, is there a bad tail risk, or what could the top risk be? Then we look at their edge. What differentiates them from their competitors, from the fund next door to them; what's their edge? What's their game, their strategy? Basically, we want to know how deeply the fund manager is involved in the strategy and how much he believes in it. What kind of strategy and how he articulates it to us is very important and in some ways, you have to look at venture and private equity very differently than a hedge fund manager for example, but we look at strategy and their game as "very important" and then we look at their team.

Who's on their team? How old are they? What's their background; how long have they worked for the firm; how well did they get along together? We go to face-to-face meetings probably at least two to three times to make sure that this goes back to the relationship factor, too. We want to make sure that we can actually like them. I want to be comfortable with the way they do business and their ethics, but we also observe strongly how they interact as a team. We just want to see the vibe in the company.

Are they really a team or is there some kind of underlying unhappiness, discontent, or animosity among the team? That's the big red flag for us because we are investing in the team and like I said earlier, we would like to have a long-term relationship. We don't want to see this team blow up in a year, or see one of the key people decide he is going to up and leave in six months. We want to be really comfortable that this team is dedicated to the firm and to each other. Overall, the team is important.

Then we obviously look at their organization, their back office, how well are they set up, who is their chief financial officer and see now what he is doing and if he has experience. Then we also look at performance, which is really just one of our necessary criteria. You can have a terrific performance, but if these other criteria aren't met, then you are off for consideration.

Richard Wilson: I think other family offices will appreciate that advice. I think many do an on-site visit or they try to, but sometimes due to an inconvenience like the manager being based somewhere like Hong Kong or Singapore and the family office based in Canada, sometimes the on-site visit doesn't even happen, which is why that is valuable advice.

Since you have so many direct investments in real estate, is it correct to assume that income is not high on your priority list for your other types of investments made?

Elizabeth Hammack: That's a really difficult question because we do have these different groups with different objectives. I would say it's a mixture, and we do put a high value on capital preservation.

We want to make sure that we grow the portfolio. We don't bet the firm on outrageously risky things. Having said that, though, we do have allocations to high-risk investments. I think we have an intelligent allocation that is constantly reviewed to make sure that we have a good mixture of conservative investments that have very good appreciation potential and then more risky high return investments mixed in. We do have a lot of tax concerns and issues that need to be addressed and reviewed because we have a family that is a mixture of non-U.S. and U.S. people. There are always tax issues to consider when making an investment, so we tend to be very careful and thorough in looking at tax issues with different fund managers.

Touching on that point, we have rejected fund managers who do not have counsel or experience in tax structuring their investments, as well as someone who doesn't seem to really care about their investors' tax concerns. That is a big black spot against that fund manager.

Richard Wilson: Could you give an example for other family offices listening to this or fund managers that don't keep that in mind when they form their funds? Is it the legal structure that needs to be set up differently?

Elizabeth Hammack: Let me give you a couple: Say a fund manager tells us "we might have some foreign investments and they might be corporations, but they don't really hold anything." They will be PFIC for U.S. investors, which is a large tax issue that I do not, as an investor, want to have to deal with. Some of them I have to and some fund managers say, "Well that's just it; tough." You have to fill out the tax forms yourself and deal with that.

Instead of setting up an alternate structure for me to use that or for other investors similar to me, they just say, "That's too bad; I don't really need your money anymore, anyway." That really alienates us, not only for that deal, but any subsequent deals they put together. Say in a couple of years they do put together the appropriate structure and come to us we will say, "You know, you didn't care when we were there two years ago, so thanks, but no thanks."

The same would be the case if a fund puts together a different type of deal and they don't take into consideration a foreign investor. They will say, "Well, that's too bad that a foreign investor has to go file a U.S. tax return now." That's not going to be helpful to an investor considering whether or not to invest in your firm, so it'd be better if you would please set up what's called a blocker structure, which is very, very common. But they say "That's just too much, though" and they just can't help us do that.

We will keep that in mind in the future, too, when you come knocking because lots of fund managers are responsive. You know the investor remembers who is responsive to their issues, and even if they cannot accommodate us for our tax issues, all they have to do is just be sensitive and a little empathetic about it. Then the relationship is preserved and everything is great, but it's just an issue when they are careless and unsympathetic about that issue because taxes for family offices, for this one, taxes are a very sensitive issue.

Richard Wilson: I can imagine that the insensitivity might come once you get the 750 million or billion dollars in assets, so that's kind of goes in line with your preference or your size of managers probably.

The single family office you work for has been around for over 40 years. Can you pick out a best practice that has taken a long time to develop, but that other family offices could try to emulate?

Elizabeth Hammack: Well, I think it was about eight years ago I wrote a code of ethics for the firm. That's been surprisingly useful. When I first did it, people said, "Well, of course you know we do this already; why do we need it written down?"

Common sense stuff, but it's really effective. It turned out, from my point of view, to be good because we had a written code of ethics. Best practices, I thought at that time, which again was eight years ago or so. Part of that was to be highly aware of any conflicts of interest and to disclose them to me in writing whenever they came up. I make sure that people update it annually and more frequently as needed and that actually helps a lot because it helps highlight people's conflicts with the company and the company's conflicts with the family. It does help to be more transparent overall, so that, in the investment committee, I know that Joe sitting next to me already has an investment in this firm that we are looking at.

That's a conflict that needs to be disclosed and discussed. Before the code of ethics came out there was more of a casual thing. Just having a written code of ethics and a regular disclosure process really helped that. It just made everyone a little more aware, letting people know when they may need to be more communicative, or need to have a little more transparency here. I think that builds trust. It makes things more open and makes sure that any kind of conflicts are out in the open. I think that the code of ethics had a lot of good impacts throughout the company, and on the investment committee it definitely had a good impact as well.

Richard Wilson: That is really valuable. I have asked family offices for a list of standard documents they use while running a family office and nobody has mentioned a code of ethics. You mentioned standard disclosure is within the code of ethics. Are there two or three other parts that you think should be built in to a code of ethics for other family offices that are now taking notes? Are there two or three sections you think it should include besides standard disclosures, or is that the one primary thing? If you have that everything else is kind of common sense of what should be written in there?

Elizabeth Hammack: Sure, in the form it's not just the conflicts insofar as what you have invested in; here, I asked for any investments and private funds and security that we also have investments in, but I also asked what else do you do, are you on different boards of directors, for example, because that could lead to a conflict. I may also ask, "Are you involved in any other local organizations or vendors that could lead to a conflict?" That's part of the form as well. It's not just focused on investments only.

Richard Wilson: Some of the major standard documents that every family office should have in place include a family mission statement, a list of objectives, a risk management procedure, an investment policy, etc. Many of these things seem obvious to family offices like

	yours, which have been around for 40 years, but am I missing any major documents that may not be as obvious to a family office that has only been around for three to five years?
Elizabeth Hammack:	I don't think you are missing a major one. I think those others that you mentioned are good to have as well.
Richard Wilson:	Great. I am a big believer in documenting processes and procedures internally for family offices and investment fund managers. I believe most family offices have a core set of 20, 30, or 50 processes that are repeated daily, weekly, monthly, quarterly, or annually that should be documented step-by-step and constantly improved.
	Based on your experience in the family office industry, have you found that those types of documented processes from the business perspective and operational perspective of the family office, have you found that those type of processes and procedures are something that many family offices do have in place? Or are the teams usually so small and so closely connected that it's really not necessary, like it would be for a billion-dollar corporation being run? What is your take on this issue?
Elizabeth Hammack:	Well, I have seen family offices with a relatively small group of people who don't have policies and procedures, and they seem to be doing okay. Having said that, I am a believer in having the policies and procedures because if you have a change in personnel and you don't have procedures written down, institutional knowledge about your process has just walked out of your door, and that's a huge blow to the firm.
	I think having policies and procedures are enormously valuable. We have just gone through a whole exercise of revising ours because we are planning on registering with the SEC as a registered investment advisor. In going through ours, I found them to be extremely robust. I didn't have to do as much work as I had anticipated. But it's because we also been around for so long and we have seen the value in it and in the past we have learned from mistakes.

For example, Joe just left the firm and, oh boy, what was he doing? How did he process these documents before?

Then we have learned, okay, that needs to be documented. Over time we have documented almost everything in this firm so that when someone new comes, they start and are handed the binder. If they find something that could be done better, we ask that they let us know and we will change it.

Richard Wilson: How do you deal with the overwhelming amount of inquiries you undoubtedly receive from those trying to raise capital from your family office for their investment fund or private offering?

Elizabeth Hammack: Well, first we are pretty proactive, so we do our research and usually have a target list of managers that we want to get to know and possibly invest in, so we might have a list of, say, 15 or 20 of our top target list.

For other e-mails or cold calls that we get that are not in our target list, we have a variety of ways of dealing with that, depending on if they have come in via the private equity director or to a hedge fund director. If it's a relationship that we have already established or we know them through another relationship, then they get priority.

That's just the way it is. If it is someone we don't know, we generally do research, as we spoke about before. If assets under management are too small, we just pretty much cross them off the list because we don't want someone too small.

Richard Wilson: Sure, that makes sense.

Elizabeth Hammack: We do tend to go through every e-mail and phone call, though; we don't just delete or not respond.

Richard Wilson: Do you have any best practices to share here for fund managers who are reading this, maybe a few best practices they should follow while contacting family offices like yours?

Elizabeth Hammack: At least one comes to mind because it's a constant complaint I hear among the portfolio managers and our fund directors, and that is how the fund managers are not responsive to our questions. I am not saying that they don't respond to our e-mail or a voice mail, but their response doesn't address the issue that needs to be addressed.

They always seem to be in sales pitch mode and so we might ask a particular question and they will come back with, you know, another little pitch, but they don't actually answer our question. It's like they are not listening to us. As a fund manager, listen to the question, and answer the question. Give the sales pitch afterward, but answer the question; otherwise, we will just hit the delete button and just say, "Forget it if the guy is not listening to us."

I would rather deal with someone who is listening to me than not. Our best practice is be communicative, but mostly in your communications, be responsive to the questions we asked. I know people want to get across what they want to get across and that's great, but we want our answers or we just get frustrated.

Richard Wilson:	Right. That reminds me of Steven Covey. He says to influence others you must first be influenced. So, you actually listen first, understand, and be influenced by that other person potentially before replying. I think it's an excellent piece of advice because, even though it is something that sounds basic on the surface, like a procedure or processes document and sounds like the most boring thing in the world. Listening very carefully can make a huge difference, as you have mentioned two or three times. If you get to a billion dollars in assets and you stop listening to your investors, you are probably going to lose them even if your performance is great, right?
Elizabeth Hammack:	Right.
Richard Wilson:	Well, thank you for your time today, Elizabeth. I think everyone reading this will learn something from your experience.
Elizabeth Hammack:	Thank you very much, Richard. I have enjoyed speaking with you.

 For more resources on the code of ethics, please see the example at www.FamilyOfficesGroup.com/Ethics.

FAMILY OFFICE INTERVIEW WITH FRANK CASEY

Our next interview is conducted with single family office veteran Frank Casey. Frank, who has more than 37 years of experience in single family office management and investments, was a member of the team that blew the whistle to the SEC on Bernie Madoff. Frank served in the military until he was recruited to join Merrill Lynch in the 1970s. In the years that followed, Frank worked his way up to join Providence Securities, where he developed a bank risk management model and was a successful trader. It wasn't until the early '90s that Frank started working with high-net-worth family offices, which is where this interview begins.

Frank Casey: I started shifting back into the high-net-worth family office marketplace around '92, but in the process of doing so, I landed up with a firm called Rampart Investment Management in Boston and that was predominantly an institutional firm.

We were options experts in the equity options arena and that's where I met Harry Markopolos and Neil Chelo and began ferreting out that Madoff was a fraud in the spring of '99 and we began publishing in May 2000 to the SEC to no avail for eight years. There were family offices that were heavily investing, as well as wealthy families through private wealth management banks in France and Switzerland and so forth, and even some "hedge funds of funds" that were really nothing more than feeder funds in the United States.

I saw these institutions executing, basically, what I will call "willful blindness." They did not want to see or hear from a group of "competitors" that the emperor had no clothes and the reason that they didn't want to hear it is that they were making too much money at it as institutions feeding wealthy people into it. I didn't really get to meet a family that had actually personally invested until about 30 days before Madoff blew up in November of '08. When I found this family it was just a crying shame; I tried to do everything I could for them to convince them that they had made a mistake, but they didn't listen, as no one had listened, and they consequently lost all of their money.

Since that time, Richard, our investigations on Madoff culminated with his capitulation in December of 2008, so we had worked on it from 1998, pretty much all of 1999 through 2008. Since then, I have been increasingly moving back toward families because I think that a couple of things have happened on Wall Street that are going to change the whole structure of the way wealth is managed in the United States.

First of all, I think that too many of the Wall Street investment banks have treated their clients as prey, as "dumb equity." When I say "dumb equity," I don't mean the investors are dumb; what I am saying is that they treated them as dumb equity because they needed to have a conduit, a place to move their product and they would build a very complicated structure like collateralized debt obligations and sell these to investors, many of whom were wealthy families. Consequently I think that there is a lot of distrust, in fact I know there is a massive amount of distrust of "Wall Street and investment banks." Many of these investments banks have wealth management departments and we are beginning to see the movement of these wealth management teams out of the firms that had been tainted by Madoff and/or other debacles. They are moving into smaller, regional banks and brokers and so forth, or setting up independent registered investment advisories.

The reason, perhaps, is that these wealth management teams were at these big investment banks for three reasons. The main reason being the financial branding of course, the confidence that it exuded; number two being the balance sheet because people felt confident keeping the money there; and lastly, proprietary product, because these guys had trading firms and hedge funds that were embedded or serviced. Consequently, the deal flow was considered to be a currency. Well, the name's blown, the balance sheet is deleveraged from 33:1 to 12:1, they are getting rid of the prop trading desk to reduce risk exposures, and now the wealth management teams are spinning out.

I was invited to a dinner down in Wilmington, Delaware, hosted by three families and they brought the brightest minds—I don't know how I got invited—within various fields, scientific fields and on. It's called the Non-Obvious Dinner. What a blast this thing was! At these non-obvious dinners, each person's ticket to that free dinner was that they had to come up with an idea that was not obvious but might change the world and you argue your case with a person at the table and then table against table and the winner was selected. I argued the case that we are heading back to the future; that we are going to go back to the House of Morgan concept.

Some families are going to band together, each family having an expertise in a particular area, be it private equity, energy, financial risk management, whatever. They will form teams that band together almost as a confederacy to basically service their peers on a peer-to-peer basis and they will perhaps waive out the salaries because the families are already paying the salaries. The fees would be more of a general partner (GP), limited partner, sharing expenses but no salaries, and the GP would perhaps get paid a little kick at the end for taking the initial risk. I suspect that we are going to move that way.

Now that begs the question: How does a family office that has perhaps $200, $300, $400 million or whatever, build staff to keep its overhead down around 1 percent or less, and effectively attract talent for specialized areas of investment?

You really can't do it efficiently and effectively. So my argument is that teams of advisors, such as myself and my compatriots, will service those families to provide staff extension ad hoc (as needed) to help them basically create peer groups of the managers in the areas that they want to look at. If, let's say, a family or a confederacy of families come and say, "Listen, Frank, we need to look at some long/short specialist equity managers, some distressed managers, some emerging market managers" or whatever, and our grouping would be able to deliver to them all of the due diligence on peer groups.

We might provide a dozen names in each sector. The chief investment officer of the family would then select the top three or four managers out of each peer group, perhaps put together a sample portfolio for a conservative account and an income account and an aggressive account, and so forth. But, the family participants could select dynamically across these peer group buckets to their own liking. They may say, "I really don't care about volatility in the short-term, so I am willing to accept illiquidity; I want to do more of distressed managers and I want to be more heavily weighted on that end."

Richard Wilson: I have identified several ways that family offices are growing in numbers and size in Chapter 10 of this book, "The Future of the Family Office Industry." The source of growth you have seen and experienced firsthand is when an advisor moves from working underneath a large wealth management or trust corporation to being independent and operating within a single or multi-family office model, correct?

Frank Casey: That's correct. I have a friend, Gary Brent, outside of Toronto. Gary became the head of Canada Trust Wealth Management division at one point in his past. He quintupled the assets under management and tripled the profit margin in five years by basically firing all in-house managers, going to the best of the best. They went to the best-of-breed outsourced managers, the individual wealth manager knowing their clients' risk tolerances, time horizons and the like. These were managers that were approved by the Canada Trust platform, and Gary's team basically would ferret out the best managers and put them on to the platform.

You see a lot of "wealth management banks" or trust departments at banks that may be very good at handling traditional sponsored bonds, but how do they expand their operation into alternatives or specialized investments? In order to produce an excess return for a given amount of risk, or what we call alpha in our business, one really has to have an ability to ferret out in the capital market structures global inefficiencies. The markets are generally efficient the more liquid and deep they go, so the inefficiencies usually come from finding areas that are less liquid and therefore less covered.

Now, that means that experts in that area and maybe even industry specific—healthcare, energy, micro-cap, gold mining micro-cap—those people that deal in a rather inefficient sector where there is not a lot of liquidity and that have a specific industry knowledge, they go for an alpha potential. How does one distinguish the good managers from the bad? How does one determine whether it's fraudulent or if there is a good due diligence process in place? How do you do that with limited staff?

Even if you are a wealth management team that spun out a big wealth management division of a trust company, the chances are that you do not have enough people to do the job efficiently. I believe that the wave of the future, and what I am positioning myself for, is the ability to deliver talent that I have vetted, first as a manager of managers and an advisor to create a staff extension very efficiently at a low cost and then allow the internal CIO of the organization or the patriarch of the firm to basically work with us and so we become, in essence, a sous chef and they are the main chef.

Richard Wilson: Right, that makes sense. So you help bring resources to the teams, they don't have to hire somebody full-time that has a lot of experience in kind of vetting managers because typically analysts have relatively little amount of experience, otherwise they are extremely expensive to keep on board full-time, right?

Frank Casey: That's very right; you hit it on the head. For instance, in my manager of manager association on the hedge fund discipline side, I deal with a fund in Shrewsbury, New Jersey. They ran $2 billion and mostly broker or customized portfolios, predominantly for the general accounts of insurance companies; they also ran a fund-of-funds. These guys have tremendous pedigree and depth and, like most great managers and analysts, they are really not necessarily great at relating or marketing. People like myself, not a third-party marketer but a special principal or partner, are basically in charge now with the responsibility of building those businesses. In our case, for instance, none of us are drawing salaries. We are basically building this company out and building broker or customized relationships with families.

Richard Wilson: I want to move into the topic that you are often asked to speak about at conferences and dinners and seminars, and that is your risk framework for approaching fraud risk, which is sometimes referred to as headline risk. I believe you call it TIPS. Could you explain how you came up with that and what TIPS stands for?

Frank Casey: Sure. It's an acronym. I am ex-military guy, and we all
                      had acronyms, like long military phrases. The acronym
                      TIPS, to me, covers all of the salient points of due dili-
                      gence. The "T" stands for Third-Party Verification, the
                      "I" stands for Internal Controls, the "P" stands for the
                      Pedigree, and the "S" stands for Strategy. I'll go over each
                      in a moment, but of the four components, T, I, and P
                      are predominantly qualitative. Strategy, the "S," is maybe
                      three-quarters quantitative but still has a qualitative piece
                      in it.

                         In the old days, around 1998, I remember when we
                      discovered Bernie Madoff. First of all, he was doing a
                      strategy that he claimed could produce 1 percent a month,
                      consistently, and he had no draw-downs. That strategy
                      was one I was using in '74 through '78 covered call writ-
                      ing. I knew darn well what covered call writing does not
                      do, and it does not produce 1 percent a month. It is a path
                      dependent strategy; you still have to pick the right stocks
                      to go up, and that's how you made your money.

                         The option income coming in was just considered an
                      extra dividend, right? Maybe back in the inefficient days
                      when options first started in '74–75, I could write cov-
                      ered calls to 12 percent to 15 percent call. I buy stock at
                      30, sell at 35 or whatever, and make 15 percent to 17 per-
                      cent a year on balance on the portfolio. As the markets
                      became more efficient, covered call writing didn't pro-
                      duce those rates so I knew it didn't produce 1 percent
                      a month. The first thing in TIPS is the Third-Party Ver-
                      ification. I was a third-party verifier knowing that that
                      strategy didn't work, right? You have to have somebody
                      who understands the strategy that you are potentially in-
                      vesting in, first of all. The Third-Party Verification really
                      comes down to checks and balances.

                         Consider it just like you would a normal good busi-
                      ness. You would want a good administrator who is sepa-
                      rate from the manager. You would want an auditor that's
                      a high quality auditor and, more importantly, an auditor
                      that actually understood the business they are auditing.
                      If you were doing brokerage work, you would want that
                      auditor to be third party; you wouldn't want the manager
                      being the broker because there is a potential conflict in the
                      custody of your money. Why would you even want the

money at the brokerage firm? Why not keep it at a trustee bank separately and have a delivery versus purchase arrangement? With the collapse of Lehman and Bear and so forth, many people have moved to a third-party custodian now. You want the net asset value, whether it is daily or monthly, to be struck and verified by third parties, not just provided by the managers. Bernie, by the way, failed on every one of those things. Bernie was a self-administrator; he was supposedly having his father-in-law doing the audit and he was basically a man and a dog in a strip mall in New York state. It wasn't even his brother-in-law; he did his own brokerage and trading, he did his own custody work and his NAV (net asset value) client statements were totally bogus. You should understand what the strategy is and what it should produce.

Richard Wilson: Right. So it sounds like it's what you referred to earlier. They somewhat willfully looked the other way because they wanted to impress their boss, their ultra-high-net-worth family, or their clients with these consistent returns that make them look good, right?

Frank Casey: Yeah, that and there was tremendous conflict; people were conflicted all along the pipeline. What happened with some of these funds of funds was that they had analysts inside of these funds of funds with Chartered Financial Analyst designation or Financial Risk Manager designations, etc. Whether they did their homework or not, I don't know, but I suspect what happened was that when they were first hired they were asked to do checks and balances and to do due diligence. They came up with a whole bunch of questions and the boss basically buried it with willful blindness because they were just making too much money at it.

Talk about a conflicted arrangement! The wealth management banks, the funds of funds that invested in Madoff, they were charging their clients a percent, let's just call it a percent or some basis point to basically run that client's money. They were then paid an extra 2 percent to 4 percent by Bernie per year for providing the capital and without disclosing it; so they were conflicted all over the place. So what does an investor do? Well, I wouldn't trust the statements unless I had my own auditor doing something and double-checking. The way Bernie used to handle that, by the way, was that on the bottom of his statements it would say, "Not to be used for your tax return." Auditors that were hired by wealthy clients would call Bernie's office and say, "Hey, I need to check on this or that" and he would say, "Listen, if you want to check on this or that, we are going to give you back your money" and then the client would waive his own auditor off because he didn't want to be kicked out because it was the goose that was laying the golden eggs.

Richard Wilson: So in TIPS, Third-Party Verification is the first part. Let's talk about the second part.

Frank Casey: "I" is internal controls. When you look at a manager, you want to look at his record of compliance. Does he have a compliance manual, does it specify checks and balances inside of one's organization? You want segregation of the responsibilities. You don't want the trader also running the books. Baring's went down because the trader was running the book and could play with the numbers. The trader had a shadow account that no one even knew about for which the bank's balance sheet was at risk. You want to double check everything.

One of the management firms that I worked with in the past, a bank in London I was a consultant to, had a fellow who ran the due diligence side. He was at one time a brain surgeon and he basically discovered hedge funds in his 30s. When he began studying hedge funds he said to himself, the qualitative side is missing in the due diligence regimen on a lot of these firms and on top of that, those that have the qualitative side don't apply it in any systematic format. He created a whole checklist, and each item had to be initialed off by the person doing the due diligence with date, time, and comment. Now, there was a standardized procedure on everything. A good part of this whole TIPS concept I gleaned off of him over these years, and what he always demanded (which I found very interesting) was a CFO in the linkage. Bigger hedge funds might have their own CFO and the funds of hedge funds should have an internal CFO, but a smaller manager can't afford a CFO. They maybe should contract with a CFO instead. The idea of the CFO is you want all of their pedigree basically at risk; they report to no one. It's a series of internal checks and balances. They are going to make sure that the back office has depth to it, there is complexity in the firm's structures, and that not just one or two people are controlling everything.

Madoff, believe it or not, was running his whole fraud off of the third floor of his office in the Lipstick Building and no one was allowed down there except the people that were phonying up the documents. It was quite naïve the way they were doing it. After the fact, Harry Markopolos, my investigative partner on that case, wrote the book *No One Would Listen* (2010, John Wiley & Sons) about our story and now the documentary *Chasing Madoff* will be released in late August 2011 across 15 cities and we will see if it gets traction. It's basically a story behind the story of what we were doing, and it's built as a financial thriller.

We were a little paranoid because we were dealing with one of the most powerful people on Wall Street and nobody was listening to us. On the other hand, when you look at this thing, what came out after the fact, each bank has a clearing number and the same clearing number would show up in multiple banks, which made no sense. In other words, such and such bank supposedly you were using had the same exact clearing numbers as another bank, no. No one ever doubted, including the SEC; no one ever got a hold of the Depository Trust Company number (DTC) number and basically checked the counterparty of any one of his trades. They could have asked for his options trading desk. He used an option strategy, so someone should have said to him, "Give me your options trading desk." He didn't have one.

These are red flags that we laid out for the SEC; we had 29 red flags and 26 pages, all documented case studies of who to call, when to do it, and what to look for, and they failed to pick up the phone on any of them because we were "a competitor." Who better to blow the whistle on a fraud than somebody who understands the business, right?

Richard Wilson: The next part of the TIPS process is really the part that kind of blinded everybody because of Madoff's connections and his kind of professional background. People didn't look at the other parts of the system that you are setting forth here, this whole pedigree section, right?

Frank Casey: Absolutely. The next part is pedigree. That is the one that got everybody and the pedigree on a couple of levels. One, professionally in his business, he was a chairman of NASDAQ; he was the developer of the Electronic Trading System. I mean, he was a bright man. I asked one of his major competitors in the earlier days who was a founder of a major trading firm, "Was your business profitable, and could Bernie make a lot of money doing it?" I already knew the answer, but I wanted to hear from him. He said, "Oh, it was extremely profitable when the difference between the bid and the offer was at least one eighth of a point, which is 12 and a half cents, right? So sometimes on certain markets it was a quarter of a point. We would buy on the bid side, and sell on the offer side all day long; we could make that spread, so that was very profitable." I said, "Well when did it turn unprofitable?" He said, "When we went to decimalization and the bid offer spread dropped to pennies." He said, "We sold our business and we sat there and watched Bernie make money year after year after year and we said, 'How is this guy making money?'" I believe personally, that if you ever find a clean set of books, you are going to find that, in order to maintain his position as king of Wall Street, he was moving money from the Ponzi scheme over to his execution business to continue to build himself out as the biggest on Wall Street. Everybody was blinded by his pedigree.

The answer to pedigree is that when I am speaking with a hedge fund manager, we'll try to figure out if we can come to somebody we both know personally within the first 15 minutes of conversation. Everybody is kind of linked in this field; it's not that big of a field. If we can't come to some common ground that I can make a few phone calls and check that, I am going to start digging. No matter who it is, even if they have great pedigree and even if we know someone in common, I will never move forward without a background check by an FBI type of guy, and it's not that expensive. I mean, if you are going to make a major investment in a manager, what in the devil is $750 to $1,500 to do a background check on the guy? You would be surprised what you find.

Thierry De la Villehuchet was the poor gentleman that committed suicide after losing a billion with Madoff.

Thierry De la Villehuchet...that's how I found Madoff in the spring of '98, and Thierry De la Villehuchet was the ex-president of Credit Lyonnais USA. Here is a man that is connected and he knew most every private wealth management bank in Switzerland and France; he was royalty himself in a way. He was a French nobleman, and his family, I figured out later on, bailed out Louis XIV. This man was well-connected and I found him when he had $320 million with Madoff. We warned him, Harry and me, all through the years and the reason we stayed in touch with him is because I built another business with Thierry not related to Madoff; we tried to build the business with him.

I had hired a floor trader, took him off the floor of an exchange in the options pits and moved him to Boston, and in the process I became very uncomfortable because of the arrogance of this individual. Before he ever got a hold of a client dollar, I called Thierry and I said we need a background check on this guy and he said, "Oh, we checked him out. There is nothing on him; he is fine." We hired Bo Dietl, the guy on *Imus in the Morning*, a top cop out of New York. He came back and said, "Well, we can't find anything yet." I said, "Keep digging, Bo; I just feel it."

The hair on the back of my neck was standing up. I didn't like the guy. Bo came back and said, "We got him." He said, "It took me sending a guy on to the West Coast to dig through the local court records, and buried in court records was the fact that this guy was connected for interstate wire fraud; he became an FBI informant and hence the case was buried." Immediately, we held a summary court-martial and we fired this guy, but we protected ourselves because we were willing to hire a private investigator. Some people loathe doing that because they feel, "Well, I won't get into the club, this guy won't take my money if I start sniffing around." Do yourself a favor; if the hair on the back of your neck stands up at all, walk away until it lies back down again, or keep digging.

Richard Wilson: That is great advice. Lots of people do a very basic criminal background check, but not an investigative background check in my experience.

Frank Casey: Absolutely, and sometimes cases get buried.

Richard Wilson:	Right. The last part of the TIPS process is on strategies or structure. This is the part that you said does have a quantitative component to it, but is still qualitative.
Frank Casey:	Yes, but still has a qualitative side. For instance, if I gave you a chart of returns and it had very few blips and it was going up from the lower left to the upper right rather consistently on a 45-degree angle or a 30-degree angle, you would probably tell me that that's the investment you would like to invest in, right?
Richard Wilson:	Right.
Frank Casey:	Now, I can develop that chart by writing out of the money options with no underlying equity in it. In other words, I can create for you a line that looks like that and I will be, 90 percent of the time, picking up dimes in front of a steamroller. One day, I will open lower, 30 percent to 50 percent, because I am basically selling the equivalent. The same goes if I were an insurance company underwriting catastrophic risk insurance and collecting premium; that's the line you're seeing, the premium intake, and I am not reinsuring so the margin's nice and fat. I'm also not diversifying my portfolio. One of these days, hurricane Katrina hits and I haven't bought reinsurance. You're just gone, wiped out. Looking at the metrics of math and saying, "Oh the reward, the risk is very good, and the Sharpe Ratio approaching 1.0, which is very good, or 1.5, that's extremely good." But once you start approaching 5 or 7 on the Sharpe Ratio, something's wrong and you have to find where the underlying risk is.

The other thing is that each return profile has a certain volatility structure to it and pattern of return that is commensurate with its strategy. If you are doing an equity options writing program, it's more of a steady line. Even if it's a legit one, it's more of a steady line with no big swing, no big returns. If a guy told you he is doing dynamic global tactical asset allocation or global macro work and he is getting a steady rate of return, something is wrong. That is a pattern that looks like the tooth of a saw, up and down, up and down, because there are tremendous swings in that marketplace and they come on your blind side. You have got to understand what the strategy is and what the pattern of return looks like. If you are hunting bear, it should be a bear print that you see, not a doe print, you understand? As a hunter, as an analyst, you start by first figuring out what game you are hunting and what the track should look like. Then, it's a matter of matching the sign to the animal that you are tracking. It's not just the metrics, it's the quantitative side; you have to understand what premium you are being paid for illiquidity.

I saw this happen; I helped build funds of funds tenfold, over six years, to about 2 billion. We moved from predominantly an 80 percent family office basis to 80 percent institutional basis during that period of time. In that process, because we were all risk managers, even me who was a marketing guy, we would study the illiquidity of things. Let's take something called asset-backed lending; it sounds simple enough: You basically provide liquidity or financing for assets. The asset has got a loan to market ratio of 50 percent or less, so it seems like a very secure loan, and so forth and so forth. They were being embedded inside our hedge funds that were providing monthly liquidity when the loan run off was 18 to 24 months. So, guess what happened? They get inside fund-of-funds that are offering monthly liquidity.

When I was competing on a funds-of-funds basis in finals, I was just amazed; these funds-of-funds competitors are offering monthly liquidity to institutions investing $150 million per. I feel strongly that they have 25 percent or more of their money in asset backed lending managers, so sure enough when the illiquidity hits and people demand their money back then these loans are sold not . . . it's the joke of Wall Street, when you are a manager and you call up the trading desk of the various firms for asset backed lending or any illiquid structured finance, like a CDO or whatever, or a collateralized debt mortgage obligation, and you say, "I need a mark" and they will say, "Oh, for the book or for a trade?" The reason is for the book it's 98–102 bid offer. Oh, you want to sell 30 million? 70 bid.

That's what happens, because they couldn't hedge off the other side of the trade efficiently. Everybody is selling and that's what happened to a lot of these structured finance fields that even the government is buying out paper at 60 cents on the dollar when the actual market value of that paper is even 38 cents today. It's amazing because you can't move that much paper that's illiquid, so you have to understand the liquidity of the trade—not what they tell you in the documents that they are going to provide you, but the actual underlying liquidity of the instrument that they are invested in. The liquidity of the instrument must match the liquidity of the structure. I guess what I am saying is if you are going to go into a military conflict, if your job is to charge the hill, you don't do it without proper support from air cover, artillery cover, ammunition and supply; you must have the proper talent to protect yourself and achieve your mission.

Some people say, "Well, I never do alternatives." Guess what, even as a pension manager, say you have an assumption of 8 percent and bonds are yielding you two and a half or three and a half and you are not getting it there, then you are going to tell me that you are going to get it from the stock market with consistency 10 years, 11 years, it's a zero return. Pick your assumption on the stock market. Some people say I can't get there from here without alternatives; I just don't want more of the same, thank you. They want more transparency, they want delineation on the liquidity and the potential risk of illiquidity; they need help in advisory in building their own personalized portfolios and they don't want to buy off-the-shelf products. They don't get the level of transparency and the due diligence regimens under what I call TIPS—Third-Party Verification, Internal Controls, the Pedigree flags, and the Strategy metrics, both qualitative and quantitative.

Richard Wilson: Right, and that makes a lot of sense. Most people focus on that almost exclusively, yet even though they are kind of playing in that sandbox during maybe 80 percent of the due diligence process. I don't think oftentimes they look at deer tracks as deer tracks and bear tracks as bear tracks; they just look for something that falls in this ratio with this track record with this amount of assets under management. They want to check all 40 boxes on their check list, and if those 40 boxes get checked then we move them up to the next level of the investment committee, etc. I think that's an interesting approach.

Do you see that governance boards are being built that are external and look out for the greater good of those families within the family office? Are they separate independent governance boards? Do you see more governance processes and boards in place or do you think that people are just going to be a bit stricter on their DDQ processes than they were before Madoff? What do you think is the reaction right now?

Frank Casey: Now, I think you are on to something very interesting here in governance boards and providing stewardship for the money. Family offices are more akin to corporations. I was a corporate risk manager for many years. Family offices don't have a homogenous portfolio. Family offices have short-term liabilities and intermediate-term liabilities and long-term liabilities. Short-term is to keep the family going, educate the kids, whatever. Intermediately must be that you want to do XYZ until you get a liquidity event or you have had your liquidity event; you want to create an environment where you can fund certain charities and so forth intermediately. Long term might be when you want to liquidate your wealth and endow a museum or whatever. Whatever those liability streams are, they had different horizons and because of that they can accept the various levels of illiquidity and volatility matched to the time horizon. What you need to do as a family office is not chase the hot dot and look at the manager and then say, "Oh, this man is up, or he is down, and how does he do against his competitors?"; the more important question for the family office is what type of strategies managers should I build within each one of these asset buckets that match the liability bucket?

You want liquid alpha or liquid alternatives perhaps in your stocks and bonds for your short-term liabilities. You can go a little more illiquid such as distressed or event-driven things, activism and things like that, or reshaping corporations in your intermediate bucket. In your long-term bucket you can look at emerging markets, emerging managers, and other things where you can hit the long ball, perhaps, and you know you are going to accept illiquidity, more private equity, and so forth in those buckets. That sounds like a CIO function only but no, it's actually a governance board function, too.

One of the things that family offices struggle with all the time, I believe, and wealthy individuals, too, is they go to their accountant and their accountant says one thing; then they go to their lawyer, they take that back, and they sit there trying to triage that. Then, they go to their financial advisor and they are getting feedback and they are triaging that. Take all of your advisories, your brokers, your asset managers, your legal guys and your accountants, put them on a continuum, and they come to a quarterly meeting just like a board of directors. Decisions are made at the quarterly meeting and they battle it out there. They have to be brought into the floor and argue it out for the good of the family.

Richard Wilson: That is some great advice for family offices. Thank you for all your time today, Frank.

Frank Casey: My pleasure. Thank you very much.

FAMILY OFFICE INTERVIEW WITH JOHN GRZYMALA

Our next interview is with family office veteran John Grzymala. John has more than 20 years of industry experience and is based in New York City. He has worked as the chief financial officer of a family office and has helped multiple single family offices with their investments, including the acquisition of more than 20 companies. To provide you with a bit on his background, our interview starts with John sharing some details of how he got into the industry.

John Gryzmala: In July of 1988, I was with a privately held company in Connecticut and things weren't going the way I wanted them to go in the company. I started doing some job searching, and I looked in the *New York Times*. I found in the Help Wanted section, which I guess not too many people use anymore, a CFO position. When I interviewed for the position, clearly it was something I was interested in, something I could handle. After I took the job, though, I quickly realized that the position was much more than just CFO for this family-held business. I have to say prior to this, I really didn't have much in the way of family office experience, but I had good business sense.

The family was hiring a large number of household help. They weren't doing any background checking. Some of the people were just paid by check. No 1099s were issued, no payroll taxes were being deducted, but not because of any issues with doing that, they just didn't think of it. The same was true in other areas like art collection. The patriarch was developing a large art collection. When I got on board with him, he might have only had 20 pieces. He would say to me in passing, "No one could tell me what this piece is." That got me thinking about the insurance; were they insured properly, were appraisals done on a regular basis? Because of all of these different issues, I, in effect created a family office to manage all of these issues of the family.

Richard Wilson: Was the family office started because someone sold a business?

John Gryzmala: No, that wasn't the reason here. When I came on board, the patriarch was still in the process of developing different business areas. He was more focused on just getting the controls in place, a CFO-type position for all of these various entities.

Richard Wilson: How did you and your team split up the investment portfolio and the capital that you managed between individual securities that you could buy and sell versus mutual funds and ETFs, versus kind of hard assets in real estate as well as fund managers such as private equity and hedge fund managers?

John Gryzmala: First of all, there was no investment committee outside of the patriarch and me. We would look at various investments that came to us—and by the way, I have to say our basic model was a PE (private equity) model. We were looking to buy relatively small companies that had, as my boss would say, "billion-dollar potential."

There were no formal guidelines, as I was saying; we only wanted to put 50 percent of money in the PE space, and it was on a deal-by-deal basis. We might have a very high percentage at any one point, and then we look at the overall investment portfolio and say, "We are a little bit too heavy here. Why don't we go to a VC firm or maybe a hedge fund or maybe some angels and sell pieces of the business to bring the percentage down to what we are more comfortable with?" There were very rough guidelines that we kind of tooled around with on a monthly basis.

Richard Wilson:	Did your single family office ever invest in a private equity fund or you just acted as a private equity fund yourself?
John Gryzmala:	We acted as a private equity fund; we never invested in another fund. The portfolio was very rough numbers, with 20 percent art; a very large art collection. At one point, it was 900 pieces. Maybe another 60 percent or so was in the private equity area, and the balance in more traditional marketable securities. He wasn't really interested in hedge funds. When we discussed that, for some reason, he always talked himself out of doing that. It was more of a plain vanilla–type stock and bond portfolio that we put together with our leading bank.
Richard Wilson:	With the companies that your team would acquire, was there a research process? Would you then actively reach out to them? Or, did you work with an M&A consultant or some sort of business brokers professional to help you?
John Gryzmala:	Yeah, M&A consultant, business broker, etc.; there is never a shortage—even going back quite a few years ago, there was never a shortage of deal flow. At one point, he wanted to have someone on staff to do that, and I convinced him that that didn't really make any sense to pay someone salary when we had the ability of getting those deals without having to pay a salary.
Richard Wilson:	Do you think that's actually relatively common? I was asked to speak last week at an angel investment conference. Their interest in me was that I had experience in working with family offices. I'm finding more connections every year between family offices and angel investors. Do you think this is a common type of investment for family offices?
John Gryzmala:	Yeah. I have met a number of families through the various family office organizations that I have joined. I would say a fair number are definitely using the same type model that we have used. I can't put a percentage on it but definitely, there is a good percentage of them doing just that.
Richard Wilson:	Do you think there is anything unique that companies should be doing to reach out to family offices in terms of attracting capital from that pool?
John Gryzmala:	I think the answer is yes, but as we spoke earlier, because of the privacy issue alone it's very tough to get in the door. I found the best way is to just do good old-fashioned networking. That, I think, is how it works. I have met quite a

number of business type brokers over the last year or so, and they really have good interesting deals that they are working with. Many of these business brokers are working both sides. They are looking to help their family sell a business, but also looking to raise money for other businesses. There is really no conflict of interest as far as I am concerned. They are the business brokers in effect, and I think they are doing a good job with it. I think that's a good way to go as well as networking. Reaching out to families directly I think is just difficult. I am not so sure that's the best way to go.

Richard Wilson: Was there kind of a family constitution or an investment policy or a values or mission statement that guided what you did? Or, because it was a single family office and really just the patriarch and yourself making up the investment committee, were there just loose guidelines that your team worked off of?

John Gryzmala: Going forward, I am a firm believer in a mission statement. But the way we ran our operation, it was loose, very loose; more oral agreements on how we were going to proceed.

Richard Wilson: It sounds like to me that growth was very important to the patriarch given your private equity investments. Was it more about growth than capital preservation?

John Gryzmala: That's 100 percent right, growth ahead of capital preservation.

Richard Wilson: And about how many different investments would be made at one time? Would it be something like 15 or 20 at one time, and were they are all very long-term? Or would it be more like two or three at a time?

John Gryzmala: Yeah, smaller number; we would focus on those, get them developed and then look to others.

Richard Wilson: Can you provide any hard lessons learned to other family offices that are actively making investments?

John Gryzmala: Well, keep your finger on the business on a daily basis. I think that's the most important comment or advice that I can give. Things change so quickly, not only the personnel but also technology. We have bought a lot of technology companies. I remember one that didn't work. We invested in a company that was making a very small storage device. This was before CDs came into the marketplace. Well, if we had done a little bit better homework, we would have found out that another company had a similar device, and they beat us to the IPO and ours basically just died. That's just an example of how you just have to keep your tabs on the marketplace and the business.

Richard Wilson: Somewhat related to that, how many people do you think should be on a single family office team? I have heard that many family offices being run with three people, sometimes five people. I've also heard some others that have teams of 50 to 70 people for a single family office.

John Gryzmala: Yeah. I actually interviewed for a family office that had a staff of 50. It's a large family. We were fairly substantial. At one point, we did have a very large staff. Very large by my definition is upwards of 20 people. My philosophy for the last 10 or 12 years being with the family was lean and mean.

I believe in outsourcing for all of my decisions basically. On my staff was an art curator. Why? Because the art collection was many hundreds of pieces. I needed that person on board. I had a couple of bookkeepers and basically a personal assistant to me and the patriarch and the family.

At one point, we had an attorney on board. If I asked the attorney a question related to a trusts and estates issue, his response would be, "Well, I think this might be how it should be handled, but let me go and check with our outside trusts and the estates attorney." Using that as a prime example, it didn't make any sense to me to have those people on board to incur those expenses when I could get best-of-class service by going to our outside trusted advisor. Be it a wealth management person, a tax planner, or a trusts and estates attorney or other attorney, that's how I ran the show. I am a firm believer of lean and mean.

Richard Wilson: I am wondering for single family offices who are listening to this interview or reading this, and from your knowledge of working for a single family office for 20 years, do you think there is some sort of rule of thumb that a middle-road single family office could kind of judge themselves on? Is it for every $50 million they should have three to four people on board, or is there any type of rule of thumb like that?

John Gryzmala: It's hard to answer. I think it's a function of how much you are investing in different vehicles. If you are worth a billion dollars and your mind-set is, "Well, I don't want to invest in anything that's less than $100 million," well theoretically, you only have 10 investments. But if your logic is to invest no more than $5 million, well, you are going to be faced with dozens and dozens of investments that need more monitoring and therefore need more staff. I don't think there is an easy answer to your question. It depends on the family. As when you meet with Angelo Robles in the future, I think you will hear from him the phrase "if you know one family office, you know one family office." I mean, everyone is different.

Richard Wilson: I think that's a recurring theme that people are hearing in these interviews.

John Gryzmala: I was always looking for best-of-class service and advice, and the only way that I found that I could get that is to rely on outside consultants, not on the internal staff.

Richard Wilson: Sure. What should family offices budget for while looking to bring in someone who is slightly more junior than yourself, perhaps?

John Gryzmala: Well, that's a good question, for a smaller family office, maybe under a $100 million, someone to come in and get it up and running might be in the $150,000-a-year range, which is a ballpark obviously.

If the assets under management are closer to $500 million, it might be in the $200,000 to $300,000 a year range. In the billion-dollar range, well, the sky is the limit depending on the responsibilities and whatnot. I think it's pretty hard to bring someone in for too much less than $150,000 in this part of the country. In the greater New York area, I think that's a good rule of thumb. In other parts of the country, it might be a little bit different.

Richard Wilson: Do you think there should always be some sort of performance-based measurement based on measuring risk or helping manage risk or manage investments or making the PE investments to work out in the end?

John Gryzmala: My answer to you is yes, and the experience I have there is just with my own personal agreement with the patriarch. My overall compensation package was highly incentivized with the bonus. So the salary was, relatively speaking, modest. At the end of the year, though, we had a very good and detailed analysis of what was accomplished, and I was paid accordingly. I think that's definitely key.

Richard Wilson: Great, well thanks again for your time, John. I know that the tips provided here will be very valuable to those who listen to this interview.

John Gryzmala: Great. Thanks a lot, Richard.

FAMILY OFFICE INTERVIEW WITH MATTHEW ANDRADE, DIRECTOR OF INVESTMENT ANALYSIS AT KINNEAR FINANCIAL

Our next interview is with Matthew Andrade, director of investment analysis at Kinnear Financial, a commodities-focused single family office based in Calgary, Canada. Matthew Andrade joined Kinnear Financial in 2010. Before doing so, he earned roughly 12 years of experience in the investment industry and investment analysis already. As an investment analysis director at Kinnear, he provides financial, economic, and capital market analysis for investment initiatives.

Richard Wilson: Matthew, you are very experienced, but running investment analysis for a single family office must keep you busy.

Matthew Andrade: I could say quite confidently that there is never a dull moment.

Richard Wilson: I just gave a two-sentence overview of your background and the single family office you work for, but could you explain a little bit about how you got on the family office side of things? Also, what makes your single family office unique maybe from other single family offices?

Matthew Andrade: Sure. Initially, I had known Jim Kinnear, our founder for a while, but I had gone and done a stint with my prior employer in Scotland covering oil, gas, and oilfield services, and merger and acquisition work. When I came back here, I sat next to Jim at a dinner and he said that he was trying to build a business, doing a number of different things, including oil and gas royalties, which is what he had done in building his prior company, Pengrowth Energy Trust. He took that public in 1988 at about a $12.5 million IPO and to-day it's somewhere between $4 and $5 billion in mar-ket capitalization listed on Toronto and New York. He was in the process of retiring from there. He actually officially retired in late 2009 and he was spinning up Kinnear Financial, reactivating what was primarily a holding company and converting it into a true fam-ily office. He had started a next generation Canadian oil and gas royalty trust, this time on a private basis. He was looking for someone that could do both M&A analysis work as well as run the investments for the family office.

Richard Wilson: It seems like an amazing opportunity to work for that successful of a team, and even though it's very large corporations connected, I do see that your investment team has five or six people, and you are basically head-ing up that investment analysis team, right?

Matthew Andrade: That's right. The investment team, per se, is myself and one analyst here. We have a fully functional and sep-arate finance team and several accountants and a ded-icated CFO as well. We work quite closely with them to make sure we have the capital where it needs to be at any particular moment in time.

Richard Wilson: Is there a formal investment committee that meets pe-riodically, or is it basically you leading the team?

Matthew Andrade: No, we don't have an investment committee, per se. I do have team meetings with my analyst for idea genera-tion and to make sure the tasks aren't slipping through the cracks, but my investment committee is a simple phone call to my Principal, and if he likes the idea, we go forward; if he doesn't, we don't.

Richard Wilson: I see. How does tax efficiency fit into your priorities when you are analyzing things versus income growth or capital preservation? Is tax efficiency number one, or is it farther down the list?

Matthew Andrade: It's much farther down the list. Our general view is that the tax tail should not wag the business dog, so if the investment makes sense and we believe we can make 50 percent or 100 percent return on our money because it is a junior oil and gas or a junior metals and mining stock, then we will take that on in the knowledge that it may also not work. Tax would be a very, very ancillary consideration for us.

Richard Wilson:	Okay, that's interesting. Your team has, I'm sure, a global span of investment with an institution as large as yours, so you are probably investing all over the world, is that a correct assumption?
Matthew Andrade:	We are, although it is a different animal, the Canadian capital markets, in that most of the assets that we invest in on the portfolio front are domiciled in Canada. The neat part about the Canadian capital markets is that they understand natural resources quite well, no matter where they are in the world, whether it's oil and gas or a mining project; it's very, very common for a Canadian company or Canadian listed company to have a copper mining project in the DRC in Africa or an oil and gas project in Argentina. In terms of global diversification, I can get an awful lot although we are still buying a Canadian listed entity.
Richard Wilson:	Okay. I would guess the answer to this next question is no, but I am interested. Does your group ever work with CTAs or commodity funds that have some super-specialization in something that you need a partnership with? Would you like to have someone who is watching that small marketplace very, very closely to get partnered with a fund manager who manages commodities, or is that pretty much what your team does and you are excelling at it, so that wouldn't make sense?
Matthew Andrade:	It is the latter; we don't put money to external managers. Period. Our view is fairly simple. I would say that I don't mind being held responsible for performance, but I do very much mind being held responsible for performance I don't control. We don't put money in external managers, especially not in the commodity space because the CTA or some other commodity futures fund just doesn't make sense to us.
Richard Wilson:	Do you see any other trends related to private banking structures or family office industry growth in the area?
Matthew Andrade:	I don't know about the private banking structures here; I mean, we do deal with some private banks, like the private banking arms of some of the Canadian banks for a variety of reasons. But I think as it relates to building of structure itself, at least in Calgary in particular it is a very relationship-based town.
	Guys remember the guys that they dealt with when they didn't have a lot of money, so they tend to be very,

very loyal to those guys, whether they are stockbrokers or legal advisors or that kind of thing. While the family office concept is an interesting one, I was very mindful when I joined Jim that he had a number of relationships across the brokerage community on the sell side, for instance, that they weren't just going to replace. As a family office executive, you have to be mindful of those relationships and remember that it was his relationship that built up over 30-odd years.

Richard Wilson: Sure, that makes sense. It seems like a smart way to go when you are so specialized. A few family offices I met are really specialized in commercial real estate or one or two operating type businesses that are still operating.

What about when it comes to family office training? Are you so specialized that you just train them in-house with experience and they cut their teeth by watching your team manage investments, look at them allocate capital, and they just learn from that strictly? Or are there a couple of family office conferences or web site training portals or other resources that your team kind of relies on to teach your team the family office side of what's going on inside your family office?

Matthew Andrade: In terms of conferences, I have been to a number of conferences and actually spoken at a couple for a group called Camden out of the UK; a fantastic group of people. What I liked about those conferences was that they were driven by content as opposed to sponsors. It's difficult if I wanted to find, for example, a UK large cap manager. I could find a consultant that would help me do that. I don't need to be pitched on that when I go to a conference because I am looking for the content of the conference, I am looking for the ideas. Camden did a very good job at that.

In terms of other sort of training for the team members of my team, it's been more us teaching them at a very, very basic level because this is for both the undergrads and the graduates. It's their first real job, so explaining how, for example, merger arbitrage works, you have to spend an hour or so explaining the concepts and detailing them via live example, but that's how everybody learns at some point. I didn't come out or you didn't come out as a fully minted professional;

you just have to learn them, so a big part of my role is teaching them in the hopes that if they understand the "why" then the "how" and the "what" will fall out from that.

Richard Wilson: I think that in a few ways some time and money gets misplaced in conferences in the industry just because there is so much pitching and selling done when the content is so valuable. If you are spending all your time traveling to, say, London for one of those conferences, hopefully by the time you get there, you are spending your time learning something that's critical to your business or growing some critical relationships. I think that is a great point to make.

What would you recommend to someone who is reading this or listening to this and they work inside of a family office?

For example, I interviewed one person who had worked at a single family office and the patriarch died and the family office was shut down. He was kind of left without a chair and hadn't had to market himself in 20 years. He had a hard time getting his foot in the door at other family offices. Do you have any suggestions for people trying to get their foot in the door somewhere new?

Matthew Andrade: You know, it's funny; I had somebody reach out to me as a result of the posting that I had made on the LinkedIn Group that sort of generated this discussion. He was just asking me, "I would like to learn a little bit more about this, I am currently a portfolio manager overseeing U.S. large cap equities, but have thought about getting into the family office space." It was just an e-mail saying, can I take 20 minutes of your time and can we talk about this? I would encourage anybody to do that. If you say, "I just want to learn a little bit more," nobody is that busy that they can't spare half an hour to talk to somebody about it. For other family office executives, I would say please make the time for somebody that is trying to learn a little bit more about this and trying to develop a relationship; just like a university intern that's coming out trying to get their first job, they just want to soak up as much they can.

Get to know somebody and then in the event you get to a point where you do need to hire somebody that is a little more experienced, maybe you have already developed a relationship as result of one of those contacts. If you are somebody trying to break into the family office business, don't be shy about sending an e-mail to someone like myself or another executive. The worst that happens is they don't respond to the e-mail or they say thanks but no thanks, in which case you're no further behind than you were today.

Richard Wilson: Right, I think that's excellent advice.

Matthew Andrade: The answer is not suffering from sort of 9,000-pound phone syndrome; sometimes you just have to pick up the phone and reach out to people.

Richard Wilson: Sure. I think that some people who may naturally have the technical analysis skills or some of the deepest risk management knowledge or financial modeling knowledge, for example, may be more introverted and then less likely to be those people who pick up the phone even though it might be the more valuable candidates to speak with. I think that's great to hear from someone who is a director of investment analysis that you should take a proactive approach like that and not wait for something to kind of fall into your lap kind of by accident.

Matthew Andrade: Now, if you are afraid to pick up the phone, then send the e-mail, right? Quite often you can. If you are smart you will re-read the e-mail, make sure that's exactly what you want to say, and then when you hit Send, there is no personal interaction, for lack of a better term, so it goes nowhere. Then it goes nowhere and you don't get embarrassed; you don't get flustered. So yeah, send the e-mail if you are not comfortable picking up the phone.

Richard Wilson: Many family offices are overwhelmed with capital-raising inquiries; how does your team deal with that?

Matthew Andrade: Sure. What I would say is on the investing side, when we have capital looking to deploy, we have a pretty rigorous due diligence process. When we speak to management teams, we want to crawl all inside of those companies and understand exactly what the prospects are and what are the risk factors involved. With very few exceptions, for good or for bad, what's happening is companies just get tired of us asking all the questions. They say, "Listen, you know what, I don't know if we are the right partners for you," which in a funny kind of way actually validates our process, because if we are not going to get the cooperation and support and the engagement from the management team that we are investing with before we make the investment, it's highly unlikely that's going to happen after we make the investment. In fact, it's probably going to get worse. So, on the flip side, we do see an awful lot of ideas looking for capital.

I would say if somebody was looking for capital, do some research on the family office. Sometimes they have web sites like us, sometimes they don't, but if they do have web sites check them out. Anyone can go to our web site and see that we are commodity guys, so we are not tech guys; we are not real estate guys. If somebody pitches me on a real estate deal, it's not impossible that we could do it, but it's very difficult. It would be very difficult for us to do because it's not where we have core expertise. If you are pitching a tech deal to a family that's made their money in the farming business or the agri-business sector, you have got to know that it's a long shot at best. When the family office says, "It's not a fit for us this time, thanks very much," then take that for what it is and just move on. If they say, "You know, it's not a fit for us today, but we'd like to stay in touch," then you can put them on a mailing list or a press release list, but you have got to be careful because quite often that's a very polite way of saying thanks but no thanks; take it for what it is.

Richard Wilson: That sounds like safe advice. I have had an experience myself where a lot of times I might get asked to be put on a mailing list, but then nothing will happen and they are very busy and they are only allocating to one or two managers a year, so chances are you should probably move your focus somewhere else.

Matthew Andrade: Right.

Richard Wilson: Do you think that sending things in the mail is definitely more effective than just sending an e-mail or leaving a voice mail, if you also send something in the

	mail, it can't hurt you and probably helps a lot or do you think that's probably a waste?
Matthew Andrade:	I would go in the opposite direction. I would say the problem with sending something to me by mail is that I just get so many calls during the course of the day; all it's going to do is land in the pile of pitch books that I receive that I don't look at. If somebody is looking for capital in the commodity space, they are better off phoning me. If somebody is going to phone me, I try to be professionally courteous enough to phone back, even if it's a "thanks but no thanks." If they have taken the time to phone and leave a message, then I will find out what it's all about. In one particular case, an individual phoned me on a project and it looked interesting; had I not returned that call after I dug a little bit further, then I wouldn't have known that it was an interesting transaction to look at. You never know where something is going to go.

As an investor, deal flow is your lifeline, so you don't want to turn off your relationships with the sell side, be it either investment banks or brokers or that kind of thing. If they phone you with an idea, you should at least give a cursory look to all of them and provide your honest feedback to the broker or the banker and say, "Listen, interesting deal, here is why this doesn't work for us" or "Here, if you made this tweak here or you change that bell or whistle over here, it might become a little more interesting to us." That feedback is also useful to them. |
| Richard Wilson: | With one analyst assisting you, are you enabled to do that? I ask because I think some family offices might be listening to this and say, "Wow, you know if I return every call? It could be an extra 60 hours a week with all the volume we get." Does your team help you complete analyses that you know need to be done as well as maybe help take a few of these phone calls? |
| Matthew Andrade: | Most of the calls tend to come to me just because they are sort of the proverbial gray- or no-hair perspective, depending on your outlook. Very often I travel a fair bit, so what I will end up doing is if I get an e-mail with an idea or a pitch, I will forward it over to my analyst just simply saying "Your thoughts." They will write |

a quick sort of e-mail response to me and they might spend an hour or two looking at that. Then based on their response, I would say, "Okay, we should learn more about this" or "Okay, somebody go back to this guy and say this is going to work." You have to trust your team members; you have hired them for a reason, so let them go do their job and in this particular case, it doesn't matter whether the team members are a year out of school or 10 or 15 years out of school. You hired them generally because they have got good instincts.

In my case, I can't read every pitch book; I can't talk to everybody. If my colleagues here can act as a first line of defense, then they should do that. Empower your people to go try to do those kinds of things and then back up, when they say, "No, I don't think this is a good idea" and the individual pitching the idea basically tries to go around them and say, "Well, you know you are not a decision maker, I know I need to talk to somebody that's a little more senior to listen." If it wasn't good enough for them, then it is not good enough for me.

Richard Wilson:	Right.
Matthew Andrade:	You have to really back your people because if you don't then your people are going to wonder what they are for.
Richard Wilson:	Right. Do you have one or two comments you didn't get to work into one of the questions, something you may have wanted to communicate to other family offices or family office professionals or did we kind of cover everything that you are hoping to get across?
Matthew Andrade:	Well, I think the only thing I would say to folks is understand what you are good at, but also understand what you are not good at. The difficulty I think where a lot of investments go wrong for folks is somebody did not want to be the one asking the very basic question in the room, that everybody else probably had, but nobody wants to look a little bit silly asking; maybe it's because I don't have any shame, but I don't have a problem asking those kinds of questions. If I still don't get the answer, then we just don't make the investment because ultimately as a family office executive, your primary job is to protect the wealth of

your Principal or your family, and if you can, grow it a little bit along the way.

So I get up every morning thinking, "How do I protect Jim's money, and how do I make sure that we don't lose it?" On that basis, it's actually a pretty simple discussion. If we don't understand the project or the investment, then we don't make it, because ultimately I have to then turn around and advocate for that for Jim to make an investment. As executives, understand the investments, whether they would be in fund managers, understand who the managers are, what their track records are, you know, go meet with them.

There is no substitute to face-to-face meetings. I spend the vast majority of my time either on the phone or in meetings trying to get to the bottom of all of these people that you want to invest with because, quite often, investments are driven around management teams. Go do that, but rely on your junior people; hire young folks out of university. They want to learn; they want to make a difference; they want to build their skills. Take a bet on somebody because you were a young professional once, too, looking for your first break, so try to build that. You are not going to hold on to them for 20 years; you know that, they know that. But, you can teach them to become a better professional and along the way, you maybe have some fun too.

Richard Wilson: Excellent. I appreciate you spending that time with me here today and sharing your advice with thousands of people in the industry that will read it.

Matthew Andrade: Very well. Thank you very much, Richard.

FAMILY OFFICE INTERVIEW WITH ANGELO ROBLES, PRESIDENT OF THE FAMILY OFFICE ASSOCIATION

The final interview in this chapter is with someone I've known for several years, Angelo Robles. Angelo runs an association of single family offices called the Family Office Association and has over 20 years of experience in investments and working with family offices. He was an Internet pioneer in retirement planning for Fortune 1000 executives, and he has also written several books and many independently published articles. He is the author of the white paper "Lawsuit Lottery and Protecting Assets" and "Structured Solutions: What Family Offices Need to Know."

The reason this interview is valuable is that we interviewed more than 30 single family offices and multi-family offices in this series, and almost all of them work inside of family offices. They see a very granular view of the industry by working inside of it. The single family office space is diverse, though, and hard to understand. Angelo has a 10,000-foot understanding of the industry today because he works with hundreds of family offices day to day.

Richard Wilson:	Thanks for allowing us to interview you today, Angelo.
Angelo Robles:	Richard, the pleasure is all mine. It's great to have a chance to talk to you again, and I look forward to our conversation.
Richard Wilson:	Could you add just a little bit of extra detail on exactly how you came to run the Family Offices Association and become so specialized in helping single family offices?
Angelo Robles:	I am happy to. I know you are focused on the part about Family Office Association which is of more direct value to your audience. We are now in the summer of 2011, and it was three summers ago in 2008. Talk about good timing, though; who would have known that about a month later in September, the world would feel like it could be coming to an end. At any rate, I had an opportunity three summers ago to really believe that there was a tremendous opportunity to build a global membership organization that would be dedicated exclusively to the single family office community. There are certainly a limited number of organizations that may have that perspective now, but I felt the timing was right for an organization based in Greenwich, Connecticut, that was very sophisticated in investing in global opportunities. The timing was right for families to join an organization that was really dedicated to the concept to believe the thought leadership of single family offices.
	I had a chance to really get together with many single family offices that I have known for a while, weigh my decision, get great feedback from them and have a chance to officially launch. You are testing my memory now, but that was October 14th of '08. I have been off and running ever since then. I have been very, very blessed and fortunate that our organization has been incredibly

successful, and really so simple. We don't advise; we don't consult. We are simply a private club, a membership organization, dedicated exclusively to single family offices around the world. What started modestly with maybe initially a dozen or a little more single family offices, we have been very blessed at this stage to have hundreds and hundreds of single family office relationships and members around the world. This proves to me my initial concept going back a couple of years ago that a single family office for a family that has the resources is a tremendous opportunity to have control, privacy, and customization.

I think those families, meaning the wealth owners and the single family office executives, needed an opportunity where they could get together, share ideas with their peers, and have detailed peer discussion on investing, on philanthropy, on family governance, etc. They also needed a place to have a chance to hear from amazing outside experts. We have been very blessed to have had John Paulson, Ray Dalio, Steven Cohen, Michael Milken, David Einhorn, Bill Ackman and many, many others, often in an intimate setting, to really provide our audience with an opportunity to interact with some true investment and other thought leaders around the world.

Richard Wilson: From your perspective, what would be your best guess of the total family office industry and, even more importantly, the number of single family offices in the world?

Angelo Robles: If you are more broad in your definition like you are and I'm becoming more a fan of and in favor, I think you are right. I think the definition, as you define it broadly, may very well be into the thousands. I don't know that 10,000 are in existence, but I do agree if we define it globally and as broadly as you are, I would say it's definitively more than 5,000.

Richard Wilson: Have you identified a few places or locations that seem to be hotbeds for family offices, particularly single family offices? Or do you think it's just extremely diverse geographically because many business owners want to stay in Virginia where they were running their business and sold their business and now they are in Virginia, or they are still in Texas, that's where they run their business, etc.?

Angelo Robles: I think it is very diverse and that really is both the joy and sometimes, for those on the outside, the challenge of a single family office, besides the fact that they should be very secretive and hard to identify. They certainly want to have a level of control, which is why there is an entity in place or, so to speak, a buffer between the outside world and the wealth owner or the family. A great choice as a single family office could be anywhere. I will be domestic here for a second, but we have single family offices or family Principals as well as the operations and executives in more remote areas, in Vermont, in Maine, in Wyoming, in Utah and Montana.

That being said, I do think there are a couple of unique pockets, and relatively that's going to be where some level of wealth is concentrated. I do think there are some nuances to understanding the wealth owners and the single family offices based in those locations. One of them—I will start in my own backyard here in Greenwich, Connecticut, which—being a greater suburb of New York City—obviously has a significant level of wealth and specifically nuanced or niched in hedge funds and private equity and Wall Street tycoons. It tends to be people that are highly sophisticated, specifically from a global perspective on alternative investments.

One of our other hotspots is Greater Palo Alto, where you are going to have a lot of angels and super angels, venture capitalists, tech entrepreneurs, a little bit of a younger persona, very entrepreneurial, often a big believer in really taking a direct stake and doing direct deals. It's a little different perspective to what they do. They may not be as frequent of an investor as, say, an East Coast family would be in, say, hedge funds. We have noticed nuances in wealth from Greater Greenwich that I noted in New York City, Palo Alto, in San Francisco, from city real estate families and media moguls of LA, to a combination of everything, and I would say Greater Palm Beach, to a little bit farther south from Palm Beach, in Miami, there is a unique aspect of a lot of Latin American families that set up operations in America.

I think you also hit upon a couple of other key areas in Asia. We have many families in Greater Singapore and Asia, in general. I think areas in Switzerland, as you noted, still the UK. I wouldn't discount areas in Dubai and Kuwait as being opportunities for certainly a lot of families that have wealth. I do find a lot of the Latin American families look at opportunities either currently in Europe or potentially in greater Miami as a hub. Certainly, there is significant wealth in the country where you are in right now, in Brazil, in Colombia, in Mexico, and Chile.

The hard thing for those from the outside to sometimes understand about single family offices is that they are all snowflakes, meaning they are all different. Sure, you could go to pockets of wealth in Greenwich, in Palm Beach, etc., and there is going to be more single family offices there than there would be in a small town, a less populated, or a less wealthy state. Again, single family offices and wealthy families are everywhere.

Richard Wilson: That's in line with what I've heard over the years. What percentage of single family offices do you think still own very large successful operating businesses versus being cashed out. It could be that their company went public, they sold the company, and now they just have the single family office. Now they manage their wealth, and may have some investments, but they are no longer the chief executive officer or chairman of a very large operating business. Do you get a feeling for what percentage are still operating fully versus those that have cashed out and that's why they've formed the single family office?

Angelo Robles: Well, I hate to go so much down the middle; it almost seems like a copout. But I would say potentially, given that I have said that, it still could be about 50/50. I noted the nuances in wealth where I am, in Greater Greenwich, Connecticut, or the areas like Palo Alto and Miami. If you ask one of my traders or hedge fund managers who are still active in what they do, and several of them are on the Forbes 100 list, they may give a different answer. We all heard the story about George Soros really changing the whole structure of his fund to basically be just a giant single family office for his own wealth because of the issues pertaining to registration and all those other aspects. People in that realm may look, after reaching a point in their career, at that whole aspect a little differently.

There are so many entrepreneurs and businesses and opportunities to create wealth and cash flow and still have a chance to create the inner workings of the beginning single family office, growing out of "the family business or the operation." That's another thing, though. That's what makes our world of family offices, and in my case specifically single family offices, so exciting. I used the word before, but they are all different; they really are like snowflakes. Every one that you meet is different. Of the hundreds and hundreds that I know, sometimes you get a little bit of familiarity with general concepts that may be applicable to some of them, but they are all different. Even the ones that look like they should be alike because they are located in the same town, they come from the same industry, the same generation, etc., they can still be so different. It's just exciting and like I mentioned earlier, sometimes challenging to those looking in from the outside.

Richard Wilson: At multi-family offices, investment committees are oftentimes made up of five to eight professionals, sometimes on a high end of 12 or more. Internal team members are normally part of the committee, though sometimes it may be an external risk consultant or chief investment officer brought in for another objective opinion. At least that is usually how I found it works.

At single family offices, some large ones may have 50 or 100 people on a team, but most that I found are smaller to medium-size teams with five to seven, sometimes 12 to 15, professionals within the single family office.

I am curious about investment committees at single family offices; have you noticed how they are typically structured? Does it mean that with a smaller team, they might bring in two or three or four external experts to supplement their team? Or how do you see investment committees working in single family offices?

Angelo Robles: Well, you are hitting upon a topic that I find exciting and unique among the single family offices. So much wealth has been created around the world, and it's new money. It's opportunities for these wealth creators, these family Principals, to really look at their single family offices differently. The same goes for families that have multigenerational single family offices that were created 20, 30, 40, 50 years ago. This is a new breed, and they are really taking a hands-on approach to what I will classify as a modern single family office, which tends to be very hands-on, very efficient and lean in terms of the level of talent comparative to maybe older or past single family offices, and partially that's due to their intellect and knowledge on investing and their hands-on approach as well as the technology. The way the world is changing makes it easier, if I can use that word, to have a more streamlined or lean single family office and be every bit as efficient, if not more efficient, than "a single family office of old."

One single family office I spoke to about a week or two ago noted to me, "Angelo, if I had to give a suggestion to other single family offices moving forward, don't get bogged down by layers of committees or management. Then we are going to lose what made you a single family office, a lean, mean machine that makes investment decisions quickly and decisively and is able to act." If you start to have too many layers, you are going to start to look a little bit like the entities that you are trying to get away from because of your perception of a level of conflict in what they do, however you perceive that to be.

I would say, again, there is no one right answer. Sometimes you have a wealth owner or a family that's very involved in the process; sometimes you have a really, really sharp, intelligent chief executive officer or chief investment officer, depending on how the single family office may be structured. Sometimes you have an investment committee made up of those within the single family office, wealth owners, as well as potentially some outside trusted resources, whether they would be bankers, attorneys, accountants, consultants, etc. By the way, they are often billion-dollar-plus families, so we are not talking small single family offices. They are very sophisticated. For them to make sharp decisions on what's going on now in the world, they have to be. Offices are presented with many options and challenges. Look at the last month where the markets were down, down, down and then up and down; look at 2008; look at how complex things are in today's world; look at the opportunities or challenges in different parts of the world like Latin America and Asia.

I think a single family office needs to use as much intellect as they can get from the outside that it trusts, but I think it has to make quick and decisive decisions internally. The office has to trust in the talent that it has to help make those decisions. I guess you could say, if the talent doesn't come through, then maybe you want to head in a different direction. The talent is going to have their feet to the fire, getting compensated properly, but they are also in the position where if they don't perform up to expectations, then the single family office or the wealth owners obviously could always go in a different direction. I have become less of a fan because of the feedback I am getting from our members of multiple layers of decision makers and looking to make that much more streamlined.

Richard Wilson: The next question is actually connected to that. In working with family offices, I have seen that many family offices don't invest in mutual funds. They sometimes invest in ETFs, but they often invest in the industry that they made their money initially, or in real estate, alternatives, and sometimes in direct investments to companies.

I am wondering, then, if you've found how single family offices invest the money within their portfolios. Has it been invested in one, two, or three areas on average? What have you found there?

Angelo Robles: Yes, I would like to comment on that. Again, simply being a global membership organization, being the founder and chief executive officer of it, for single family offices we don't get involved at all in consulting and advising; we are simply perhaps nothing more than an observer. I do have really, like you said, a 10,000-foot view with hundreds of global single family offices and I get a chance to learn. Still, I am so much in the learning stage myself in terms of what I am doing and I really love what I do. This answer falls a little bit within the notion that all single family offices are snowflakes; they are all different, and that's what makes them both exciting and challenging.

I do have, that being said, some comments to make, especially as we are going through our series of the modern single family office and how sophisticated—simplistic in some ways—but how sophisticated they are in their "investment approach." First of all, opportunities like 2008 and even currently what we are going though, families are going to be on the lookout to hedge their portfolio. They don't want to bleed 30 percent or 40 percent. They also understand that they are not a pension; they are not a Taft-Hartley foundation and/or an endowment that has certain tax and other advantages. If they are going to be looking at a goal like, "We want to net or we want to gross 8 percent or 10 percent," but when we factor in the potential high taxation of a lot of investments, including hedge funds of taxation, that may only net 2 percent or 3 percent or 4 percent maybe in today's market; that may not actually look half bad.

That's not the way that a family long term is going to be able to preserve the entrepreneurialism, the spirit and wealth, long term for decades or for multiple generations. They are going to have to do better than that. Now, everyone is going to make their decisions and have their own goals and values and a direction that they want to head. I am seeing a lot of single family offices that are very active in the process of investing and that are very active in alternatives, in direct deals, in emerging markets and exploring opportunities to hedge portfolio risk using options and derivatives, being strategic or, a better word, being tactical. That's what we are seeing with a lot of families, especially 2008 and later; they are being very, very tactical in their investment approach. They are almost, I could say, scanning the globe, looking for opportunities, narrowing down those opportunities and then selectively making a strategic bet on "markets or opportunities," micro, macro depending on the situation, how it flows out, etc.

We are also seeing a lot of families that are very active with emerging managers, probably more than I would have thought initially. I am being too generic, and my comment is, you know, "Angelo, anyone can pick up a magazine or a profile of the top 20 to top 50 hedge funds by AUM." I am not discounting those are managers that are great entrepreneurs; they have obviously been successful. A lot of their big money now comes from the big boys, the big pensions, and the people that could really move the $100 million-plus or more blocks. They rely on the pension consultants, meaning those organizations, the pensions are using the consultancies that are going to want a little bit of the safety in picking big blue. It's easy to pick a top-20, a top-30, or a top-50 manager; maybe that's going to grow 8 percent or 10 percent. Let's check the box and move on.

I think for a lot of families that are entrepreneurial, that are more aggressive, that are more tactical in their approach—I think they are going to want something different than that. They know that the research proves that a lot of the significant returns with "hedge fund managers" happen very early on. How do you identify, how do you source and vet, how do you diversify, how do you get a strategic edge? Do I then make an investment and get on the board of that smaller manager? Do I get favorable terms, "most favored nations" that would be very favorable to the early or the larger investor? How do I know who to choose that's maybe even a little bit off the radar? I want to make sure they have a pedigree. I want to make sure they are still really, really hungry. So they are motivated more on the two part of the 2 percent and 20 percent management and performance fees being charged, because once you get $2 billion, that 2 percent adds up. Maybe that takes a little bit of the edge off some managers that are "playing it safe" and, boy, I'm being way too broad, but I am giving you some of the feedback I am getting from my families.

We are seeing a lot of those people saying, "I want a real talented manager that is hungry, that has a niche in the market, and that has their money heavily tied up in what they are doing, so they really have their mouth where their money is, so to speak." How do you find that talent? Is it as simple as using databases? Sometimes, and sometimes that at least provides a generic opportunity. These are really, really small people that are connected, whether they are wealth creators or the right single family office executives. They are looking into the institutions that they work with, the banks, the prime brokers, even others to help identify.

They are looking inside those institutions, not as necessarily with the rainmaker—but that's no offense to the banker. I was a rainmaker; you were a rainmaker. It's a valuable role. They are looking for the intellect, the researchers, the traders, and the people that sort of speak in the know; they are using their old college connection. They are using everything they can to help the constant task of sourcing and vetting talented managers that could really give them an edge in a niche and give them true alpha. They are diversifying their investing on favorable terms.

                     Now again, I am being very broad in a response, but this is probably far more thought and attention for a really detailed complex answer. If you would ask me in terms of what families are doing, the families I know, they are smart; they are very tactical; they are diverse; they are trying to play on a playing field that is favorable to them as much as they can make it.

Richard Wilson: That's in line with a lot of what I'm hearing from other family offices, but that definitely adds a lot of color. Related to your topic of how to find some of those managers, that's basically what I'm betting on for the next few years as I'm looking to expand Richard Wilson Capital Partners.

                     We're focused on providing best-of-breed fund managers exclusively to family offices because I do believe that they do have unique needs in the industry. Sometimes they are marketed to as if they are not different from other investors. But they do have a lot of unique characteristics and needs, right?

Angelo Robles: There are a lot of things different. It's not just broadly equities, though, that I somewhat alluded to indirectly through hedge fund managers, opportunities for long-short, especially people like to be very talented in the shorting situation. There is still tremendous potential opportunity in credit and mortgages here domestically in the U.S., but especially in certain countries in Europe and opportunities in Latin America and Asia. You are starting to get into an area where the families, even if they may have 50 or 60 employees, may not necessarily have enough internal intellect to be able, if they are based here in America, to know every little nuance that's going on around the world.

                     Some of them open up an office and hire people that are local in those communities to help them better understand and invest, but that's really leveraging on the right centers of influence. I noted some of them, political thought leaders, traders, researchers inside institutions "in the know," are all valuable resources.

Richard Wilson: Great. I just have two more questions.

The first is that I recently spoke with a single family office that wants to form a fund around its commercial real estate investing expertise. They are experts in managing assets but they have never tried to raise capital before or work with other family offices. What would be your suggestion here? Most single family offices just get bombarded with communication all day long and a lot of it is not really catered to exactly what their needs are. All of these people are approaching them, trying to get access to the capital for every type of project you can imagine. Do you have any insights you could share with other family offices that have structured funds in the past?

Angelo Robles: Privacy is first and foremost as a membership organization. Even to fellow and the most pure single family office members, we do not publish our list of members. We don't make introductions. We occasionally have some single family offices that are members that reach out to us and say, "You know what, we are looking to get more involved in energy, in XYZ, or in Asia and in Latin America. If you happen to know families that potentially may be more open to meeting other single family offices, we would love to learn more and share research and information."

We are noticing a bit of an uptick with a more modern, slightly more open single family office with families trusting other like-minded families, always looking for peer advice or guidance. I guess you could say that would potentially be an organization like mine. We are not the only one, though, and our organization provides value to families in learning in a safe environment by sharing peer dialogue and having a chance to meet families on a favorable basis and learn that others are doing oil in Texas, or energy, or real estate in California, or direct deals in China. Then they can ask, "How is it working out, what's successful, what's not successful?"

It's a great opportunity for the right people like that on proper protocol, not someone on the marketing side or the fund side, but on the single family office side to be involved with an organization, whether it's local, regional or more global like we are and have a chance to collaborate with like-minded families. I would say from a legal perspective, especially domestically here in the U.S. with all that is going on with the SEC and with single family offices, make sure that they are setting up what they are potentially looking to do more carefully than ever. It would really need to have a separation among the single family office and maybe more of the commercial entity or operation. We have to get a little bit of a legal disclaimer there, especially domestically in the U.S.; there is just so much going on with that.

I think simply the opportunity of building a private network (whether it's through an organization like ours or their own network) is that they get to know people, to develop relationships and friendships, and get to talk a little bit. They can say, "We made our money in XYZ. Here is what we are looking to do." A lot of families that have that level of money still have multiple operating companies or are starting companies that potentially could make them more money. That's what makes the world go round, and makes people entrepreneurs and successful. There is money to be made in areas related to finance and real estate. It's not surprising that already wealthy families may head somewhat in that direction.

I have had, especially multi-billion-dollar families, tell me—which I thought initially sounded a little bit arrogant, "Angelo, we are doing multiple projects in real estate, in this and that around the world. We give a truckload of money to providers that we deal with, multiple global banks, one or two significant real estate firms, attorneys, accountants, big accounting firms. Maybe there is nothing wrong with us putting a little pressure on them. We pay you guys XYZ seven figures every year, and we are happy with the relationship, but we know that you are not the only person that could provide that level of whether it's custody in research or legal advice. We are doing big things around the world. You know where their family is. Is there anything wrong with you making strategic introductions to us, both locally on a political level, to other families, to other entities that may be interested?"

Now, again, that may be a little strong for some people to squeeze the arm of a provider that you are dealing with. You know what, though? If you have earned the right to be in that position, maybe there is nothing wrong with potentially exploring that and seeing what people you deal with as a provider or a center of influence may be willing to be a little bit more valuable to you as really truly a strategic partner moving forward.

Richard Wilson: Is there one or two things you come across within the writing of your books and white papers and all these conversations that alone, if a family office were to do this, will probably, over the long run, make or lose $100,000? Is there anything that comes to mind that's just like very, very important for single family offices to be doing almost across the board?

Angelo Robles: It's important to have your legal entity set up properly, although we did speak about how a lot of family offices are informally run out of a company business. Theoretically, that may be pushing up on certain Department of Labor, state law and other laws. It would also be pushing on ERISA laws if it's a public company or something along that line. In today's world, that would not be the smartest thing to do.

I would say spending money on proper legal counsel that has a familiarity with operating companies and with family offices would be now, more than ever, a very, very important thing to do. Also, as the family office is being created, you want to make sure the legal entities, and normally it's more than one operating company, are set up properly. There may be opportunities to set up a private trust company. We are seeing significant interest in families, even though that may be a little smaller than expected on the family office side, see the value and the benefit of setting up a private trust company, of looking into multiple offshore entities and of considering the captive insurance company to hedge against certain risk. That insurance company may also act as an estate planning vehicle under certain circumstances, receiving families or single family office executives more than just on the investments, but also looking into the infrastructure and the estate planning and asset protection opportunities so they could better understand how to leverage our expanded exemption that we currently have to be of benefit to the family.

I think those dynasty trusts, private trust companies, as I noted, are all areas of interest on the investment side.

Understanding global market, hedging against downside risk, potential opportunities with long, short, young, or up-and-coming emerging managers are also areas of interest. That's all the combination of eight or nine things that may be nothing overly specific that we are seeing families that are smaller with their single family offices what they are doing moving forward and how they are being successful at it.

Richard Wilson: That's great. I think that that is very valuable to family offices listening.

Angelo Robles: If I had to give one little parting comment: single family offices are absolutely on the increase. Not just domestically here in the U.S., but unquestionably around the world; in Asia, in Latin America, in other parts of the world, in Australia and even in Europe. This is regardless of what's happening with families that may or may not potentially have to register here domestically in the U.S. with the so-called downturn in assets in 2008 and maybe parts of this summer, anytime families have wealth—and we leave that definition up to people to define what wealthy truly is—and they desire a control then the opportunity to create a single family office has never been better and will always be interesting to people.

People, if they are newer to money, lack the resources and knowledge to understand the single family office. There are so few professionals that could help them in creating and setting up a single family office that it often becomes discouraging or it's easier, to go to a multi-family offices or private banker, and that's no offense to the multi-family office or private bankers. Many do a great job, and many single family offices deal with the multiple of those to help supplement what they are doing inside the single family office. I would say, though, for families that have that kind of money, strongly consider the opportunity to create a correct, modern single family office moving forward; it's never been a better time. Right now, there is so much opportunity with talent, with technology, and with opportunities out there in the world for a single family office to provide truly tremendous value to a family short and long-term.

Richard Wilson: Great. That's an excellent point to end the interview on. This will be a great addition to our newsletter book on family offices. I really appreciate your time today.

Angelo Robles: I always enjoy our conversations, Richard, and I'm a big fan of what you are doing with the Family Offices Group association and training resources. I wish you continued success in what you're doing. Thank you for the time.

CONCLUSION

These interviews were a rare peek into the mind of single family office executives. Single family offices are some of the most secretive organizations in the field of finance. Unlike multi-family offices and wealth management firms, single family offices exist only to serve their one family client, so there is less incentive to market their services or participate in traditional public relations opportunities. That is why it is so rare and so valuable to gain the insights from these single family office executives and learn how they serve their clients.

To create this family office book and our *Family Office Monthly Newsletter,* we interviewed 36 family office executives. If we included all of those interview transcripts in this book, it would reach more than 700 pages in length. We would like to share one additional bonus single family office interview with you in MP3 audio format.

 To access this bonus interview, please visit www.FamilyOfficesGroup.com/Bonus.

CHAPTER 7

Multi-Family Offices
Interview Transcripts

Experience is the best teacher, but the tuition is expensive.
                                                    —Norwegian proverb

Chapter Preview: In this chapter, we provide you with a sample of the transcripts of interviews we have conducted with multi-family offices around the world. Many of these family offices are global, and several have been listed as top-30 most successful family offices.

This in-depth chapter provides transcripts of interviews with multi-family offices, many of which you may recognize from lists of top-30 family offices in the industry. As touched on in the previous chapter, I recently completed 36 interviews with leading family offices. This chapter will provide you with detailed interview transcripts of seven of these interviews. Due to limited space, we are not able to publish the full transcripts of all of these interviews. They would take up well over 700 pages of text and be too much information in one package for most busy professionals to consume. We know, however, that these seven interviews will be informative and useful to you.

FAMILY OFFICE INTERVIEW WITH CHARLES GRACE
OF THRESHOLD GROUP

Our first interview in this series of multi-family office transcripts is with Charles Grace. Known across the industry for founding Ashbridge Investment Management, Charles is now a director at the Threshold Group, a top-50 family office in Gig Harbor, Washington. Charles's experience in the industry dates back to 1958; his grandfather was the president of Bethlehem Steel, and Charles is one of the top five most experienced and recognized professionals in the family office industry. I was honored to recently spend some time interviewing Charles.

Richard Wilson: Charles, can you provide us a short history of how you became a leader in the family office industry?

Charles Grace: Up to the point of being a leader, the history of the firm is that there were sort of two levels of wealth in my family. One was my grandfather, who was the president of Bethlehem Steel Company for many, many years, and then my father and uncle, who created a metal-bending company that was successful and was sold. Those were the two layers of assets that we deal with. The Ashbridge Corporation is a family holding company. It holds investments in various types of securities, private placements, and real estate, that type of thing. It has an affiliated company called the Ashbridge Investment Management. Ashbridge Investment Management was created to provide family office services in the manner provided to the Grace family to third-party families. We started out very small and grew it up to about a billion dollars, and then markets went up and down, that type of thing. Finally, we decided that the family wasn't involved enough to keep it, so we merged it with Threshold Group.

Richard Wilson: As a director at Threshold, you likely deal with probably the highest level of decisions, though maybe not the granular portfolio construction issues. Do you have a good feel for where clients of multi-family offices are placing their asset nowadays? Perhaps at a high level, do you see clients at Threshold having a lot of exposure to mutual funds and ETFs or hard assets and real estate, or hedge fund and private equity fund managers? Or, is it really all the above and the allocations are on a case-by-case basis? Is there no heavy weighting toward one of those specific areas right now?

Charles Grace: Richard, I can give you some distinction there that depends upon the size of the investor, of the client, for example, the larger family offices that have higher wealth families deal with different investments. We use managed accounts and separately managed accounts rather than mutual funds and ETFs. ETFs are very often used as placeholders and mutual funds used to serve as placeholders.

There is an emphasis on having a person out there that's managing a portfolio for you in a custom manner. Then, the next level is the fund. By the way, mutual funds are used primarily by the smaller investment clients; they market themselves more to smaller clients than the larger clients. If you go back to the larger client that is where we were, and where Threshold is, partnerships make sense. We use a lot of partnerships. We use partnerships, of course, for private equity and, of course, for hedge funds. Real estate is another area of interest, and managed futures, from time to time, has been an area of interest. That's basically it. I think the ETF and the mutual fund are placeholders for the very, very wealthy or investment vehicles for the less wealthy.

Richard Wilson: I think CTA managers and commodity funds often get rolled into hedge funds as just another type of hedge fund, but I think that's just splitting hairs as how you defined CTA funds. That's actually in the line of what I have been hearing from other people about mutual funds, though, that there seems to be a lot of interest in commercial, real estate, and hard assets of late. There seems to be interest in alternative managers, as well, for many reasons.

Is there any trend that you see that's really driving the industry right now, from your perspective as a director there?

Charles Grace: It used to be that we only looked through the diversification for risk control; risk control has just become a much more sophisticated process now, at least as practiced by Threshold. It has become more sophisticated in that you allocate assets in accordance with the requirements of the investor. For example, there is an income requirement; there is also a growth requirement, and the assets are allocated and segregated for income and for growth, as opposed to a plain fully diversified total return strategy.

Richard Wilson: I see. So it's much more custom risk management for the specific exposures of that family or needs instead of just trying to diversify?

Charles Grace: Exactly.

Richard Wilson: Okay. I guess that's why some of the different asset classes with a lot of downside protection or different types of risk profiles are needed, like you talked about using managed futures and stuff like that.

Charles Grace: Well, tell me about the risk control on individual asset classes; we found out that didn't work terribly well when those correlations went one-to-one. Nonetheless, the answer to your inquiry is that generally I agree.

Richard Wilson: What about the investment committee? Assuming you had a formal investment committee at Ashbridge, though I know some family offices don't really have a formal one put together, how was the investment committee run at that firm versus how the investment committee is being run at Threshold? Could you compare the two or how those worked?

Charles Grace: Well, I know more about the Ashbridge model than the Threshold model because I don't sit on the investment committee currently. The investment committee is typically managed by the chief investment officer and it has a breadth of in-house people involved. It has research and also research people; typically it has client-focused people, and very often it has outsiders who sit in. I think that's a newish point, in that very often, people look outside of their own organization for investment expertise and they have outside members of the investment committee. They also have an outside investment board that they talk to and which helps them to define the investment strategies that they use.

       The investment committee varies in its activities depending on how individuals lead the accounts and manage. For example, some family offices and banks and trust departments have models that they manage from and allocate from, and some do not, so there is a difference in that. It used to be thought that that model was a bad thing because your clients weren't getting particularly personal attention, but it's become such a useful tool that the Threshold people, for example, started with a model and then vary and customize that model to the needs of the client. The investment committee also has managers as well dealing with asset allocation. It passes on, it approves, and it disapproves suggestions of system managers that might be offered to clients.

Richard Wilson: One thing that's come up several times in these interviews is that at single family offices there are oftentimes investment committees where people vote on things such as whether to select a fund manager or not. However, at the end of the day, the investment committee is a nice sounding board for the patriarch, and the patriarch is the person who is going to make the decision. Even if people vote against him, and he is outvoted by everybody, he is going to do what he thinks is best for his money in that single family office.

In a multi-family office, do you see it as a bit more democratic where the number of votes really matter or do you see it as whoever is chief investment officer is going to make the decision at the end of the day and he is just looking for kind of a sounding board for other people's opinions?

Charles Grace: That's a question of influence of the chief investment officer or chairman of the investment committee. That's how forceful he is. I think that they try to create some type of a consensus and if it doesn't come to that, they hold an up and down vote. At least that's what I have seen in the organizations that I have been associated with. There are various levels of influence on the committee. It might be the chief investment officer or the president of the company and for various reasons, he might have a very strong influence. It might be the client that feels a specific manager or a specific strategy would be more or less appropriate for that client.

Richard Wilson: Okay. It's really going to depend on the politics of the individual multi-family office whether there is a forceful chief investment officer or not in place, is what you are saying?

Charles Grace: Yes. Also, the strength of the client and if the investment person is willing to listen to what the client wants, rather than just selecting his own favorite manager. That's a hard one to answer, but there are various constituencies that should be heard on the investment committee. Those are the client-facing people, the research people, and probably the overall strategist, which could be inside or outside people.

Richard Wilson: You talked earlier about how an investment committee often helps choose fund managers; I was interested in asking you about that. For other family offices listening to this, what types of fund managers does your family office really look for? Does your office have certain types of criteria in terms of their team size, their track record, or their assets under management that your team really zeroes in on very quickly? What types of criteria is your team looking for within a fund manager?

Charles Grace: You have three levels with this. You start out with statistical screening. Nobody is going to hire a guy that's a little bit of fourth-quartile manager. You do a statistical screen based primarily on measures of risk and measures of return. Then there is sort of a quantitative analysis for a manager where you go through an awful lot of the ratios, risk and reward oriented. That's all stuff that's spit out by the computer. Next level, and the most important level, is the qualitative analysis where you go out, you sit down with the fund manager, you sit down with the whole organization from compliance to analysis to the various activities so you get to know them. When you come back you make a decision based partially upon the statistical characteristics of the past performance but primarily upon the character of the people that manage that business.

Richard Wilson: So the team is absolutely critical.

Charles Grace: It's the team that's the important thing in selecting a manager. What's important is the quality of the team and the confidence you have in them and their ability to articulate a strategy.

Richard Wilson: Does Threshold have a set level that if the manager doesn't have X dollars of assets under management they are just not worth your time to look at because you can't put enough into their fund without being 20 percent of their fund?

Charles Grace: We haven't run into that problem with Threshold. Where we do see the problem is with the big investment banks and the big commercial banks. They are allocating assets to individual managers. They cannot access, for example, small cap managers the way the smaller company can because they have to give it so much money. They drown them in money, and it becomes somewhat useless because they do all this work and they can't use it because they want to give it more money than that manager could or should have.

Richard Wilson: I see. When you see a very talented team that has track records from other places, and perhaps a few of them have worked together in the past and you like their investment thesis, is there a certain number of track record years you like to see within that fund? Do you like to see three, five, or seven years?

Charles Grace: That's an interesting subject. You would like to see a track record, not necessarily in numbers of years, but through various cycles in the market. You like to see a track record in an up cycle and a down cycle. Having said that, the issue of a younger firm that has a track record elsewhere and how you credit the track record as to what they can be expected to produce in the future is a tricky subject. That depends on how long they have been working together, what resources they used to have compared to what they have now, and the incentives that they have now. For example, in a big organization or a small organization, they are more apt to be highly incentivized because they own the company. At times, we do splice the old track record with the track record of the new or younger company, but very carefully, Richard, with very careful scrutiny of what the situation was in the different situations between the two vehicles, the two companies.

Richard Wilson: I assume that if the team is very important to you that you may sometimes wait and get to know a manager over several years before investing with them. Is that correct?

Charles Grace: It is better if you can do that. Sometimes you can't because sometimes you need a manager in a particular slot, so you don't have the time to, "I want to work with them three years before I will hire them," but obviously the longer you know them, the better you know them. The preferred practice is to simply know them longer rather than shorter.

Richard Wilson: What if you had a family member, a cousin, a brother, or a son who came into wealth who wanted to hire a multi-family office and they wanted to go out on their own, do their own due diligence and hire an independent multi-family office. What advice would you give them on choosing an excellent multi-family office that would really look out for their full financial picture and take care of them long-term and their specific needs?

Charles Grace: Sure. I would provide the advice that one should select a family office that has a history and that has all
of the resources required. Once you get past that, there
are a bunch of them that can do this. After that, it's a
question of the relationship that you are able to develop
and what you can accomplish, you feel, in your communication with an individual, primarily with an individual in the organization like a very senior individual
in the multi-family office. That level of communication
is the most important. So many people can provide excellent investment advice, Richard, but the most important thing to know is if he is going to communicate it
to you in a way that you can understand it. You need
to be sure that you can understand what he is saying to
you and that he is giving you all the information that you
need in order to approve his decisions or to hire him to
represent you.

Richard Wilson: Your focus on the importance of listening is interesting.
It ties in with the answers you gave earlier in this interview, and I think that's something for people listening to
take away from this. It's not all about a yes/no checklist
whether you are selecting a multi-family office or selecting a fund manager. It seems like you have a wealth of
knowledge and experience in this niche and it seems like
so much is based on the team and the history behind it,
right?

Charles Grace: Well, yes. I mean, there are so many places where you can
find experience and resources and track records and all
of those things. However, the thing that's most valuable
is the fact that they are able to listen and communicate. If
the guy is not listening to you, don't hire him. If he can't
communicate to you in terms that you understand, don't
hire him. It's very rare. Every individual is different and
they build different relationships with different people in
different ways. You have to feel that your relationship
with the point man in that organization that you are going
to hire understands you, listens to you and communicates
with you clearly.

Richard Wilson: That is interesting. My family has a long history in capital
raising; my father actually raised well over $1 billion dur-
ing his 25-year career, and he insists that listening is the

skill most undervalued by every business school, and almost every business and investment professional as well.

I just interviewed a billion-dollar-plus single family office out of San Francisco earlier this week, and they said the same thing that you just said. If a manager comes to them and has a billion-dollars-or more in assets, oftentimes they don't even want to work with them because they find those large managers sometimes have a bit of hubris and they don't really listen carefully or communicate as often. I thought that was really interesting because many times I think when family offices think of hiring a fund manager who runs an institutional quality fund, they don't always consider that they might get so institutional that they might not listen to your needs anymore as a family office, right?

Charles Grace: Absolutely. I mean I think that's right on. I am not sure about the correlation between size and ability to listen because the ability to listen is a part of the individual that you are dealing with. If you are hiring a multi-family office, you are really hiring an individual because you are going to talk to one, two, three, four, five people, but there is going to be a lead guy. The lead guy is the guy that has to listen to you, understand what you need, and be able to communicate clearly in language that shows he understands what you want to do.

Richard Wilson: That's a great distinction.

Charles Grace: It could be a one-man family office, probably, not because there are certain resources that you would expect to have, but the communication is the most important thing.

Richard Wilson: What one lesson do you want to leave with other family office executives reading this advice?

Charles Grace: Listen to your clients. It's a little repetitious of what we have been saying here, but it's worth repeating: Listen to your clients, and understand what their needs are. As you and I both said, it's not everybody that does that. That was reflected in your interview, in your conversation with the boys in San Francisco.

Richard Wilson: I think part of that ties into how diverse this whole industry is because one family might have an operating business that's still running that represents certain types of risks and assets in certain countries that might have embedded currency risk, or lawsuit risk, while other families might have inherited wealth and that's a different type of diversity or risk challenge. That's part of why listening is so important, right?

Charles Grace: Yeah. I mean the person maybe found money and, though he shouldn't have different objectives, he is going to have different reactions of the various programs that you offer than the person who inherited the money. We used to divide the business up into new money and old money, and that distinction between new money and old money has been narrowed down; it's not as important as it used to be. But, there were old-money firms and new-money firms, and Goldman Sachs did a great job with new money; others were good with old money. People like Threshold did a great job with both, in fact; they have a lot of entrepreneurs as clients, but entrepreneurs think differently about their investments; they come to their investments differently than people that have inherited money.

Richard Wilson: I think definitely we have touched on some great points here during the interview; we dug in to the history of how the family office industry has developed about the open kind of infrastructure model that your firm helped pioneer. We have been talking about how family offices are allocating capital and about how listening in relationships are at the core of what's important to running a successful family office or choosing a successful family office. I think those are all really valuable points.

Was there anything else that you were hoping to fit into this interview and I didn't get to ask you about?

Charles Grace: Well, if you are running a family office of any size, you have people working for you. There are some people who manage well, and some people who don't. It's very important if you have an organization of any size like Threshold. However, there are human relations issues or management issues and that gets even more magnified when you get into big organizations where you have, like in the banks, you have layers of management; it's two different things, so you need to, in a multi-family office I think, encourage individuality of your people, but you need to understand them and make them work as a team. That's sort of a general outline of the requirements of having

	a team that works together, listens to the clients, shares information, and are happy together in a way; you have to be.
Richard Wilson:	Do you find that is a natural hurdle and common challenge among family offices? Perhaps they started the family office because they are excellent at portfolio management or excellent at risk management, but maybe they don't have people who have managed medium-sized businesses for 20 years. They may be excellent at portfolio management but maybe not naturally excellent at team management. Is that something you think is a common issue?
Charles Grace:	There are managers that the family office has communicated internally and externally to the clients, to and from the clients, therefore, those people need to have a certain amount of respect for each other and respect for the clients in that they are able to communicate with them and not create friction with the client or in-house. I can be very specific about this but I don't want to.
Richard Wilson:	No, I think that that helps. I think that one thing that's common in the hedge fund industry as well is that same problem. People come to the table with excellent trading skills, portfolio management skills, or the ability to see where some macro trends are lining up, some shorter term trends in the marketplace, etc., but most of them have never run a small or medium-size business before. All of a sudden, they have six people on their team and it's critical, like you said, for their team not only to have great backgrounds and pedigree to work well together and listen to each other and actually like where they work. It's not just a chop-shop of producing returns; they actually have to operate as a team. I think that's one of those things that kind of sneaks up on hedge fund managers and I think that's a common issue, I guess it seems, within the family office industry as well.
Charles Grace:	Your analogy is very, very valid; however, don't forget that the family office is a service organization, whereas a hedge fund creates a product. Therefore, the family office needs to be very careful about how they are communicating with their clients more critically than a hedge fund, which is judged basically more on performance than on relationships.

Richard Wilson: Which I guess is critical you bring that up because that kind of makes a difference between the family office versus a more brokerage type firm or traditional wealth management firm, right?

Charles Grace: It's all relationships, Richard; all relationships. The numbers are one thing; the performance is another; providing service is what the client wants, and that's what makes multi-family offices prosper.

Richard Wilson: One thing I am trying to get more family offices and alternative investment fund managers to do is document their processes and procedures internally so that they can improve them, become more institutional, manage operational risk, and train new team members more rapidly. This is really a low-cost way for a family office to become more consistent in serving their clients, and more profitable at the end of the day.

Do you find that at Ashbridge or at Threshold or at most family offices that everything that's done more than once is often documented almost like a large corporation would so it's run like a very consistent system? Are there procedure-based operations, or have you found that either it's not needed because each client is so diverse, or that the team is so small it's not like a big corporation, so you really don't need that type of process documentation and that it is overkill?

Charles Grace: I think it's essential. I agree from a couple points of view, the most obvious one being compliance. That aside, because that's not what we are talking about, you need to record what you are saying to your clients and what your clients are saying to you. Also, in turn, you need to share information with other members on the team. There are various people that are involved in servicing any one client. There is an investment person, there are the accountants, there are the performance people, and the client can access more than one person. Those other people need to be kept up to speed as to what's being said to and by the client. Also, the organization will profit by more people benefiting from the thinking of their colleagues. So, collegiality is the word that comes to mind when we are talking about this and documenting it is an important thing.

Richard Wilson: Great. Well, I want to thank you for doing this interview with us.

Charles Grace: You are very welcome.

FAMILY OFFICE INTERVIEW WITH LUKAS DOERIG OF MARCUARD FAMILY OFFICE

Our next multi-family office interview is with Lukas Doerig of Marcuard Family Office a top-50 family office based in Zurich, Switzerland. Lukas is senior portfolio manager at Marcuard and was kindly introduced to me by my existing contact at Marcuard Family Office, Samuel Hochuli, vice president, senior tax, legal and compliance officer.

Before moving to the Marcuard Family Office, Lukas was deputy CEO of GI Global Invest AG from 2002 to 2007. GI Global Invest AG is an investment boutique specializing in multi-manager mandates for Swiss pension funds. There, he helped with fund selection and portfolio management in many operational aspects of the group. This interview begins with Lukas sharing his background and where and how he gained his insights into the industry.

Lukas Doerig: After working at UBS in asset management and private banking, I joined GI Global Invest, where we would run multi-manager mandates for Swiss pension funds and really give them access to the best active managers available on a global scale and really with the idea of an open architecture. Unfortunately, manager selection is still very much biased by concerns and rationale about how profitable an allocation is, not for the client, but for those people who make the selection, basically the banks. It starts with the right theme of "you should be paid independently of your allocation." And that is what I was able to do at GI Global Invest and I then joined Marcuard Family Office in 2008, because they had exactly the same concept, but it's the additional advantage of running large family moneys with less restrictions whereas in the pension funds world everything is rather slow and they have many restrictions.

Richard Wilson: Many people have said that their hands are tied at a larger trust or private bank, or that there are just conflicts of pushing clients into a fund when really they could go out-side the bank and get a better quality manager, with better risk management, and better returns, and a better team. The problem, though, is that they don't have that option open to them because of where the assets are being held. It seems to be a very common reason for why people like yourself of talent move out to a place where they can add more value to their clients, right?

Lukas Doerig: Absolutely.

Richard Wilson: How does your family office typically split up the in-vestment portfolio between individual securities, mutual funds, ETFs, real estate, and hard assets versus alterative managers like private equity and hedge funds?

Lukas Doerig: First of all, as a standing policy, we do not buy any single securities with the exception of single bonds, so we really subscribe to the idea of collective vehicles and collective management. However, in equities we are also kind of pragmatic; about half of the equity allocation goes into index products where the focus is cost and flexibility, and the other half goes into very active equity managers.

Richard Wilson: Are you also light on the private equity side of the port-folio then?

Lukas Doerig: No, no that was just speaking of the equity, but if you now ask about the overall allocations, a typical portfolio, sort of a balanced portfolio would be about 10 percent in cash for flexibility, about 45 percent in various bond areas and fixed income areas, because we think there is value in bonds and certainly a lot of flexibility. We also like the idea of buying single names of very high quality, but corporates, so no government issues. We also like some very active fixed income strategies in emerging markets, in high yields, short-term high yield, etc. There is a big play-ing field there for active managers. The risk assets, as we like to call them, are split up in two halves. Of 45 percent, 22.5 percent are in equities; we allocate and we have al-ways allocated one-third to the U.S., including its emerg-ing markets like Latin America; one-third to Europe in-cluding its emerging markets; and one-third to Asia.

By definition, we have always been overweight Asia, about neutral in Europe and underweight to the U.S. Then, the remainder of the risk assets, the other 22.5 per-cent, is split up about one-third in hedge funds, about one-third in private equity, and then one-third in precious metals and commodities. We just recently cut the allocation to precious metals; that used to be even more, about 10 percent.

Richard Wilson: How important is the use of managed accounts within your investment portfolio?

Lukas Doerig: We are not focused on managed accounts. When we allocate to managers, we like to use the public vehicles; obviously the institutional share class is very cost efficient and access is paramount. We do not like to set up managed accounts because it's rather complicated, and you also have a certain tendency not to terminate the manager. It was cumbersome to set it up, so you might feel biased to just continue with the same manager.

We also have exposure to the managed accounts, but that is via fund of hedge funds because within the equity buckets, we also allocate to equity long and short funds, but any other hedge fund strategy we do not allocate directly to, but go via fund of hedge funds. We do not think it makes sense for us to build up an expertise into every exotic single hedge fund strategy, but really work with specialists who have much more resources to focus on the various strategies and do the allocation decisions within the hedge fund area.

Richard Wilson: Right, that makes sense. Many times when I speak with family offices, it's kind of an industry joke now:If you go to hedge fund alternative investment conferences, everybody says the fund-of-funds model is dead and it gets kicked around as an old business model. It doesn't work anymore. But does it work for Marcuard because of some very minimal extra fee that those funds of funds are layering on top of those fund managers fees, or does it work for your team simply because you don't want to be experts on 20 different hedge fund strategies so it's worth paying that extra fee?

Lukas Doerig: It's basically both; first of all we have very cost efficient access to funds of hedge funds, so you certainly pay less than the standard fees. Obviously there is kind of a washout in the funds-of-hedge-funds area and many of these providers have a big problem. They might even cease to exist and that makes perfect sense. There is still value a good funds-of-hedge-funds manager can add by not just buying sort of the obvious names and allocating to Paulson in his heydays, but can maybe look for the next good talent. As you mentioned, you develop some deep expertise and then add value in the allocation and maybe do a carve out of large multi-strategy managers and really sort of work with the portfolio, and not just buy the 15 most well-known large single hedge funds that everyone reads about in the paper.

Richard Wilson: Right. I think there will always be room for funds of funds in the industry not just for family offices, but also for many different types of investors. For example if there is an ultra-high-net-worth individual that doesn't want to work with the family office, but they want to allocate to alternatives, how is that person, a busy business owner, going to do all that research on funds by themselves? They just can't; they pretty much have to hire a fund of funds, if they want to do it in an intelligent way and that's not their full-time job. So, I think that funds of funds are here to stay and that's just interesting how their public image has changed so much in the past seven years.

When it comes to running your investment committee at Marcuard, do you have a formal investment committee that meets every day, week, or month, or is it more of an investment process that you follow, and that you probably help lead, there at the family office?

Lukas Doerig: We have an investment committee; it meets every quarter, but it really only sets the broad guidelines and then the implementation is bound to a portfolio management committee, where we discuss ideas and then make decisions.

Richard Wilson: Okay, that makes sense. Within the investment committee, and I guess in your case more specifically the portfolio committee, are there a few best practices that you could share with other family offices or ultra-high-net-worth people listening to this? Hopefully, they can see how investment committees operate inside of a typical family office there in Switzerland.

Lukas Doerig: In our case, since we like to work with collective vehicles, it's first about the asset allocation decision; say we want to be in precious metal equities, for example. In the second instance, you have to find a manager that adds value in the space. Selecting managers, I mean it's not really a science; it is also some kind of an art because contrary to a fund selection operation within a large bank, we do not need to know one thousand managers in a space, but we need to have about five good ones. We always start with what we have in the portfolios and then optimize at the margin, and it's not that we need to reinvent everything every month, but we like to constantly fine tune the portfolios and not create too much activity, which is unnecessary in our independent and unbiased approach. We make exactly the same amount of money whether a client is in cash, in physical gold, in a fund of hedge fund, in a single bond, in an equity fund, or in an ETF, so we have no incentive at all to trade around in the portfolios.

Richard Wilson: Do you use a standard investment policy, risk parameter, or investment objectives document set with new clients?

Lukas Doerig: Absolutely; we have an investment policy questionnaire. As a result, we are able to include in the investment policy statement on a very broad level and also on a very detailed level what the family really wants and what the next generation wants. That is the most important thing to come up with, an investment objective. It's also important to set up a benchmark to allow the family to be clear about what they want and also, risk-wise, what they can stomach. The worst thing that can happen is that you set up an investment objective and in the middle of a crisis the family says, "We cannot stomach it any longer; we need to take out risk" because then you really lock in the losses.

What we like to do once we start setting up the investment objective is to really show the families what it can mean. We have worked with the standard deviations and we have worked with worst draw-downs, and now having lived through the great financial crises, we really have those clear numbers of what the specific strategy can mean just based on the benchmark allocation. That helps a lot to really set the parameters right from the very start.

Richard Wilson: That is interesting. One family office we interviewed from Australia has a client base made up of roughly 80 percent first-generational wealth and many of them are still operating their businesses; they are still investing in new businesses; and they are pretty young wealth compared to a lot of the wealth that is found in Europe, particularly in

	Switzerland. With your clients, based on the knowledge I have of other family offices that are operating in Switzerland, I would guess that capital preservation is the number one most important thing above growth and income, right?
Lukas Doerig:	Yes, it is absolutely true; I have to add, though, that we have both. We have single generation and second generation, and it is kind of different. Then comes the aspect of whether there is still an operating business or not. For those clients who still have an operating business built around them, it is basically the safety bucket. They do not want to be positioned to a great degree to shoot out the lights, but it is really about preserving the purchasing power, so we do not take any undue risk on their liquid wealth.
	Then again in the first generation, the entrepreneur who made it himself, he oftentimes has a kind of a thinking that he can control the markets and his investments as he can control his company, or used to control his company, and that's often a difficult process to realize that you need to follow diversification; you cannot influence the market, but you want to be set up also in a professional way as you are in your operating company.
Richard Wilson:	Right.
Lukas Doerig:	Sometimes, second generation is even more about preserving capital and just producing what is necessary for the spending pattern of the given family. It can sometimes be hard if they realize that once they have sold the company, there is no longer a cash flow available from the company itself; they sometimes really depend on the financial assets to produce the returns they need for their expenses.
Richard Wilson:	Are there one or two surprising things or very important things that are very different about working in a multifamily office in your position as a portfolio manager versus working for a small trust or private bank or wealth management firm that is not a family office? Are there one or two big differences?
Lukas Doerig:	I think the biggest difference is probably the breadth of your challenges because you have come up with a situation where there is a holding in the private company and you need just to find a solution; you come up with

structuring issues. The advantage that we have as a multi-family office is that we also have experience from other families, which we can then bring in for yet another family; that is the big difference in a multi-family approach. Also, the difference as compared to a bank, where you have much more regulation and it is more standardized, at a multi-family office it's more sort of the custom craftsmanship option in asset management.

Richard Wilson: Managing the global taxation issues that come with running a multi-family office has to be one of the most challenging aspects of those firms with global clientele, right?

Lukas Doerig: Absolutely. I mean, typically, our clients live in various jurisdictions and/or have family in various jurisdictions; you really want to make sure it is all in compliance with tax laws but still tax efficient. That is also bringing a lot of value because oftentimes we see clients before they come to us; they have very good tax advice and very good legal advice. They might even have very good asset management, but it's not linked to each other and thereby they lose the benefits of all the various single providers. What we have is the advantage of having 23 people; we have tax specialists, legal specialists, and asset management specialists, all within one firm on one floor. We speak with each other, and our solutions are basically linked in the various areas and to each other; we make sure from the very beginning that investments are tax efficient.

We see ourselves as a multi-family office in the role of a general contractor; we make sure that everything is coordinated. We are more than happy to work with existing tax specialists or asset managers of our clients. We do not need to do everything on our own, even if we can, but the client can also pick us just to be the "general contractor" to make sure everything runs smoothly and that the various parts talk to each other and the solutions are linked.

Richard Wilson: Could you give ultra-high-net-worth people an idea of what they should estimate in terms of the costs of hiring a multi-family office, so they know what they are getting into before they do a bunch of research and sit down with three or four family offices to decide which one to join?

Lukas Doerig: The structure we are offering is in four areas. The first is what we call the "cockpit," where we provide an overview to make sure the accounts are set up in an efficient way and that the various mandates are coordinated. We then do a reporting where we can include everything, whatever value or asset is owned by the family, from real estate to equities, and what have you. That is basically the first step and for that we charge roughly between 0.25 percent and 0.3 percent of total assets. The second step of our offering is called *invest* and there we can really do the asset and risk management; we pick the managers, we run the assets, and tax them, depending on size, an additional 50 basis points. The third area is *project,* where we are hired to do specific projects, say in the area of private equity engagement the clients might have. They may need to set up trusts, and there we charge based on the time spent. Then the fourth area, which is oftentimes the most important, is called *family,* where it is about family governance, succession planning, education, etc. There, we often coordinate external specialists, but we can also run the projects in that area on our own, as far as it is allowed by the regulatory background. We charge for those services based on the effort spent.

Richard Wilson: I am a big proponent of more governance in the family office and fund manager spaces. I see that on your web site that you mention this several times as something your team focuses on as well. Can you go into a little bit more about how family governance is important and exactly what that is referring to?

Lukas Doerig: Family governance, in a nutshell, is basically how the family and its members are linked to each other and how their fortune is passed on. The thing is, people care less about a few basis points of performance; they care much more about what will happen once they are no longer there. What will happen with the son; what will happen with the daughter; can they deal with the amount of money they are going to inherit? Are philanthropic issues taken care of? There is an advantage for a multi-family office; the first thing you have is experience, and the second thing is that you are really independent. You might also be in a position to bring up an inconvenient truth about the family and be open and communicate problems you are seeing that need to be addressed, while maybe in a single family office, the people in charge might not

	bring up the sort of thorny and difficult issues a family might have.
Richard Wilson:	It's interesting, you know; I have spoken with several family business consultants that work with multigenerational businesses like some of the largest global businesses in the world actually, and they stated that at least one-third of their job is just listening to everybody in the family and being a conduit of common ground in trying to figure out how everybody can work together toward congruent goals that don't conflict with each other. I would imagine your team plays that role as well at times with large families.
Lukas Doerig:	Absolutely; we offer the platform and are the independent party in the whole process.
Richard Wilson:	Right.
Lukas Doerig:	It is interesting; some families say that one of the few instances where they meet and speak with each other is when they have an investment committee meeting that is run by Marcuard Family Office or when they have a family meeting organized by Marcuard Family Office. We are kind of in the middle, bringing the various family members together.
Richard Wilson:	That is interesting. To change the subject a little bit here, are there a few types of consultants or service providers that you really rely on heavily?
Lukas Doerig:	Yeah, we are certainly able to bring in specialists for such issues and we never have a problem in working with these external specialists. On the contrary, we like to also use their experience in bringing their knowledge for the various families. We have situations where a family, say, has an investment committee that is not only family members, not only people from Marcuard, but also people from the outside, like former bankers or what have you who also bring in their perspective. That is a good thing because we are open; we like to work with external specialists. It is also interesting that most of our new business often comes from references within our network; for example, there is a lawyer who has worked with one family who again brings to us the next family because he thinks what we do makes sense for another family, too.
Richard Wilson:	When it comes to tools that you use as a portfolio manager at the family office, are there one or two tools that

	really have made your job easier or more efficient? Any tools that have given you a more robust overview of risk, or something else that you think every family office should be considering? Or, is it really just your experience and in-house proprietary tools you have built up over time?
Lukas Doerig:	No, we have a very strong IT platform; out of the 23 people here, three people work in IT. We have a very good chief information officer who has been working for the firm now for the last eight years, and he has really had a clear vision in how everything was set up. Especially on the investment side; we basically have one central database where we can put instrument returns of any instruments available and bring it out in a unified format. That allows the clients, and us, to make an easy comparison and analysis. We also work with Markov Processes International, a regression-based analysis tool where you can put in a fund manager's return data and dissect it in every way possible.
Richard Wilson:	That IT Department sounds like it might be one of your competitive advantages, at least in terms of being efficient in providing all these services to your clients. I haven't heard of a team with less than 100 people having three people being just focused on IT, so that is pretty interesting.
Lukas Doerig:	Yeah. It was a huge investment, but it has paid out well because as you say, it allows you to be efficient and it allows you to be on top of things. It's what our clients like, especially that they have a backup, because we also have an Internet-based platform. We are obviously very well protected. There is access to any document and they can also give access to certain areas to other people who work for them, so say the legal people, the tax attorney, can access the tax statement for various investments and just that. Or, they can have their art dealer, the person who advises them on their art, access just the catalogue of various paintings and the related insurance policies, etc.
Richard Wilson:	That is interesting.
Lukas Doerig:	Many clients rely on a laptop, and if that laptop gets lost, they are in big trouble. We also offer backup services and IT services within a project, which is part of our

	offering that has become more and more important, because technology is everything.
Richard Wilson:	Interesting. When it comes to your job as a risk manager, I know being able to manage risk as close to real time as possible is important. You often need to be able to create reports for your clients during volatile times. I am sure it becomes important, so this kind of makes your job a little bit easier that you can actually answer clients' questions accurately and in a timely manner, versus everything being paper based in five different systems halfway patched together. That scenario has got to make your job a lot harder, I would believe.
Lukas Doerig:	Absolutely. We know we do not depend on Excel sheets, but we have an integrated solution, which brings together statements from various asset managers. Basically, you can fill in any information and then bring out a standardized format and report, which the client can work with.
Richard Wilson:	What are your requirements for getting to know an investment fund manager such as a private equity fund, hedge fund, REIT, or managed futures group before you will make an investment? What if they are 8,000 miles away from you, based in Singapore?
Lukas Doerig:	We generally meet the fund managers we invest in, but there might be an instance where as you mentioned, you have a manager sitting on the other side of the world and you do not really go there, as it's just not worth the effort. What we prefer to do is always make sure that any allocation to any manager is not too high because that is just the best risk management tool, diversification. Then, the fate of your portfolio does not depend on one single manager.
Richard Wilson:	Sure, I think that many times family offices don't like to be too big of a percentage of the fund manager as well. Does your team keep that percentage at 3 percent, 5 percent, 7 percent or 10 percent? What percentage of a manager's portfolio do you like to be at the most?
Lukas Doerig:	Certainly not higher than 10 percent. Also, in manager selection, we have a conservative approach; we like to see a track record. We like to see a certain minimum size of assets, and we do not need to jump into the most exotic and most daredevil kind of manager, but we can be conservative.

Richard Wilson: In my experience, I found that family offices prefer funds that have $100 million and more in assets and a five-year track record or more, but some like seven years or more track record, and 250 million or more. Does your team look at emerging managers under 100 million or you are looking for really large managers who have seven-year-plus track records, etc.?

Lukas Doerig: We do not need seven years plus, so three years is fine, but it is always a tradeoff. I mean, if a manager is much better and only has three and a half years, you allocate to him while if you have exactly the same performance record for the manager who has already had six years of track record in the 300 million instead of just 150, you obviously go for the second one, so it is kind of a tradeoff.

Richard Wilson: If all else was equal, you would obviously rather have somebody with a longer track record and more assets in place, right?

Lukas Doerig: Yeah.

Richard Wilson: Okay. Even though you are flexible, is there a really minimum where somebody calls you and says, "We have 30 million in assets," do you tell him just to wait and call you back when they are in 80 or 100 million? I have found that a lot with family offices; is that how you operate as well?

Lukas Doerig: Yeah, absolutely. We do not need to be the first soldier on the beach; it's just not necessary.

Richard Wilson: When your team is working with identifying fund managers, do you use external sources? Do you work with other family offices to get many of the leads that you end up investing in or do you work with third party marketers and placement agents frequently? What's your experience with finding really good managers?

Lukas Doerig: We work with both, so we have our network in the industry. We obviously have a lot of capital placement agents calling us, so it is also experience. You read about the manager, and it is kind of an open process. Then again, you do not need a huge universe of managers to run your portfolios, and as I initially said, we like to optimize at the margin. There is no need to find 100 new managers every year, so you know your universe and if a new manager pops up in that universe, you will certainly become aware and you will crosscheck what you have in the space and then reallocate or not.

Richard Wilson: My last question is about the family office industry both in Switzerland and just in general, from your perspective, in Europe. I see the industry growing pretty quickly and becoming more diverse; every family and family office has different needs and services it seems. Do you see strong growth there in Switzerland, or do you get a feeling that the family office industry is really growing rapidly now because more people are realizing how valuable the multi-family office formation or structure is? Is that the perspective there in Switzerland? Do you see any trends going on right now in the space?

Lukas Doerig: I think there is a growing demand for family office services, but it will probably take some more time. On the other hand it is interesting that in Switzerland, just in the recent past, there have been many single family offices also set up because Switzerland is quite liked for its advantages; it is a growing trend. Also, more people realize, and unfortunately only after having lived through certain crises, that you want to have an independent provider who is really able to provide you with advice without any conflicts of interest; if not just over the long run, problems will come up.

Richard Wilson: Thank you for your time here today, Lukas.

Lukas Doerig: You are welcome, Richard. Thanks for having me.

FAMILY OFFICE INTERVIEW WITH JEFF COLIN, FOUNDER OF BAKER STREET ADVISORS

Our next interview is with Jeff Colin of Baker Street Advisors, a top-50 multi-family office based in San Francisco, California. While Jeff started this family office just eight years ago, it is already nationally recognized, and we chose to interview him to learn more about what makes his firm unique and so successful.

Richard Wilson: Inside the wealth management industry as a whole, the percentage of wealth managers who truly focus on serving ultra-affluent families is relatively small. Could you share a little bit about how you became specialized in this area?

Jeff Colin: Sure. One of the unique aspects of our geography being near the Silicon Valley is that the creation of wealth here over the last 20 years has been dramatic. Most of the Bay Area wealth management has taken place within the large banks and brokerage firms and over the last 15 or 20 years, the technology has developed that allow independents like ourselves to compete from a product offering perspective. It also allows us to have a true, unique, and completely open architecture where there is no conflict of interest because your advisor, maybe for the first time for many of these folks, is actually offering advice free from conflict and free from compensation conflicts in particular. We think this is our unique advantage versus the large brokerage firms.

Richard Wilson: When you first started your family office, it must have been challenging to provide such a complex solution when the business was first starting in its first year or two. Could you share a little bit about how that process worked and what your first one or two hires were to the team that kind of led to this fast growth track you've seen?

Jeff Colin: Again, I would focus on the advent of technology as a backbone. It used to be in the old days that you had to spend a tremendous amount on infrastructure. One of my advantages in starting Baker Street is that I had worked at a large brokerage firm for over 10 years and had been working with ultra-high-net-worth individuals. I had gone to a startup multi-family office and built out the infrastructure. I had worked at two major investment banking firms, running infrastructure and the investment management pieces of their business.

When I started Baker Street, I really had the advantage of new technology being available at very low cost, but importantly the experiential background to know what high net worth or ultra-high-net-worth individuals would demand as far as services and products were concerned, as well as the network that allowed me to go out and build it very quickly. We were up and running in a very short period of time with a competitive offering to the types of things being promised at the major brokerage firms. But again, I would stress the fact that we were able to do it from an independent platform and we were also able to do it in a truly holistic sense where we look across estate and trust, tax and investment managements

	to come with a holistic solution on behalf of our clients, and that's what has resonated with folks in the Bay Area.
Richard Wilson:	If I understand correctly, it's basically a combination of taking best practices, in terms of systems and processes from large institutions, and combining them with the fact that you're not married to some in-house product. You can be truly independent, right?
Jeff Colin:	That's a major thing. The other thing that I would focus on here is the name Baker Street Advisors. Just by way of background, the name comes from Sherlock Holmes's fictional address, which was 221-B Baker Street. I'm a childhood fan of Arthur Conan Doyle literature. For me, Sherlock Holmes was the world's first consulting detective. As I was thinking about what high-net-worth individuals really wanted from an advice standpoint, I defined it as someone, an investigator, to keep the analogy going, to look through all the facts, and to reach the conclusions that a normal, rational person would reach. I really focus on what I would say is the truth. The truth, in our instances, are costs matter, taxes matter, and independent advice is the only way that we believe that you can ethically get it at a low-cost, tax-efficient, absolute-return-oriented strategy.
Richard Wilson:	Interesting. Since you run a top-50 family office and have a diverse range of clients, could you share with us where assets are being invested in your client's portfolios between things like mutual funds and ETFs, which are very traditional versus hard assets, and others investments like real estate versus private equity and hedge fund managers?
Jeff Colin:	I'm happy to share. We're actually very open in regard to this. We believe in, espouse, and execute on a multi-asset class approach that is strategic in nature as opposed to tactical. When I say that, I mean that you won't find us making lots of switches from our asset allocation model. We run the gamut in the wealth spectrum, although we focus on $10 million to $100 million-plus. Those folks as families tend to have children and/or grandchildren or nieces and nephews who may have needs to invest as little as $10,000 or $13,000/year from their annual gifting. Our asset allocation model allows us to do that. The tools with which we accomplish it in that case vary; we run the

gamut from using ETFs and index funds, mutual funds for the small accounts, to separately managed fixed income and equity accounts for our larger clients. On the highest end, allocations for us would include things in hard assets, such as timber funds or other types of private real asset funds, including real estate, private equity, venture capital, etc.

We take our guidance from the endowment type of models, but we adjust those models to fit taxable individual investors. If you look across the endowment models for Harvard, Stanford, Princeton, and Yale, you'd say, "Those are really smart people. They've done very well over 10- and 20-year periods." And you peer back, if you want to; you can open up the annual report at Yale, Stanford, Harvard, or Princeton and see that they own 5 percent to 7 percent of their portfolio in fixed income. They are not taxable and they have meaningfully large alumni from whom they can model their annual contributions. To us, that looks like a big off-balance-sheet bond portfolio. We adjust an endowment-like model for taxable individual investors, and that serves as a base starting point for how we drive our allocations and how we make our decisions.

Richard Wilson: Which makes a lot of sense, I think, since most families who employ a family office have enough wealth that their time horizon is really 7 to 10-plus years. Most of the time I think there is not a big need to access that cash in just the next couple of years, at least as it's been in my experience working in this space.

Jeff Colin: We're not quite as illiquid as a university endowment would be. At the $30 or $50 million level, the majority of our clients have an endowment psychology, meaning they have a pool of assets from which they look to receive a certain dollar amount for the rest of their lives and maybe intergenerational for their children, their grandchildren, philanthropy, etc. They want to access that cash flow stream in a way with as little volatility as possible. In 2008, when the markets were down meaningfully, although everyone, including our clients, was nervous about what might happen, they may or may not have changed their actual spending patterns. Obviously, we know from the literature that Harvard, Stanford,

Princeton, and Yale went off and they sold bonds. They had too much illiquidity, so these multiple $10 billion-plus endowments were in liquidity crisis.

We navigated through 2008, not that our portfolios weren't down. They were, but we didn't get any of our clients into a liquidity crunch, and for us and the majority of our clients, 98 percent, 99 percent were able to hold through the downturn both psychologically and from a pure portfolio perspective. They are now back at or near their all-time worth.

Richard Wilson: Some ultra-wealthy individuals may want to invest in the industry where they created their wealth, such as technology, commodities, or biotech. Should those individuals go start their own single family office, or are some multi-family offices flexible enough to work with those niche interests, even if it takes up their whole portfolio?

Jeff Colin: We are completely flexible. We tend to focus on the risk aspects of that question. In most cases, when individuals understand the risk that they are taking, and again, it may be modeled risk; we can build a portfolio to suit their needs. They may truly have expertise in technology venture capital and/or real estate but we can quantify that. I would take a step back, though, and say that we are a data-driven wealth manager.

We focus very much on using an academic backdrop of bringing practical solutions. If you came to me with $100 million and said you were going to put $60 million of that into technology venture capital, meaning you have $40 million left, we'd start to get into questions like, "What do you need that $40 million to do for you? Does it need to provide you with 100 percent of your cash flow because you're tied up for maybe five, seven years in illiquid venture capital? Do you care about the risk around the $60 million?" I can tell you without running the numbers that the 60 percent of your portfolio in any one thing, regardless of how low the correlation is on the 40 percent piece, will become probably 90 percent plus of your risk and therefore will drive a very high percentage of your returns. We walk through processes, and ask the client, "Tell us how you think about it." This is how we think about it. "Let's come up with a portfolio that makes sense for you and we'll construct and execute on it."

Richard Wilson: Cash management is an important component of family office capital management; could you talk about how you approach that area of your portfolio?

Jeff Colin: I'd be happy to, and I would also maybe distinguish between cash management and liquidity management. Cash management would, in our minds, be access to capital that you may use or are highly likely to use in a very short time period and let's call that six months or less. You know that you're going to be buying a piece of real estate, or you know that you have a cash burn rate of X. In that case, unfortunately in our opinion, there are no magic bullets. Interest rates are set at 0 percent right now and there is not a lot that we can do about it, so you have to make two choices when investing cash and/or liquidity today. Are you willing to take duration risk? Are you willing to take credit risk? How much duration, and how much credit? A lot of that again gets back to the riskiness of this overall portfolio and how one views it.

We are big fans—again for clients with appropriate-sized assets—of going to, in our case, the world's largest fixed-income managers. Just like if you ran a privately held company, you would have a treasury department; we'd go to them and have them build customized liquidity management portfolios to meet our client's needs. For example, I've got $100 million. I want to keep $25 million of that highly liquid, but I'm interested in earning above a 0 percent rate of interest. What do I need to do to get it; what type of risks in duration and credit do I need to take? Then we allow some folks that we believe to be the most sophisticated managers of short-term liquidity out there to execute. With our consulting hats on, we will help our client grade the performance.

Richard Wilson: Many ultra-wealthy may wonder why every family office they meet with talks about investing in alternative investments, like private equity or hedge funds. Can you explain the argument for why that is so often the case?

Jeff Colin: They are looking for a magic bullet. In many cases hedge funds tended to be very popular in the 2000–2002 meltdown when we had that tech wreck. When you looked back and you said, "Oh my goodness, the NASDAQ plummeted by 50 percent, as did the S&P (or close to), and hedge funds had positive returns. That's magical,

I want to own that." I want to own something with, again at the time as promised, fixed-income-type risk with equity-like returns. And, by the way, they don't make the mistake of just owning the capital markets. They are sophisticated traders and they avoid that. 2008 proved that to be wrong. In 2008, hedge funds as an asset class as measured by the HFRI (Hedge Fund Research, Inc.) index dropped by over 20 percent and generic hedge fund investors said, "Well, that was really terrible; you told me you could make money in up markets and down markets but you didn't. You failed." Well, I think what the investor failed to understand, is they did 50 percent better than the stock market, which was down 40 percent across the world. Hedge funds were down just 20 percent.

We come at it, I'd say, from a slightly different perspective. Can you get correlation benefits, positive expected returns, and correlation benefits to equities and fixed income and improve the overall efficiency of your portfolio? When we think about alternative assets—it's somewhat longwinded, I suppose—we break them between public and private. Public alternatives are hedge funds where they are typically liquid securities underlined and private alternatives where you may end up buying a building with the intention of holding it for 10 or 20 years or a portfolio of real estate where you anticipate holding for quite some time.

So, unfortunately I don't think there is a single answer. I would say with our detective eyeglass out, we try to help our clients really understand what it is that they are buying when they are buying a hedge fund and we discourage them from thinking that there are magic bullets out there, whether it's a manager who made a call and did extraordinarily well by making a concentrated bet or someone who apparently has the magic touch in venture capital. Our belief is that if you can get access to skilled managers with low correlations to publicly traded securities, it's worth thinking about.

Richard Wilson: Can you share how your investment committee works at Baker Street Advisors?

Jeff Colin: We do have a formal investment committee. It's comprised of the partners here at Baker Street, plus we have brought in a panel of outside advisors with expertise across different markets: public equities, public debt, hedge funds, private equity, private real estate, as well as an expert in asset allocation to help us inform our decisions. We really start at the asset allocation part of the conversation.

We drive and inform our decisions about how much one client or a particular type of client would own in alternative assets by looking first within our models at the percentage of hedge funds that are relevant for a moderately risk-tolerant individual with $50 million, and then we move on from there. Do they want to own less liquid or illiquid assets in that pool? Then we talk about due diligence process, and here we have favored investors or investment vehicles that we then put client money into.

Richard Wilson: The problem I see at many family offices is that there are hundreds of incoming pitch books and pieces of marketing materials coming in to their offices nonstop; they are overwhelmed with their search for best-of-breed fund managers with top-quartile returns, institutional-quality teams, and great track records. Have you developed an efficient process for selecting fund managers and dealing with that flow of information coming towards your firm?

Jeff Colin: I actually don't think it's that hard. There is a lot of noise out there, I do agree with that. But, if you're informing your decision making from a top-down perspective, you've determined what the strategic allocation is, whether it's us on behalf of the client or another family office. Then you don't have to listen to all the noise. If you're full up on real estate or you're full up on hedge funds, it's only anecdotally interesting to continue to view new hedge fund offerings or new private equity offerings. If you're looking to replace something or fill a gap in your allocation, it becomes a shopping exercise as opposed to a buying exercise.

If I know that I need hedge funds exposure on behalf of a client—and clearly at this point, we've gone through the selection process and we're comfortable with our choices—we don't have to recast the net and say, there are 8,000 hedge funds, who am I going to pick today? From our standpoint, we are not a believer, at least in the public equity market, that trying to identify long-only skill-based management works. When we get folks who say "I'm a great picker of stocks in the U.S. equity market," we say, "That's really great, but indexing and indexing using tax loss harvesting will beat you 90 percent of the time." So I'm not going to worry about what those folks say; we have to screen them, we have access to the databases etc., I don't care; not interested.

Richard Wilson: Right. That makes sense.

Jeff Colin: It cuts out a lot of noise.

Richard Wilson: Right. I think you're basically saying you take it from a top-down perspective and sure, for a three-month period you might be looking for global macro managers with seven-plus-year track records that meet some risk profile, but you're not looking at the whole world of hedge funds. You're always looking out for some interesting idea though, right?

Jeff Colin: Here is what we know: We know for a fact because academic studies have been done over the past 50 years showing that outperformance reverts to the mean; looking at a three- and five-year track record and saying, "This manager has been top four for the last three to five years, has got great this, has great people, etc.," it's almost assured they will revert to the mean.

When I say almost assured, I mean you can look anytime you want at the S&P performance persistence; there is an extraordinarily high correlation with folks who live in the top quartile reverting to at least below the median, quite frequently. So the odds of picking someone who has been in the top quartile who will stay in the top quartile over an investment timeframe is pretty close to zero. It's certainly below coin-flipping kind of luck. We turn the whole consulting industry on its head to look at the academic work that's been done and say, "I'm wasting my time, but we're going to tell him they are wasting their time and we can prove it."

Richard Wilson: I think it's a strong point and it is interesting that so much of the academic work is rigorous and statistically relevant, while observations on a personal basis are not and gut feelings are not. Could you explain what investment criteria you use while constructing your portfolio?

Jeff Colin: One is, without being I guess derogatory of the process itself is, I would say they are wasting their time. You can free up a lot of time, energy, and human capital by actually doing the academic work. This is somewhat self-serving but, coming to the conclusions that academicians have reached over the past 60 years, we think that if you go from the 31,000-foot level, you need to start an asset allocation. If you can control your risk from the top down, the bottom-up part is only anecdotally interesting. Meaning, manager selection and security selection, if you're right and I would argue that no one is right consistently, but if you're right, only has a small value incrementally or the ability to add slight incremental value; I can give you the numbers. For most people, though, it's a massive cost-sink both in transaction costs and tax costs, which are not quantified by many people. Then there are the human capital costs.

We look at the asset allocation and we say okay, let's look at mean-variance optimization, which is Nobel Prize–winning work; it created something we call the efficient frontier. It's highly sensitive; it's a garbage in–garbage out model. I'm not disparaging the work that was done. We modified that with some academic work that was done called Black-Litterman. In the '90s, Fisher Black (had he lived he would've won a Nobel Prize) and Bob Litterman modified mean-variance optimization with something that they called the equilibrium portfolio. The equilibrium portfolio looks at the capitalization weighting of all investable assets and says, that is an efficient portfolio. Everyone in the world has voted and that is how they have allocated their capital; all voters come to the polls and have allocated all investable capital.

We got the global market cap; it's in equilibrium almost all the time, so security prices are clearing and therefore someone like Bill Sharpe out of Stanford would say that's the null hypothesis. Are you going to make a non-consensus bet against every gambler, every investor out there? And how are you going to do it? It's clear to us and could be clear to anyone that if you look at equilibrium portfolio that is the global market cap and if you look at Harvard, Stanford, Princeton, and Yale and say they are making very large non-consensus bets. What do they know that we don't know? Why do they have 5 percent fixed income and the world is at roughly 50 percent? Why do they have a lot of illiquid and the world is a tiny portion of illiquid? Well, they've done a lot of work and identified that there are opportunities for them.

We, Baker Street, use the mean-variance, use Black-Litterman, adopt the endowment-type model for taxable individual investors, and then use another model called Sharpe-Tint, from Bill Sharpe and Larry Tint. Then we ask, "Do we have liabilities that we need to spend for and what are those?" We actually can and we would advise any individual, any family office, any client to use some sort of asset liability match, just like the large pension funds do; they call it LDI, liability-driven investing. I have a known set of obligations, meaning I need to spend a million dollars a year and I don't want to work for the rest of my life. I don't want to have to care about what happens in private equity markets or venture capital or China or anywhere else. I've got this known liability, cash flow liability. I may be overfunded to that liability by a large amount, but again, I have $100 million of assets; I can put it all in 10-year treasuries. Unfortunately it's now at 2.5 percent.

I could easily spend a million dollars a year. I'm completely asset–liability matched. We married a model to our process, but we would encourage anyone to do that. If you can drive that, you would come up with an asset allocation that's rational for you or for your family or for your family office and the execution becomes an exercise in controlling what you can, like taxes and cost management fees, etc. and letting capital markets do their work for you. So, I hope that answers your question. I think it's not directly what you were looking for, but I think a lot of people start off on the wrong foot. We're Americans and successful ones at that, and we like to believe that people can win and we like to believe that someone of skill can pick winners. But we know, and I mean conclusively know, "the debate is over" kind of conclusively know, that it doesn't exist; that skill set does not exist. If you believe in capitalism and want to own equities, you should index. Period. Outperformance doesn't happen and you can look across any timeframe and say, "Well, what about him, he won." True, but what happened to the next 5 years? What happened to the next 10 years, anyway?

Richard Wilson: Right. It seems like you have got another level of depth.
                  Either you have another level of depth or you're very
                  good at speaking as if you have another level of depth
                  beyond what I think some heads of family offices have.
                  I don't mean that to say anything bad about anyone else
                  I've interviewed or worked with, but the sophistication
                  that you're speaking with at your level is in line with
                  how endowment portfolio managers often speak. What
                  about your background or experience got all of these
                  things ingrained into how you think about running a
                  portfolio?

Jeff Colin: I'm a student of this industry, and I'm a student of the
                  process. When you ask about ingrained, I'm inclined to
                  share my screen saver. There was a television show called
                  The X-Files and my screen saver says, "The truth is out
                  there." I grew up in a place in this business of major bro-
                  kerage firms where I don't think I knew what the truth
                  was. I knew what to sell because my bosses in New York
                  told me what I should be doing and I felt that I did it eth-
                  ically; I felt that I did it honestly. But the more layers of
                  the onion that I peeled back, the deeper I got into what
                  you can call the "white paper" in the university world, the
                  more I came to the—I wouldn't say conclusion—because
                  we hold these truths to be self-evident.

                  Like I said, I'm a student and I'm curious, but there
                  is not a single piece of academic evidence in the past for
                  close to 70 years of computing power that shows in the
                  equity space that the pursuit of active management is
                  worthwhile. We know from time to time that there are
                  winners; we know, let's say 10 percent after tax, that in-
                  dexing outperforms five and seven years, for 90 percent
                  of active managers, $80+$ for sure, which means that just
                  10 percent wins. The concept is "find me that 10 percent."
                  You're smart, find me that 10 percent.

                  Here is the deal: You have a 10 percent chance of
                  winning, which by the way is not much better than flip-
                  ping a coin or throwing darts at the *Wall Street Journal* on
                  mutual funds from Morningstar. You have a 10 percent
                  chance of winning and if you win, you win by 100 basis
                  points or less. So the margin of victory, if you're really
                  good, you might generate 100 basis points of outperfor-
                  mance for your client or your investor. If you lose—and

there is a 90 percent chance that you will lose—you lose by 300 basis points.

If you do the math, and it's not that hard, your expected return of playing that game is minus 2.5 percent every year, forever. You compound a negative 2.5 percent return in this environment, but in any environment, and you are literally destroying millions, if not billions, and certainly when you look at it as across all the investors, trillions of dollars in net worth. Guess what? Fees on the average active equity mutual funds are 150 basis points, so that's 150 of the 250. Transaction costs, which you don't see, because if I'm going to outperform my index and I don't care if it's emerging market, mid cap, small cap, international, you name it, I'm going to incur transaction costs. I'm trying to beat the market and those transaction costs will be about 50 basis points. If you look at most mutual fund turnover you're going to see 30 percent to 100 percent and in some cases 300 percent turnover, meaning they are buying and selling stocks all the time, crossing bid offers, and paying transaction costs. Those add up to 50 basis points you never see.

You also pay taxes. The perversity in the mutual fund world is that, for taxable individual investors anyway, they can pass through gains but cannot pass through losses. So you will have years and we may know 2011 as one of those years where your mutual fund has dropped in value and they hand you a tax bill, because in order to meet redemptions they were selling low cost basis stock. That, on average, is about 100 basis points worth of tax expense every year forever. And that's about the 200 basis points that you're 90 percent likely to capture. You can't win; don't play the game.

Richard Wilson: Nobody has explained it at that level of detail during this interview series, but I find that a very low percentage of family offices invest in mutual funds while a pretty high percentage of investors who don't work with family offices do invest in mutual funds.

Jeff Colin: Separate accounts are no different, to be honest with you. They'll tell you that they are tax sensitive and their expense rate shows certainly in the ultra-high-net-worth arenas not 150 basis points, it's 65 to 75 basis points. So instead of losing by 250, you lose by 200 basis points.

Richard Wilson:	Right, but you still lose.
Jeff Colin:	You lose, and the money you're losing on a $100 million portfolio is a lot different than the money you're losing on a $10,000 portfolio. It's real money with a big denominator.
Richard Wilson:	Right. You have a pretty large team now, and you leverage technology. You obviously have a top-down perspective on where you're allocating. Would you rely on a couple of institutional consulting firms or outside fund manager screening type experts or is everything done in-team in-house because your team is large enough?
Jeff Colin:	It's all done in-house.
Richard Wilson:	Okay. Even though I don't believe those who have outperformed for a few years are going to continue to do so forever, do you have some institutional objective criteria requirements you can share? For example, a certain number of dollars, a certain team size, a certain number of years of a track record?
Jeff Colin:	Yes, in general, but let me back up. We are attracted to investment management firms that are large and, when I say large, in general I mean multibillion dollars, if not tens and in some cases and many cases, hundreds of billions of dollars. The reason is that at any level of scrutiny, the place that I never want to make a mistake is in the infrastructure piece of it, meaning a Vanguard fund will track the market. I generally don't have to worry about whether Vanguard the firm is going to survive, even if I pick poorly, or if the fund I participate in drops dramatically in value because emerging markets have dropped or some asset just dropped.

I'm not really worried that Vanguard will fail. If I invest in just an emerging market fund and I've got a great multiyear track year and I'm pedigreed and all those things—I've got a couple of hundred million. If my fund drops by 50 percent, my business may fail. I don't want to take that risk. I'm willing to take the beta part of risk and I'm willing to look at the skill side of it where I think it's appropriate to look at the skill side of it. What I don't want is the infrastructure risk that drives us to think about investment management firms that are large and sustainable. It drives us to only a small number of providers and it prevents us from investing in general in startup firms. There is an exception to everything, but it prevents us from investing in seed hedge funds or seed investment management firms. We know how hard it is to start a business and I don't want to invest in a great manager whose business fails because they can't manage the business.

Richard Wilson: Right, that makes a lot of sense and I'd imagine for some areas, for some types of safe hedge fund managers, that really does narrow it down very quickly to five options or seven options, especially when you're looking at one's strategy.

Jeff Colin: Yeah and look, we're smart shoppers on behalf of our clients. So, one of the biggest hurdles for us is cost.

Richard Wilson: That does go in line with some other studies. I think they've come out saying that half of all funds shut down due to operational failures and business failures and not the portfolio doing poorly. I think what you're saying is you want to cut that out of the equation almost completely so that you can break out.

Jeff Colin: Right, 50 percent of hedge funds fail in the first five years, 50 percent attrition rate.

Richard Wilson: Yeah, that's an amazingly high number. Can you help those ultra-wealthy who are looking to meet with and interview several family offices and select one themselves? Do you have one or two questions that everybody should be asking a family office to really get at the heart of what they are doing for you?

Jeff Colin: Absolutely. First one would be, "Can I have a written copy of your asset allocation methodology? What do you do? How do you do it?" That would be the very first question I would ask.

Richard Wilson: Okay, so just make sure that they actually have thought through it enough that it's been diagrammed and it's consistent in a sophisticated way. Some people won't even be able to send you anything that looks more than some nice graphics and a colored one pager, right?

Jeff Colin: Most people wave their hands around and say, "You look like you're a 60–40 investor to me." Everybody can show a pie chart, but how did you get there? What was it? I think I did some of this verbally. What was your process that gave you confidence that this is the right allocation for me? What process did you use to get me here? How did you arrive at that?

The other thing that I think is extraordinarily important, and we're calling this structural alpha, is to ask, "Where are my costs?" We know for a fact there is a one-to-one relationship with, if you can save costs you will keep more money. It's the only thing we can guarantee in our business. If I can save you cost, you will keep more money. Show me where the bodies are buried. Those are the two things I would ask.

Richard Wilson: Okay, great. You have managed to start a family office from scratch and in eight years turn it into a top-50 family office in the world. What's the number one piece of advice or best practice that you could leave with single or multi-family offices that are listening to this?

Jeff Colin: Well, I'm going to go back to Sherlock Holmes to finish this interview, and one of his favorite quotes of mine is "When you eliminate the impossible, whatever is left, no matter how improbable, must be the truth," and I think for me the one thing that I would leave everyone with who is in pursuit of building, starting, or utilizing a family office is to get to the truth.

Richard Wilson: I think that brings us full circle here. Was there anything else you wanted to add?

Jeff Colin: No, I think you got it all. Focus on after-fee, after-tax, risk-adjusted returns; have a process that leads you to that conclusion; and again, just bang on the point, focus on the truth. There is a lot of new information out there. There are a lot of great salespeople to be perfectly honest with you. It's a highly compensated industry with a lot of talented folks. Understand what the truths are and where you can make an impact in your portfolio and your portfolio management, and you will be able to guide your client or, if you are the beneficial holder, will guide yourself to a very successful long-term investment program. It's sophisticated, but not that hard to do.

Richard Wilson: Your multi-family office has emerged as one of the top 50 in the world, so I think it's quite an accomplishment and actually puts a lot of weight behind everything you're saying here. Thank you for your insights today.

Jeff Colin: Perfect. My pleasure. Good luck.

FAMILY OFFICE INTERVIEW WITH THOMAS MELCHER OF HAWTHORN MULTI-FAMILY OFFICE

This next family office interview was conducted with Thomas P. Melcher of Hawthorn, PNC Family Wealth, a top-50 family office that manages over $21 billion in assets and serves more than 500 ultra-wealthy families in the United States.

Richard Wilson: Thomas, can you explain how you got to your current position, basically running one of the top family offices in the world? How did you get so specialized in the family office field specifically?

Thomas Melcher: Well it's probably like most people who find themselves in the multi-family industry; it was a planned accident in some ways. Luck and timing get you far in life, but in all seriousness I took an interesting path to the current role that I have. I actually started as a corporate banker 20 some years ago, for what was then Pittsburgh National Bank. It was the merger of Pittsburgh National and Provident in Philadelphia that created the PNC Financial Services Group. The old Provident Bank was a very well-known trust company. After being a corporate banker for a handful of years, I felt that working with families was probably more up my alley than working with institutions and I moved over to what was then the trust department.

When I was 26 years old or so, I had the opportunity to be introduced to what was then, and still is to this day, one of the wealthiest families in America, and quite frankly I attribute some of my success to the fact that I actually didn't quite know who the family was or what their background was; I wasn't seasoned enough to know that I should have been intimidated as I went in to meet them the first time. I started working with the family and the challenges that these large families presented to me were very interesting because they are not just solely financial challenges, which are obvious, but the non-financial and behavioral issues that go with great sums of wealth are equally intriguing to me and I think it's becoming a strong area of focus in the industry as we move forward. So I started working with that family—fast forward, we had some changes occur within PNC, and I was tapped on the shoulder seven years ago, almost eight years ago now, and asked if I could take over Hawthorn and perhaps change the trajectory of the business and really make what was up until then a very well-kept secret within PNC a little bit less of a well-kept secret going forward and to size out the opportunity. Today we have roughly $21 billion in assets under management now serving just over 550 families and when I took over Hawthorn we had about $9 billion in assets under management.

We have nearly quadrupled the number of employees in the firm; we have doubled the number of offices; but it's been very disciplined growth. While aggressive our focus has been on making sure that we have the appropriate resources in place ahead of time to give the highest quality service, attention and advice to any family that chooses to use us as a partner going forward.

Richard Wilson: Wow, that's really aggressive growth over the past seven years. It seems like if your team keeps that up, you might be in the top three to five family offices in terms of size. Do you think that part of that is the strong backbone of PNC behind all of the ideas that you are implementing, or is your team doing something really innovative? Obviously if it's very innovative and proprietary you probably can't speak about it here, but is there something that's happened there?

Thomas Melcher: I think it's a combination of things. First, quite frankly, you have to look at the environment. The last seven years probably have been seven of the most incredibly daunting and challenging years for any financial services firm. Interestingly, when I first took over Hawthorn seven years ago, being at a family office that was part of a large financial institution may have actually shown up somewhat in the negative column, instead of the positive column, because banks were thought to be sort of stodgy and a good place for widows and orphans, but not a particularly good place for a dotcom entrepreneur or real estate entrepreneur.

Richard Wilson: Right.

Thomas Melcher: Then the industry went through this tremendous turmoil. Through the really outstanding management of Jim Rohr and his management team of PNC (and the fact that as a bank we have long held that PNC is a moderate risk profile company—we didn't just say that publicly, we actually behaved that way) we were able to navigate the crisis exceptionally well. When many of our peers found themselves blowing up because of subprime or any of the other variety of things that negatively impacted financial institutions, PNC was very much viewed as a rock in a storm. I think the fact that we are part of PNC certainly is a significant positive today because of how our institution weathered the financial crisis. Clearly, when you talk about a bank with the reach of PNC and the number of a corporate clients and the number of retail clients, it turned into an interesting referral source and I think PNC as an institution is incredibly committed to teamwork. Many of our peers are interested in that type of teamwork and the idea of cross-selling, but I think at PNC it's a different level of teamwork. It's not just about cross-selling; it's teamwork that's really about doing what's right for the client. If a family has a closely-held business and our corporate banking area has been servicing that family and they have come to a point in time where they decided to sell the business, the corporate bank doesn't call up Hawthorn because they have to call Hawthorn, the corporate bank calls Hawthorn because they know we are going to take extremely good care of those clients. They are looking at those people as if they were members of their own family; they know that if they refer them over to our line of business that we're going to take care of that family also as if they were a member of our own family. There is a real culture at PNC that certainly has been helpful to Hawthorn's growth and obviously the industry issues have contributed to that.

I think that's clearly one thing that's helped Hawthorn's growth. I think the second thing that's helped Hawthorn's growth is our model. Since 1991, our model has always been to provide objective and integrated advice; I guess pretty much everybody in the industry has now adopted that approach or some form of that approach. I think what was innovative in the '90s may not be innovative today, but sometimes being innovative isn't necessarily as important as doing something that is going to produce successful result.

We always put our client's best interest first in every situation and we try to be extremely thoughtful, not just with issues that pertain to investments, but with issues that pertain to estate financial planning, tax planning, and life in general where it's appropriate for us to offer some thoughts. I think that type of partnership and objectivity really resonates well with clients. This business is fundamentally about trust—and you don't sell trust, you earn it.

We take earning trust very seriously. We have a good track record of doing it. We don't rank ourselves based on assets under management. It's nice to have more assets versus less, and it's nice to have more clients versus less, but the single most important metric for Hawthorn is our client retention rate. How many clients who hire us stay with us? It is extraordinarily high, well above 95 percent. We measure that religiously and we are very proud of that metric. People still want to know the performance composite and how much the portfolio returned, but what we do is so much more than just investments and to me the ultimate measure of success is if people stay with you year in and year out, in good years in the market and in bad years in the market and across generations. Then you have a very relevant business model that's delivering value for clients who want what you have to offer.

Not everybody wants what we have to offer and that's fine. I would rather figure that out sooner rather than later, but I think it's just critically important that as an institution you understand who you are, what your resources are, what you are good at, and what you are prepared to do for your clients. I think it's important that you are very clear about that and I think it's important that you execute on that. When everybody knows the full lay of the land, expectations are set appropriately, evaluations are done objectively, and everybody has the information they need to make an informed decision. I think that more than anything perhaps, has been the key to our success: the clarity around what we promise and then the delivery stacked up against it.

Richard Wilson: Can you explain to me what the elevator pitch is for a multi-family office to an ultra-wealthy individual? Why should they stop using their networked individual advisors and start using a complete portfolio management and financial management solution through a multi-family office instead?

Thomas Melcher: I think it's a great question and I guess I would respond by giving you our elevator pitch and then you can sort of decide how it fits. At Hawthorn we talk about four specific points. Our feeling is, when dealing with families that have more than $20 million in investable assets, for many of them they have already gone through the blood, sweat, and tears required to actually earn that type of wealth. Whether they realize it or not, most of our families are a lot less sensitive to making another dollar versus losing a dollar.

I am not sure that all people necessarily appreciate that, so we spent a lot of time thinking about that and it may sound blatantly obvious, but the headline for us is we really believe that it's our job to "Keep Wealthy Families Wealthy." We chose those words very carefully. It doesn't mean that we don't want to grow their assets. Their assets signify that they have achieved a level of success in their life where they have to think a little bit more about what can go wrong versus planning and trying to figure out what they need to have go right.

Below that first-point headline banner of "Keeping Wealthy Families Wealthy," we really try to put into very plain English what that means. What we settled on were three more points. Point two was easing the complexities of wealth. For people who don't have great wealth, it's easy to look at the ultra-wealthy and say "Gee, I wish I lived in that beautiful house and was able to fly private instead of commercial" and all those trappings of wealth that are self-evident. But many people don't understand the complexities that go along with wealth; whether it's having the right insurance coverage or being adequately protected, or just worrying about whether or not your children will grow up to be productive citizens versus people who feel entitled to everything that the world has to give them. What we saw is that our families worry a lot about those issues; so we thought if we can make it easier to deal with the complexities of wealth, then we are making our clients lives better.

Point three: If we can deliver peace of mind—which certainly has an investment angle to it, but it's broader than just investments—that those two points would be two really important things. So Keeping Wealthy Families

Wealthy, easing the complexities of wealth, delivering peace of mind, and then the fourth point, which we think its highly aspirational, not only for us but also for our families and the industry is the following: to help our families define success in words as well as numbers. More often than not the traditional wealth management industry is geared toward what portfolio you build and how you perform versus the S&P 500. While that may be a very relevant measure, it may also be an irrelevant measure.

For perspective, let's think about something outside of the investing or multi-family office industry. If you were going to build a new house, you would do your homework. You would find a beautiful lot, perfectly placed to build your dream house. You don't then go out and buy the building materials and a hammer and just start pounding in nails. You hire an architect; you try to figure out the plan, what are all the different things that I need to think about. Do I need to grade the lot? How deep does the foundation need to be? Where should the pipes and the wires be? Where does everything need to be structurally to ensure that dream house of yours is built correctly and is safe, sustainable and will last for generations to come? That's what you do before you simply start hammering.

Too often in the wealth management industry people don't do that initial homework. They go right toward hiring the interior decorator and they don't ever think about the foundation and the structure. I think it's really difficult for most people to say "This is what I want to do with my money" in plain English. It's very easy for people to say "I want to beat the S&P 500 and I want as much income as possible." We take those things—keeping wealthy families wealthy, easing the complexity of the wealth, delivering peace of mind, and helping our families describe success in words as well as in numbers—to heart and we execute on that promise.

Whether you are at Hawthorn or at some of our very capable competitors (it pains me to say, there are other people besides us who are good at this business but I respect many of my peers because they are good at the business) you can connect with virtually everything we do, whether it's tax planning, whether it's family governance, whether it's multi-generational education, whether it's investments, whether it's philanthropy; all of those different terms that get thrown around directly connect to the four points of keeping wealthy families wealthy, easing the complexities of wealth, delivering peace of mind, helping people define success in words as well as numbers. The key is to execute on that client promise.

I think if you say it over and over again, if you live it and if you get people to connect with it, then those are good clients. For families who hear what we have to say and don't connect to it; that's okay too, maybe we are not the right place for them. There are a lot of different people with a lot of different priorities, but if people do connect with our message and it resonates, then those are the type of clients that usually end up coming to us and staying with us for generations.

Richard Wilson: When you say that you get more first generational wealth clients or more second-, third-, fourth-generation clients?

Thomas Melcher: You know, I think the composition is changing, so if you looked at our aggregate book of business, many of the clients that make up our book of business are second, third and fourth generation. If you splice the data a little bit differently and try to take a closer look at the new business being generated or new clients who are hiring us, we're much closer to the first generation for new clients who are engaging us versus some of our older clients. Again, that makes perfect sense. We have been around a long time and our client base tends to season just as each of us tends to season over the years.

Richard Wilson: With over 500 total clients, how do you manage global taxation challenges?

Thomas Melcher: It's actually a very interesting question. We have been very specific about our client base so virtually 100 percent of our clients are U.S. residents. We are not out trying to grow our global business or focus on non-U.S. families, so in and of itself, that eliminates some complexity. Clearly when we are investing with a global manager, or things along those lines, it does matter, and that's where I think our infrastructure, the PNC infrastructure, helps us.

Within Hawthorn, we have individuals who are purely dedicated to preparing fiduciary tax returns and we also have a group of individuals that is purely dedicated to doing personal tax returns. Beyond that we have additional PNC tax resources that are significant resources, which assist us as needed.

The other piece is that many of our clients retain their own accounting experts. I should highlight a point that is perhaps different about Hawthorn. Even if it's not different, it is who we are and it's the right way, in our opinion, to do business; we believe very much in partnering with whatever resources our clients currently have in place that are serving them well. That includes outside investment advisor(s) as well. Because we are a trust company and we can serve as a corporate fiduciary, there are times when very large families will hire us to be their fiduciary and to help them with planning issues and other things along those lines. While we obviously like to be engaged for investment management, we are perfectly happy to do what is right for the family and to bring the right amount of our resources to bear for their benefit.

That kind of teamwork and collaboration has really helped us and our families—especially when we get into issues that may be beyond our core competencies. Partnering also helps us from an industry intelligence standpoint. Since we serve clients in Los Angeles, New York City, Palm Beach, Florida, Chicago and many other places beyond our core offices of Pittsburgh, Philadelphia, Baltimore, Cleveland, Delaware, we are exposed to a large network of professionals. By embracing outside resources, we have a network of tax advisors in virtually every state who have a high degree of expertise. Families who hire Hawthorn also benefit indirectly from the experience of other families within the firm. It is not unusual for an issue to arise that we have seen in a similar context with another family. In those instances we can say "You know what, Family X also had that issue and they use this person in New York City. We think we should consult that expert on your behalf as well." A lot of it is connecting the dots and knowing all of the resources that our clients are connected to, as well as the resources that we bring to bear that enable us to tackle those more difficult things. I meandered around the barn on your question, but the short answer is that global taxes aren't a major issue for us at the present time. There are a lot more

| | ultra-high-net-worth, U.S.-based clients who can benefit from our services and we can grow for a long time staying close to home executing on our core areas of expertise. |

Richard Wilson: That makes a lot sense. My role in the industry is providing institutional quality fund managers exclusively to family offices, even though there are many other types of investors I could focus on and work with. It's the same type of feeling, like this niche is more than enough for a lifetime of hard work and focus, so why make things more complex?

Thomas Melcher: Well, I think you hit the nail on the head. I think there was a real point in time, particularly in the financial services industry, where everybody, a lot of our competitors and quite frankly ourselves, asked "What are my top three competitors doing" and if your top three competitors were doing something you weren't doing, you decided you wanted to do that. But there wasn't a whole lot of rhyme or reason. We were not asking the important questions such as: Is this a good business, can I make money doing it, am I serving the client base that I want to serve? It was just sort of "they have it and we don't, and therefore that's bad."

Our goal is not to get distracted trying to do things that we are not good at—even if others are doing it. The unintended consequence of doing things you aren't good at is that you take away from your ability to do what you are good at. Pretty soon you are not spending the appropriate time and energy on the things you are good at and overall quality suffers. You can really blow up your business model pretty quickly by getting distracted.

Richard Wilson: I think that's excellent sage advice for anyone running any business, whether it's a family office or an ultra-high-net-worth person listening to this interview, they might wholeheartedly agree with what they are listening to you say right now. To redirect, how does your family office allocate capital in your portfolios for clients?

Thomas Melcher: I am going to give you two answers. Our recommended allocation is actually higher to both real estate and private equity versus hedge funds. In our balanced account, we would recommend as much as 20 to 30 percent, and in our most aggressive account, as much as 40 percent of your portfolio could be allocated to alternatives.

Somewhere between half and two-thirds of that allocation to alternatives would be, again academically and
statistically speaking, to private equity and private real
estate for two reasons—one, they tend to be more tax efficient, so when you have to adjust your taxes, they really
stand out. And secondly, if you can find the right private
equity manager that's not doing financial engineering and
leverage and all that other kind of stuff, but is really looking to take a middle market manufacturing company and
install management and do what private equity firms used
to do, which is turn the company around, deliver more
value and then sell it, you can find those opportunities
and you can make a pretty good return.

Richard Wilson: Right.

Thomas Melcher: So academically, that's what we would recommend. Interestingly, if you look at what people actually do, it's just
the reverse. They probably put two-thirds of their alternatives into hedge funds; a lot of it is that certain people still,
at least the folks that make up our client base, still have
an allergic reaction to an 11- or 12-year lockup period. I
think a lot of them, too, are also starting to understand
the math, so trying to compare time weighted returns to
an internal rate of return is apples and oranges. You hear
these private equity funds that say "Hey, we returned
an IRR of 35 percent, which equated to 2.5 times your
money over 10 years" and you kind of scratch your head
and say "How does 35 percent equate to two and a half
times over 10 or 11 years?" Well it's because you didn't
have all your money working the entire time. I think people have gotten more sophisticated around trying to nor-
malize that relationship.

So, I will sum it up by saying we recommend very,
very roughly two-thirds/one-third to longer dated, more
tax efficient pieces, but it tends to be the other way around
when people want to invest because they get the shorter
lockup and little bit more liquidity.

Richard Wilson: When you talk about real estate investments at
Hawthorne PNC, is that a percentage of direct actual investments, apartment buildings, and commercial real estate or is it almost all through fund managers?

Thomas Melcher: It's almost all through fund managers. It's through private
equity funds, which would then do the direct investing.

We wouldn't go out and recommend a direct real estate purchase, and that's only because we don't have the expertise. I mean, we know some firms that are very, very good, but deal-specific projects are not an area of focus for Hawthorn. We feel we have a much greater core competency of being able to interview managers and understand which managers are capable of delivering what they say they are going to deliver than becoming an expert in the asset class ourselves and trying to kick the tires of buildings.

Richard Wilson: Can you share a bit on how you narrow down the universe of 20,000-plus fund managers to the several hundred that you take a closer look at?

Thomas Melcher: I think there are a couple of things. One, we have a very disciplined model and it involves 10 main factors and five main categories that range from operational risk and compliance risk to their model, then into the people themselves. I think at the end of the day, if I had to identify the common traits, this is very much of an instinct business—you want to trust but verify. Again, at the end of the day, the fund managers who are willing to sit down, spend the time with us, continue to be accessible to us and who want a relationship are the best fit for us. We prefer not to work through the marketing department and sales representatives. If we can't meet the manager, we want access to senior analysts. As an aside, a great technique is to hear separately from senior people and junior analysts. If the junior people are telling you something totally different from what the senior person said, it's a pretty good sign not to invest in that firm because there is likely a disconnect between the sales pitch and the real process.

The theme we have found with managers is that the managers who can articulate their process, demonstrate that they have adhered to the process, are willing to give us access to the operational information that we need to have confidence that there is nothing inappropriate going on behind the scenes and who are willing to continue to be accessible to us, those are some of the qualitative factors that tend to set people apart.

Importantly, we don't revenue share. We don't pay to play. We don't do any of those types of things, so there is no financial incentive whatsoever for us to use one manager over another. Plenty of managers have offered to share fees with us. We are just not in that game. In the end, it's really picking up on the person's passion. Are they an asset manager? Can you tell that that it is all they think about—the valuation of their companies, the asset class—and they just love doing what they are doing? Or are they an asset gatherer who has spent 300 days on the road pitching people, trying to bring in as much money as they possibly can because then it doesn't really matter how they performance? They are getting a point or half a point of a ridiculous amount of money, and you know it's a great living for them.

I am probably not being as clear as I should be. There is a lot that goes into the selection process, but I think the core metric is truly liking the managers. There are people that are real and trustworthy and that you have known for a long period of time and you have watched them for a long period of time. They have done exactly what they said they were going to do, which by the way means in a market environment where you are expecting underperformance from a particular style, you see them underperform. In a market environment where they say they should outperform, they outperform.

It's really understanding what they are trying to do and whether they actually did what they said they were going to do. I guess the last piece that might highlight the point I'm making is that performance should not be, in our opinion, the leading statistic. Performance should be the affirming statistic. If you are sitting with a manager and they say, "This is my process and this is how I invest; these are the environments where I will do well, and these are environments where I won't do well," we should pretty much be able to say, given the environment that we either just came from or that we are in, here is how we expect the manager to perform. You almost should have performance numbers covered up and be able to say this is what we think the results will look like. If there is some really wide dispersion between actual and expected results, something probably is not right. If we interview a core equity manager when the market is down five percent year to date, but they are up 20 percent, you have to say to yourself, "How is that core equity management?" The numbers don't add up. So I think being less swayed by performance data and more rigorous about the process is important. You have to make sure that the performance is acceptable, given risk and given the process they are following. Using performance as an affirming statistic is much better than simply chasing the hot dot.

Richard Wilson: That's interesting and it hasn't come up in any of the other interviews, so that's a great point. Is there a certain AUM or number of years track record they look for? Do they only work with managers that are over a billion or over 50 million or any numbers like that?

Thomas Melcher: It certainly depends on the space. In the small cap arena, you are going to skinny down what you are looking for; in the large cap arena where the market is deeper, you are going to scale it differently. But we do in general, yes. We typically would like to see a manager who has been with the fund for more than five years so their team has been there more than five years. Even at $100 million, funds can be pretty small when you think about the capital we are deploying. Maybe more interesting with the size of the managers is when we approve a manager, particularly in the alternative space. We also approve an amount that the firm is capped out at. In other words, we actively avoid the risk of being the major investor in any of the managers we follow.

It does get a little bit tricky when you are managing $21 billion in assets, and you approve a new alternative manager but limit the firm-wide investment to $50 million (as an example). We always have to remember that we are trying to protect the clients. We don't want to get in a situation where we own too much of the fund or—as we saw in '08 and '09—gates go up due to heavy redemption requests. Managing risk has a lot of different layers to it. It's not just about verifying that the positions are in the custody account; it's how much of a fund do you own, it's watching the flows of the fund.

Who would have thought we would have to be doing due diligence on money market funds? But in the last couple of years we have had to. What percentage of the funds are invested in Europe? What happens if, you know, during the whole debt debate, or debacle as I like to refer to it, what if the government gets downgraded (which it did)? What might be the run on certain money funds? What will people do? It's a very dynamic environment, but in general it's the people, it's the process, and it is operational risk that you have to evaluate.

Richard Wilson: Well, our 30-minute call has turned into an hour-long interview; I'll let you go now. Thanks for your time.

Thomas Melcher: No, no I enjoyed the call, my pleasure.

FAMILY OFFICE INTERVIEW WITH GREG KUSHNER, FOUNDER OF LIDO ADVISORS

Our next interview is with Greg Kushner of Lido Advisors, a multi-family office in the United States. Greg has over 25 years of experience in the family office industry, and some of you may know him as the founder of the Southern California Family Office Directors Association (SCFODA). SCFODA has become one of the most well-known regional family office associations on the West Coast of the United States. Greg's perspective on the industry is unique, as his nationally recognized firm offers both institutional consulting services and family office wealth advisory services. Greg starts out this interview explaining his background a bit further.

Greg Kushner: It seems like we have been in this family office space for an awfully long time. Actually, when I started the networking group to which you were just alluding, it was 1993; it was really interesting. A lot of the people who attended that very first meeting didn't even realize that they were working in a family office and for the most part they felt like they were the only ones really in the world that were doing this very unique job working with extremely high-net-worth individuals.

The way that group originally got started, I was running a single family office for four wealthy brothers in the Southern California area and I just happened to know a number of my former Price Waterhouse colleagues back in the days when I was in public accounting who had also left accounting and were managing some very, very wealthy families here in the Southern California area. So I asked my private banker at the time, "Hey, can you invite maybe half a dozen of your largest clients to a luncheon" and I would invite these folks that I knew. He said. "Yeah,

Greg, that's a fantastic idea." So we had a luncheon in November of '93, I believe, when we started this group and like I said we went around the room, people would introduce themselves and indicate that they had worked for a wealthy family. Some individuals were the folks who wore two hats; they were the family member who also managed the wealth on behalf of the rest of their family. It was really amazing to see their level of disbelief that there were other people that were doing their jobs also and at the end of that particular first meeting, I will never forget it, Richard, almost everybody in the room came up to me afterwards said, "Wow, this was a great idea. We should do this again, Greg." In other words, if I would organize it, they would keep coming back, and that was the genesis of this first idea of the Southern California Family Office Directors Association, of which I was the original founder and chairman.

We decided at that point we were going to meet every other month. We always meet generally on the third Thursday of the odd-numbered month; you could tell I am an accountant by the background, I guess. We always meet at the same place, and it's just easy to kind of forward plan your calendar. The idea is we would ask different firms, financial firms, people in the insurance, legal, and accounting industries to host these luncheons, and they would bring maybe one or two or three of their largest clients to this luncheon. They would look around the room, they would say, "Wow, this is a pretty impressive group," and they would keep coming back meeting after meeting.

I think one of the reasons it was a success at the beginning, and still is to this day, is that there were never marketing presentations; they were educational in nature. Many of the folks who were managing family offices, Richard, were CPAs and, as a former CPA, I knew that they needed continuing education on it. We would talk to these sponsors, these folks who were speaking and say, "Look here; don't get up there and market to this crowd; don't tell people why you are the number one performing fund since March of 2000; they are not interested. But what they are interested in hearing is meaningful information showing us that you are smart, and that you know your space. Trust me, if they are interested, they know how to find you." We never gave out the list of names, we kept it very, very private and very confidential, and I guess that's one of the reasons why it worked and it's worked for so many years.

Richard Wilson: Great. Could you give us a bit of a history lesson of how you have seen the family office industry expand and maybe what one or two drivers of that growth are from your perspective there?

Greg Kushner: Sure, I would be happy to. Since I came from managing a single family office before starting Lido Consulting in 1995, because as you say, I have been there and done that, I was actually in a family office so I understand and have a lot of empathy for the folks who are sitting in that chair. These people find themselves juggling the balls of managing not only the financial affairs but the family issues as well, in addition to all those things that come along with what I call the concierge types of services that sometimes are much more problematic than they are on the financial side.

To answer your specific question, certainly there has been a great amount of wealth here in California. Of course, there was a lot of wealth generated through real estate, a lot in the entertainment industry and just in business in general and as California, being one of the largest economies in the world, clearly there are a ton of wealthy families here in Southern and in Northern California. People have asked me over the years, "Well, Greg, how much money do you really need to have a family office?" And I think probably 10 to 15 years ago, I think the standard answer was probably $100 million of assets under management; I think today the average is generally north of $200 million. I think that's also the reason we have seen the explosion over the last few years of the multi-family office model because it is a way of being able to spread that cost over more dollars to get the best talent possible.

The minute you go to work for a single family office, you might have been an expert in your field the day before yesterday, but you start to get somewhat stale because you are not seeing everything out there. You are just seeing things that are relevant to your particular family situation. I think families realize that to some extent and like the idea of collaboration and having access to other families for coinvestment, for sharing the best ideas, etc. I attribute a lot of that to the explosion that there is in the multi-family office or multi-family office world.

Our sister company, Lido Advisors, is a multi-family office and really it came out of doing this work with family offices and individual CPAs, attorneys, people that we knew here primarily here in Southern California. They would ask us, "Hey, you know what all these supersophisticated, superwealthy families are doing? Can't you do that for, as I like to say, nearly wealthy?" That seems silly to say someone *only* has $10 million or only has $20 million, but obviously compared to a $200 or $300 or $500 million family, they are just not going to be able to expend the kind of cost necessary to get the best-of-breed, the best-in-class advice. So we started Lido Advisors to really leverage all those relationships that we had developed with these families and the service providers to those families and we will take the best of and the best ideas and things that kind of cross our desk because of our relationships with these families and then bring those to our advisory clients that we manage under our registered investment advisory side of our business, which is Lido Advisors.

Richard Wilson: Family offices seem to just now be coming up in the public eye more commonly; even many financial professionals don't know what a family office is, but I think that is slowly changing.

Greg Kushner: Yeah, I think I would tend to agree with you, Richard. In general, family offices have been much in the shadows and it's certainly become much more prevalent just with the Internet and with the discussion of wealth. I was reading an article the other day; it was a study done by U.S. Trust on baby boomers and their intentions regarding inheritance and leaving money to their children. Basically, the result of that survey, which I think they found somewhat surprising, was that baby boomers are not all that interested on a percentage basis of making sure that they leave their wealth to their children.

I think when you add all those things together, the families are certainly looking for, I think the public is looking; there is always a curiosity factor of the rich. Depending on the political view, you can define what "rich" is, but I think that always sells and people are always interested in hearing how the wealthy families in the world are managing their affairs. Just with the prevalence of books on the subject that you are writing, things like the Internet where there is so much sharing of information and just the aging of the baby boomer generation and all the discussion of these trillions and trillions of dollars of wealth being transmitted and left to the next generation brings this to the forefront. So I would say in general, yes, family offices are getting more and more known and more and more involved in the daily awareness of the average public.

Richard Wilson: So I know you might not be able to share very granular details, but could you share a little bit about where you advise your clients on putting their wealth between things like securities, ETFs, and mutual funds? What about hard assets and real estate, or hedge fund managers and private equity fund managers?

Greg Kushner: As a multi-family office, as I said earlier, we try to leverage the relationships that we have developed with these very wealthy families and bring those same kinds of investment strategies and techniques to our clientele under our advisory practice or, if you like, our multi-family office practice. What we have been doing for those clients are a couple things. One, for example, is a very wealthy family here in Southern California that is acquiring a lot of real estate, very distressed real estate, very opportunistic real estate which from day one is generating a tremendously high current cash yield, cash on cash yield, and with some substantial upside potential. The family has basically said they are going to acquire about $500 million of real estate; they have allocated a certain portion of their own portfolio to the equity and what they have done is they have a friends and family situation where, for clients of Lido, we will invest side by side with this large family. They are receiving a promote, but the promote is very reasonable and that they only get their promote after our client gets a very nice preferred return, gets all their capital back, and only at that point do they then start sharing in the upside.

We would just basically not be able to see these opportunities or close these opportunities otherwise because this particular family has a deep checkbook and can just close very, very quickly. They can outmaneuver others; they have to try to find the capital and I think our clients are very happy so far with those kinds of investments. I think they are performing well so far. Obviously there is always risk associated with any of these kinds of investments and we try to clearly delineate what those risks are to our clients and at the end of the day, we are looking for cash flow.

We are looking for things that are not going to be correlated to the investment markets. We have seen a decade where the Dow stood in 2000; it was basically around 10,000 points, and a decade later, we are pretty much on the same spot with a whole lot of volatility in between, and I do believe that we are going to continue to see that kind of volatility. At least in our firm, we are not real big believers in what I call "the set it and forget it" approach to investing or putting it in other way, more of a cookie-cutter approach where, based on a client's age, they should have a certain amount in bonds and certain amount in equities; instead, we are very opportunistic.

I guess the best way to put it is "don't lose money," and if we don't lose money, we certainly don't have to make as much to get to our clients' end game or end result of their goal. We use real estate, and have been investing over the last few years because it's an opportunity in first trustee mortgages, where we are lending to borrowers who cannot get a loan the traditional way from banks. Back in 2007, if you had a pulse, you would walk into the bank and get a loan for 110 percent of your "value." Now, you can have all the equity in the world and they won't give you a loan. So, we have been finding incredible opportunities; we call it "loan to own," where we would be thrilled if we had to actually end up foreclosing and owning the property for the amount of the loan that we made. Again these are double-digit type of returns.

Certainly there are different kinds of risks than investing, say, in municipal bonds or corporate bonds but we think the risk return parameters are very, very attractive. We have a number of assets invested with what we call our hedge hybrid strategy. Our hedge hybrid strategy is kind of a result of the 2008 situation where investors in hedge funds ended up getting in gating situations or locked out to their capital and yet, we still are very big believers in the concept of hedge funds and alternative investments. So we have developed internally our own proprietary mix of publicly traded mutual funds, 40 Act funds that are run by hedge fund managers. They have hedge funds, they have the partnerships, but they run these mutual fund products. There are some different kinds of restrictions on 40 Act funds (mutual funds) versus the private partnership, but the one thing that they all have in common is that they can be opportunistic, they can be short, and they can raise cash.

They don't have to be fully invested by mandate, as so many what I will call "style box managers" must be. If the one commonality I think the family offices have and I think that Lido possesses is that we are very opportunistic in the way of trying to find ways to make money, period; end of story, on a good risk-adjusted basis rather than just trying to be compared to a benchmark. I would say in general, mostly on the offices and I know for sure on my clients, we don't compare ourselves to a standard benchmark. Sure, we will look at things like the S&P or something like that or balancing this, but at the end of the day if our clients' goals are met and their objectives are clearly being met and we are doing a good job of telling our clients what we are going to do and actually doing what we say, I think that provides for happy clients. I think that's really what we are seeing out there in the marketplace.

Richard Wilson: One area I have been studying lately is multi-family commercial real estate or apartment building investments. I find it interesting that so many of the ultra-wealthy made their wealth or keep their wealth in apartment buildings, and this holds true around the world. Do you see a lot of interest among your clients in apartment buildings, five-plexes, etc., or moderate commercial real estate office building type investments?

Greg Kushner: Well that's a really great question. Of course, I think certainly the answer depends on the experience level and the risk profile of the family. I can tell you, from our perspective, that we have definitely seen a huge level of interest in the multi-family area. We, for our advisory clients, have laid and purchased some multi-family apartments, again looking at it more opportunistically. We are usually looking at secondary markets, markets where things have gotten hit very, very hard like Phoenix. We actually just invested in an apartment building in Phoenix. We just made a couple of additional investments there in broken condo deals where we are renting them out as apartments and again provided some fairly attractive cash loads to our clients with what we believe will be some nice upside when those markets eventually recover.

We haven't invested at the moment but kind of the concept is similar where you are buying houses out of foreclosure; you are fixing them up and renting them on a long-term basis with the concept of now you have a rental pool just like you would with an apartment building, especially if you can buy that at a cheap-enough cost. These homes, for example, might have been selling at the peak of the market for $200,000; they cost $100,000 to build and you buy them for $50,000 and rent them out at that level. At some point, maybe in a year, maybe in 10 years, I don't really know, you could sell those houses eventually at the cost of replacing them, but in the meantime you are getting a very attractive cash flow in the interim while you are waiting. I think that's an opportunistic way.

The family that I had mentioned earlier that we have co-invested with has done a combination of office and a shopping center; they haven't done any apartments. Those are just two examples of where you are coming from. We have a fairly large client under our advisory practice who wants to buy apartment buildings in Beverly Hills, California. Well, apartment buildings in Beverly Hills, as you might imagine, go at a pretty steep price. The cap rates are quite low and he just feels good about the idea of owning Beverly Hills real estate. It's such a localized decision; it's such a personal decision. It's hard to make any kind of generalizations. I mean, I know we like the multi-family area right now and that's an area that we have been doing a considerable amount of research in due diligence.

Richard Wilson: Do you find that family offices are making direct investments into real estate or accessing these types of investments through fund vehicles?

Greg Kushner: Well, I think it's a combination. Depending on how deep
the pocket of the family office is and if they can have the
team of people to do their own vetting of these investments, I think there is, in general, a preference towards
individual purchases so that the family has control over
the outcome of that particular property. Yet, I am sure
there certainly are plenty of families who recognize that
there is going to be as we call them "trophy-level" type
of properties, certainly large office or apartment buildings or the kinds of deals that the large funds are going
after where it's just not practical for the family to com-
mit enough capital to control those kinds of assets. Then,
they would go through the fund vehicle in recognizing
that they don't have the same level of control that they
would if they owned the individual property.

Richard Wilson: What types of fees should the ultra-wealthy be expecting
if they are looking to hire a multi-family office?

Greg Kushner: Well, we have seen and we have tried to understand what
the fees are that families get charged. I would break it
into two general categories and that's investment-related
fees and non-investment-related fees, so things like tax
return preparation, estate planning, trust documentation
are the kind of concierge services I talked about earlier.
It's really difficult to give you an all-in number because
it really depends on if the office is focused more on the
investments, or if they are more involved with kind of the
caretaking of investments, etc.

For example, I have looked at compensation surveys
for family office executives; this might be a good window
into the question you were just asking about fees, and
that is the more investment-related the activities are, the
higher the fees, and that doesn't surprise anybody, I am
sure. The more perfunctory, the more accounting-related
the tasks are, the lower the fees are and the lower the cost
to the family. Depending on the needs of the family office,
that's going to have a large impact on the outcome, as far
as what kind of fees we are talking about.

In general, I have seen fees at 1 percent of all assets
and I have seen it down in the 10s or 20 basis points and

everything in between. I think most of the time, if there is a high level of involvement regarding investments, you are going to see a higher number for fees, but I would say it's somewhere in the half-percent to maybe 1 percent per year in that category, and again that doesn't include things like tax return preparation, tax planning, heavy-duty estate planning, and things of that nature. Many family offices outsource all of that and a lot of other offices have brought it all in-house. I have also seen, over the years, where they brought it in-house and they feel, "Oh, this was a mistake," and they outsource everything now, and vice versa. I know of a pretty large family office that just outsourced everything and now virtually there is no family office; it's all done kind of with outside providers. It really depends on the family.

The other thing that I like to always mention when I talk about family offices is whether or not there is an operating business. Is the operating business still in existence; is it still owned by the family, or was there an operating business that was the source of the wealth, the generator of the wealth; has it been subsequently sold? That's kind of an easy way to delineate the family office: operating company yes/no. Also, has the operating company been sold or been out of the family for more than five odd years because now the family business, if you will, is managing their wealth, whereas before their primary focus was managing the business and not so much their wealth. I think that's always an important factor to look at in evaluating the structure of the family office.

When you do have an operating company, many times there is not a very good allocation of costs, if you will, because many times the CFO of the corporation might also be the head of the family office. Which hat are they wearing; are they wearing the hat of the advisor to the family, or are they wearing the hat that's the CFO to the company? Those are all the things that factor into the calculation of fees. I do think, though, at some point, and certainly as we have seen with the financial crisis of 2008 and even through today, that there has certainly been a re-looking at the cost of the family office. My anecdotal evidence has shown that there certainly has been some cost cutting. I have seen a lot of changes, a lot of turnover of heads of family offices over the last couple of years, and I am sure some of that might be scapegoating, where the family office or the investments didn't do as well as expected and someone is going to take the blame and it's not going to be the family. We have seen that quite a few times over the last year or two.

Richard Wilson: Interesting. When family offices are making investments, do you see more direct investments or is most investing being done through funds of different types?

Greg Kushner: I would say it's definitely on a smaller percentage, although there is somewhat of a sex appeal, if you will, of investing in a single deal, a private equity deal. It could be a business that's maybe the cure for cancer or the next greatest retail idea or whatever it might be. I think there is a disproportionate level of work that the family office has to do when they own individual investments in private firms as compared to investing in a fund. I think without question in my discussions with my colleagues over the years with one family office, they will complain, I guess the most, about the time or effort that they put into managing and many times these are very difficult businesses; they are not something that you just put your money in and it works out wonderfully.

Sometimes there are work-out situations; you have to change the CEO or the board has to be revamped or whatever; there is a lot of time that goes into that and I don't think the typical family office investor realizes that extra level of work and effort that goes into owning an individual company. Even though it sounds kind of good on the surface, kind of sexy, exciting, and maybe these people are serial entrepreneurs, I have seen over and over again if you are successful in one business, that entrepreneur thinks that he or she can do it again and many times they fail miserably, including setting up a family office and not really knowing what questions they even should be asking. I find this happens a lot. You don't know what you don't know and there are questions that you should be asking about setting up the establishment of a family office and many times they just are completely clueless.

One of the things that we do on the consulting side of our practice is to offer our list of questions that the family member or the head of the family office should at least be considering or thinking about. Now coming up with all the answers is going to take time and a lot of deliberation, but certainly you need to know what you need to ask about as far as structure of the family office, compensation, mundane things like well, who is going to have custody of the assets, what about wiring out cash for capital calls for private equity yields for example, what are the internal controls etc., etc. There are a number of things that go into creating a family office and maybe that's one of the reasons we have seen the increase in multi-family offices, because at least it's already been there; it's not a re-creating-the-wheel scenario.

Richard Wilson: To turn the conversation toward helping an ultra-wealthy individual or family select a family office, what two or three questions or issues do you think an ultra-high-net-worth individual should really focus on when they are going to meet with family offices?

Greg Kushner: What I have done, actually, is put together a list of questions that you should ask your investment advisor. It's more specific to an investment advisor than it is to the actual family office, but a lot of the questions are just as equally germane. I will give those questions to a prospective client ahead of time, and they can feel free to ask those questions and certainly ask other firms that they might be interviewing those same questions. The thing that I think is important is, at the end of the day, it's always going to come down to one key word, and of course you know that word is "trust." Do they feel comfortable; can they trust the individuals that they are relying on to manage their financial lives? You could have every degree under the sun; you could have the greatest reputation; you could have references left and right, but unless the client really can connect with you on a personal level and feels the trust, I don't think any of those other things really ultimately matter.

I think it's a given that if they have been referred into a firm like ours or others that would be our competitor, that there is a certain level of competency and reputation that goes with it. That is assuming they have been referred in by other satisfied clients, CPAs, attorneys, or people who presumably are knowledgeable enough to at least steer that client into the right direction. But like I said, it's going to come down to trust.

One of the things that we always tell our clients is that we try to be completely transparent in every single thing that we do. There are no hidden agendas; there are no hidden fees; there are no bait-and-switches. We put our money where our mouth is. If a client looked at my portfolio, they would see the same investments that would be in their portfolio. Maybe mine might be more aggressive or more conservative, but you are going to see a lot of the exact same investments, and not on a promoted basis but on a side-by-side basis. As I always tell clients, "Look, along the way, we are going to stub our toe and everybody in this business does. At some point, you are going to find an investment that maybe doesn't work as well as you would like, and you know what, you know that if I have done the due diligence and I have put my own hard-earned money in the deal that at least we are in it together. We are either going to cry together or smile together, but we are together." I think clients really, really appreciate that especially in light of all the well-known and well-publicized conflicts of interest that are so prevalent today in Wall Street with all the big investment houses doing one thing for their own proprietary capital and the exact opposite for their clients. That's something that we are not and I think that differentiates the quality multi-family offices, the quality family offices, from others who are more of a product peddler.

Richard Wilson: Do you use a strict investment process or do you run an investment committee as well at Lido?

Greg Kushner: The answer is yes. I will give you a little bit more background. I think the first and foremost point though is that it comes from the client; it's client-driven rather than what we think. It's really more about what is the most appropriate for the client's portfolio; what kind of risk should they take based on their objective, their income needs, their tax situation, their long-term planning, etc. Once we have done that initial homework, if you will, and understand our client, it's only then that we start to develop the implementation of the asset allocation strategy. Here at Lido there are four of us on our investment committee, all with disparate backgrounds and experiences and what we do is we sit, I mean, because we are a small firm, we certainly sit down frequently together and talk about the markets and talk about our strategies. Because we are a small firm, we certainly talk about it almost on an hour-by-hour or daily basis about what's going on in the investment markets. We are always being approached by people who are in the investment business offering us an opportunity, shall we say, to invest with them because I think they find us through our family office network. We do meet on a regular basis, though; we do talk about the markets.

We have one gentleman here who sits behind 14 computer monitors all day long, and when I say 14 monitors I am actually not exaggerating; his name is Brandon. Brandon sits behind those monitors and is our eyes and ears into the world of the various markets. He is watching technical factors, fundamental factors across all the investment classes, and is just really very helpful in giving us a sense of what's going on kind of from a macro perspective in helping us develop the appropriate asset allocation for our clients. He will look at the various sectors of the market, so for example consumer staples or utilities or technology, and give us a sense on where he sees those things happening. It just helps us in determining our overall beta that we have created for each individual client.

Each client's portfolio has a designated risk profile, and what we do is we try to manage that risk level and are always looking for opportunistic ways of making money, as I mentioned earlier in the interview, more so than just trying to beat a particular benchmark or index. It's a combination; most clients have assets allocated across funds that are these opportunistic managers or what we call these hedge hybrid strategies. Some have more formal partnership investments, private equity, real estate, etc. The trustees we talked about, they will have a certain amount of their portfolio in more traditional bonds, but even there we are trying to be opportunistic and find managers who can be more opportunistic today with the 10-year U.S. Treasury around 2 percent, slightly over 2 percent. Fixed asset is not a compelling place to be; that is gone. We are trying to find any and all ways that we can add return without dramatically increasing risk for our client's portfolio. It's a basket approach. We are looking at different investments; we are looking at different ways of generating returns; and we are looking at risks and blending that all together, hopefully coming up with the right answer for each of our clients.

Richard Wilson: You have a unique perspective in running both a multi-family office and institutional consulting firm. It must provide you with a due diligence or perspective edge on some level. Can you share some of your fund manager selection best practices with our readers?

Greg Kushner: Sure. Way back when, when I was actually with the family office, I remember interviewing at that time a hotshot hedge fund manager who was up in the Bay Area and he had come recommended to me from a few folks, I think one of the brokers I knew and some other people. I interviewed with this guy and it came across very, very clearly that he was extremely arrogant and had a know-it-all type of approach and I am sure very, very smart, but I have found that people who are very arrogant in the investment world can be very dangerous. What I mean by that is they think that they are so right, dead right, that they could be dead before they are right.

What I mean by that is they get married to a stock or they get married to an idea and they are wrong and then they get more wrong and they get more wrong and yet they double down, triple down, quadruple down. I remember meeting this manager and the answer to me was, "It just didn't give me that warm feeling." It wasn't certainly based on his performance up to that point; it just was kind of these intangibles, and sure enough that manager did eventually kind of blow up. But a lot of it is just kind of by feel. Sure, I would like to say it is all statistics and numbers and all this very scientific, but I think a lot of investing is more art than it is science. Sure, science is important and if you don't have at least good numbers and good performance and good statistics as far as things like standard deviation in beta and creating alpha, you are not going to get up to bat.

But past those things, a lot of it does come down to kind of your intuition. I have been pretty successful, thankfully, over the years, missing out on some bad situations and thankfully I have avoided them. It comes down to the fact that it just doesn't smell all right; if it doesn't pass that smell test, walk away, or better yet, run away. The Madoffs of the world, those kinds of things happen when this basic rule was ignored. He had a fund and he traded with his own broker dealer. There was no separation of church and state. I always tell our clients, "Look, you could hire us, and go 'Who the heck is Lido?'" You are not giving your money to Lido, though; your money is with a third party of a prestigious well-known entity like Fidelity Investments Institutional or Schwab Institutional, a firm where they can go online, they can check their balances, they can make sure the assets are actually there.

I could print a report in my office that could say anything I want it to say, but it's nice to know there is a third party out there that's telling the clients what I am telling them is in fact the truth and that's what I mean by the separation of church and state. The Madoff example, which I looked at for a family office 10 years ago, and the number one rule was breached. You didn't even get to need to see number two or three, like who are your auditors or things of that nature; there are no checks and balances. If I want to buy something for myself, how much am I going to charge myself? There is no check and balance in this instance. Over the last couple of years, I almost always will say to a client, "Look, this is what you need to be aware of; you need to understand there is this third party out there who is going to verify anything and everything that we tell you is in fact true." That makes clients feel a lot more comfortable, especially in what I call these post-Madoff days.

Richard Wilson: That basically reinforces some other things we have heard from some of the most experienced family office professionals in this interview series. They want to work with managers that actually listen to them and that communicate with them after the investment is made. Many large family offices have emphasized that sometimes managers can get too big and too successful and become undesirable to work with. It's not always based on asset size, is what I have been hearing.

Greg Kushner: I would definitely concur with that. I mean, since we run more of a boutique type of firm, perhaps I am somewhat biased, but I just think when managers get so successful and so big, you lose that personal contact and then maybe they just don't have that fire in the belly anymore. Then they drive up in their $300,000 car and their house is in the Hamptons or they are out playing golf or whatever; I mean they are not doing the same thing they did to generate that track record that got them to where they are at.

In general, I think family offices are more inclined to go with the newer kid on the block, the smaller funds, because of the more personal connection and involvement that they are going to have, whereas the institutional players, the big pension plans, etc., they are looking at it more from a safety perspective. They are looking at it from a job preservation perspective, well so and so, kind of the old IBM example, well, I am going to hire IBM because it's IBM from the technology side of the house. I would say many families like or have steered maybe away from some of the largest. They might have some allocations to the largest well-known managers, but I would say at least in my kind of studies that there is more preponderance of families who would be interested in feeding young solid managers or investing in smaller managers that maybe are not on everybody's radar screen.

By the way, I have another more humorous approach to selecting investment managers and that's if they are really big-time golfers. So if I walk into a money manager's office and I see all these golf trophies and golfing pictures from trips to Pebble Beach and across Scotland and I say, "Oh, these people are really big-time golfers." I will ask the manager well you know what's your handicap, and if they proudly pronounce that they are a scratch golfer or their handicap is like 1 or 2, I am pretty much going to have a very short meeting because that manager is probably playing a lot of golf and is not really managing money. The nice thing is when the client plays golf with me, and those very good times I get to get out on to the golf course, they know pretty quickly that I am not playing too much golf.

Richard Wilson: I think one of the first things that David Thomas, the head of Equitas, said when I called him was that he must be working pretty hard because his golf game was horrible, so he seems to evaluate people in the same type of first-pass type of light, which I would agree with,

	I guess, in terms of the amount of free time it takes to play 18 holes.
Greg Kushner:	Yes, exactly.
Richard Wilson:	Thank you for your time today Greg.
Greg Kushner:	I appreciate the opportunity to answer your questions Richard, and I look forward to reading your book.

FAMILY OFFICE INTERVIEW WITH BOB BENSON, CHIEF INVESTMENT OFFICER OF LAIRD NORTON TYEE

Our next interview is with Bob Benson, chief investment officer of Laird Norton Tyee. Bob determines the firm's investment strategy, directs the manager selection process, and works in partnership with the client services team to deliver investment solutions for their clients. This family office is a top-10 West Coast family office that serves more than 400 families and has over $4 billion in assets under management.

Richard Wilson:	Thanks for joining us today, Bob.
Bob Benson:	Well, thank you for the opportunity, Richard.
Richard Wilson:	I was reading about your background. I know you have more than 20 years of experience in the financial industry, including several years as a senior consultant with Russell Investments Consulting Group. I would imagine that at the consulting group, you work with all different types of investors, but were you focused only on family offices at that point already, or were you really working with many different types of institutional investors?
Bob Benson:	No, most of my experience at Russell was with institutional and in fact, most of my experience prior to Russell was with institutional. The majority of my working background is in global asset allocation and risk management, essentially determining multi-strategy, multi-asset portfolios and most of that was for large-sized corporations, corporate plans and institutional investors, although part of my background includes Bank of America Capital Management and there I did work with the high-net-worth individuals.
Richard Wilson:	Many family offices emulate some of the investment moves and models of endowments because of their long-term time horizon. Could you share with us some of

	the major differences though between capital deployment and portfolio construction for an endowment fund versus an ultra-affluent client?
Bob Benson:	I would say one of the primary differences between institutional investors and the families that we are working with here at Laird Norton Tyee is that for the institutions, what they really cared about was their performance relative to the benchmark. Even if you look at a corporate pension plan, where their benchmark really should be viewed as their liability stream as determined by the actuary, what they really focus their attention upon was how were they doing with their assets relative to another asset-based index, a customized benchmark, if you will. Whereas for high-net-worth families, although they care quite a bit to select managers and funds that are beating the other managers and funds and relative to the benchmark, relative to the peer group, they care about that. When it comes right down to it, they don't care that much about the performance on a relative basis, but much, much more so on an absolute basis.
Richard Wilson:	How do your clients split up their investments between the industry where they made their wealth initially or in alternative investments, or the broader stock market?
Bob Benson:	It pretty much runs the gamut. As you mentioned, we have a few more than 400 high-net-worth families and clients. Some of those are what we call serial entrepreneurs, where they launched a successful business, so they took the proceeds from that, put that into their second venture, sold that into their third and so forth. These are very-high-risk individuals so they take that risk appetite with their asset allocation as well. So they are unwilling to tolerate low volatility. Essentially, they want to shoot for the lights and they feel very confident, if it goes against them on their portfolio side, they can launch another firm and will be fine.

So part of our problem is reining those individuals in a little bit; this is money that you are allocating for the rest of your life, perhaps for your children, or perhaps for the foundation. It's not money you necessarily want to be trying to hit home runs with. On the other side, we have some family members or high-net-worth individuals that have inherited their money and they understand the difference between producing wealth and managing wealth. They want that wealth managed with very little volatility, to make sure that they can survive through their lifetime and still have enough to provide for the next generations.

Richard Wilson: Interesting. Being based in Seattle, is there a 50/50 split of first-generation wealth versus second-, third-, fourth-generation wealth or how is it kind of split up that way?

Bob Benson: It's more along the lines of three-quarters, I would say, that are first generation.

Richard Wilson: Do you use external experts like say a risk expert, a tax expert or somebody else that's really outside your firm within these investment committees or do you have all of those people internal?

Bob Benson: We pretty much have it all internal. What we do utilize in terms of our valuation tools, on which our strategic and our tactical asset allocations are based, is they are all tied to fundamental macroeconomic data. So that we don't have too much inbreeding in terms of we build the process in-house, we build the models in-house and we interpret the results in-house, we decided to purchase the macroeconomic forecast from an outside firm to give us a bit more objectivity.

Richard Wilson: Many professionals would like to be a chief investment officer of a multi-family office, do you have a single lesson or best practice that you picked up once in that position that may be underappreciated by most people?

Bob Benson: We spent a lot of time and resources on developing what's really institutional quality manager due diligence process and monitoring process. So I think that's one area where a lot of family offices are taking some risk they may not really understand. They may not truly appreciate some of the risks they are taking with their manager due diligence process.

Richard Wilson: From your point of view, when managing the capital of a family office, what is the real benefit to the ultra-wealthy individual who is considering hiring a family office over a traditional wealth management firm or managing their investments through some online investing solution?

Bob Benson: Depending on the particular multi-family office, they can take a more holistic approach and address the fact that it's not just wealth, in many cases; it's newfound wealth.

You might have been fairly struggling along putting all of your proceeds back into the business, now you've got a lot of wealth and it changes things. There is no question that if you suddenly get $20 or $30 million in one fell swoop, you have got some issues in terms of decisions, do you put it in a trust, how do you invest it? One of the key variables that a lot of people don't take into account and they just go into a brokerage account or something along those lines, at least at first, until they realize that this money has the potential of going over multiple generations and that's a different environment.

It's not just the longer investment horizon, but how you structure the money. How you protect it from the negative consequences of taxable events. How do you decide when the children would get money? Do you set it up in the trust or do you have it based on age? Do you have it to hit them all at once, or spaced out? What kind of a legacy do you want to leave? Do you want a foundation? How much of that money do you want to remain relatively liquid, in case you get another opportunity in business to generate a new business versus, well this is not for me, business money that I earn when I sold my business, but I really intend for this money to be for the second and third generation going down the road.

One of the areas where Laird Norton Tyee really comes into play, I think relative to the peers in the multi-family offices, is that the Laird Norton families are on their seventh generation and each generation has added to the wealth pool. So there are more people, but there was additionally more wealth. They really have a lot of insights in terms of what to do badly and what to do well in managing money over multiple generations. We can leverage that with our client base.

Richard Wilson:	Right. I would imagine that your firm often gets them to the edges or into the heart of business decisions as well. If they are first-generational wealth, they might ask you about the tax consequences of buying a commercial real estate building, for example. Does your team work with a lot of business decisions as well?
Bob Benson:	We absolutely do, as well as taxes. We have business specialists, we have tax specialists, and we have a trust company here within our multi-family office. All of these

	decisions should be made together, you shouldn't make the determination of, here is how I am going to sell my business, now what do I do about the investments, now what do I do about the subsequent generations. It's best and smoothest, if you get everybody together, talk through the pros and cons and make one group of decisions and then implement it.
Richard Wilson:	Sure, okay. It amazes me how many global taxation issues come up even if somebody only owns a business in Seattle, lots of times people can have a vacation home somewhere else or they hire somebody in Singapore or something that has some sort of global taxation consequence or at least potential one. So I am wondering in your firm, how do you manage that complex global taxation kind of environment for your clients, is it all in-house or do you reach out to strategic partners elsewhere when needed or what?
Bob Benson:	Most of it is in-house; we do have in-house tax professionals that will handle most of that. Where we feel the need to get someone in an area of specialization we have the contacts within the industry to get those as well.
Richard Wilson:	Okay. If someone has just come into some wealth and they are considering forming a single family office versus selecting a multi-family office, what are some of the tradeoffs that should be considered?
Bob Benson:	Certainly I think they should consider the scope and the depth of what their single family office can do versus what a well-structured and developed multi-family office can accomplish for them. It does not take much money to start a single family office, if all we want to do is manage the assets, manage your wealth in simple means with mutual funds or maybe some separately managed accounts where it's relatively straightforward. But, if you are looking at a diversified portfolio, and particularly, if it's a multi-generational investment portfolio and you have alternatives, you have hedge funds and private equity and private real estate and maybe managed futures or some derivative hedging strategies in there, you are getting to an area of specializations where most single family offices simply lack the resources to do that properly.

Now, as I said before, one of the big areas of differentiation we have at Laird Norton Tyee is our institutional-grade, high-quality, manager due diligence and research process; it's difficult to pay for this kind of research and get the depth of this research and the breadth across the asset classes for a single-family; it's much easier to build that in a multi-family office and leverage that to all the different families.

Richard Wilson: It sounds like it really comes down to establishing if the family wants a very simplified version of a family office solution. If they are under $100 million, that's what it's going to be. Or, do they want something that's more developed and sophisticated and kind of evolved over 20, 30 or 40 or more years? Would you say that's accurate, that you have to choose between a simplified version and a full-blown one because of the amount of assets?

Bob Benson: Yes, those are your two primary options, but I think it also goes back to what I said earlier in a different question about the unintended risks or risk that you are taking that you didn't fully anticipate. In many instances, people think they are conducting quality due diligence, they think they are finding the right managers to their portfolios. But in fact, investment managers are extremely good at telling the client, their prospect, what they want to hear. And it's very difficult, it takes a definitive skill set both in the quantitative analysis for that manager's performance and strategies as well as the qualitative, being able to sit across from that manager and realize where they might be kind of stretching things a little bit, where they might be telling you, "Oh no, it's all like this, so everything is wonderful, everything is fine, this is normal." When in fact, it's not normal and you should be seeing some red flags.

Richard Wilson: Okay, excellent. Can we go into now a bit on how you complete research on fund managers and select them?

Bob Benson: Sure. The first thing we try to do is create the universe, for any new search, we try to create the universe for managers or strategies within that asset class. We try to be as broad and inclusive as possible and really get our arms around every possible candidate. And it's not as simple as looking at Morningstar data or eVestment or anything along those lines. You actually have to have some contacts as well for most instances, particularly when you are moving into alternative asset classes, having industry contacts, so you can call and say, "You know, I am looking for a managed-future fund-of-funds with this type of work."

So we start with the broadest universe possible, and then the first step is to look quantitatively at the manager. Do they have enough assets? Do they have the track record? Do they have the people, the process? We don't look at the performance right off the bat. We don't necessarily throw out a manager if their performance has been weak. If we can point to why that performance has been weak and say, "Well, they are sticking with their guns, we value that, we want a manager that is going to stick with what we hire them to do." And so we start on the quantitative side. We find out, is this a good fit for our clients in terms of the volatility, in terms of their liquidity, can we get our clients in and out in a timely fashion? In terms of the tax consequences, we look at taxes as an integral part of our manager due diligence and research and it's also part of our asset allocation. We optimize both before and after taxes for the appropriate client bases.

But then after the quantitative side is done, when we have narrowed a field that may have started at 300-odd managers down to 10 or 15, then we get on the phone, we start calling them, we start the qualitative process and get to know them. We talk about their process; we talk a lot about their risk controls. How good of an understanding does the portfolio manager have in his or her underlying securities. How are they selected? What's their sell discipline?

We bring that down to maybe three to five or two to five potential prospects that we really spend an enormous amount of time on the qualitative deep dive now that culminates with an on-site visit that lasts most of the day. We might send a couple of analysts out there or maybe one analyst depending on the type of asset and manager. Essentially we will sit in their offices, go through their books, go through their due diligence, go through their risk committee, their investment committee meeting notes, look at their trade blotters, talk to their traders. Do they have backup traders in case one person is out sick or hit by a bus? We run through everything—we run through pretty much everything that they have got in their offices for essentially a full day.

Then based on that, we will either decide none of them meet our criteria or we will select a manager and then we have a peer group where the analysts and reinvestment research group here at Laird Norton Tyee have to pitch that manager to each other. I refer to this meeting as politely harsh. We really try to pick apart the analysis that has been conducted, that led to the selection of this manager, try to find holes. When we feel we have adequately filled in all the holes, then we take it to the investment committee, which includes our operations team, our legal team, compliance team as well as the investment team and the client service teams.

Richard Wilson: It's interesting that you sometimes decide there is no manager who is a great fit and do not allocate to a certain area or asset class because of that. I don't hear that very often.

Bob Benson: Yeah, we actually choose none of the above somewhat often. It's certainly not infrequent, particularly when you are looking at alternative asset classes, where if you are looking at a hedge fund or a fund-of-funds manager, if you can't find and get access to a top-tier manager, you simply don't want to allocate to that asset class. In fact most recently, we had two candidates, a limited partnership for managed futures and we also did a parallel search for a mutual fund–based managed-futures approach. And for one of them, we found a manager that we really, really like a lot. We think it's going to be a fantastic fit for our clients. The other, much to the dismay and disappointment of the analyst, thus far he has not convinced us through the peer review process that it's worth going into that space. So it's looking now like we will simply walk away and we have invested quite a bit of time and resources into the search. The best thing we can do for our clients is just not allocate to that type of a manager and that kind of an asset class.

Richard Wilson: There is a scientific research showing that once we invest 20 or 100 hours in a project we want to see it through to completion and success. I can imagine that some chief investment officers, after doing 100 hours of research on two different fund managers, want to select one. They don't want to say "none of the above." I would imagine that's an easy thing to fall into if you are not careful, right?

Bob Benson: Absolutely, and that's one of the reasons we built the structure that we have with the internal checks and balances and peer reviews, because you do have to view that as all that research, all that time, maybe trips around the U.S. or abroad to meet with managers. You have to do that as the sunk cost, when it comes time to decide is this a manager that is appropriate for my clients and if you can't honestly say yes, I think after taxes, after fees, given the volatility, if this is a fantastic addition for my clients then you simply shouldn't do it. That is the very hard thing to keep in mind.

Richard Wilson: Interesting, okay. Are there any quantitative volatility or liquidity criteria that you look for that are in common that you could share?

Bob Benson: Well, we certainly look for performance on a risk-adjusted basis and we understand that some managers or some asset classes will only perform well with a high level of volatility when compared to alternative asset classes or other asset classes, not necessarily alternative, it could be within traditional. But I think you have to look at the peer group and you have to look at that manager and decide if they are staying true to what they intend to do. If they are small cap managers, do they start getting into the small, mid, or hold some assets that you certainly would not consider to be small anymore in terms of your capitalization. You mentioned liquidity in that given our size that could quite often be an issue that we want established investment shops, partially or in fact mostly because we really focus on the people in the process. We really deemphasize in our manager due diligence process and our manager selection process, we deemphasize the past performance and we really want to find an investment team and execution that makes the most sense. And sometimes you are looking at recent performance and that manager has underperformed the benchmark and/or the peer group, but they have the right people, they have the right process and they are sticking with it and those are attributes we find very desirable.

Richard Wilson: So it really takes to heart the disclaimer that everybody puts on every piece of paper in the industry saying that past performance is not indicative of future results, right?

Bob Benson: Right absolutely, it's more than just compliance.

Richard Wilson: Right, which I think sometimes people wonder which parts are more than just compliance, I think that's great that you brought that up. I am wondering also when it comes to, if we narrow it down to just hedge funds and maybe CTA funds or managed future funds, are there a couple of ratios that you just zero in on right off the bat, if they are not within the certain band, they are out because it's too volatile or is it really dependent on the search and there is no one or two ratios you really look at right away?

Bob Benson: It depends largely on the search. We have a core satellite approach here where we want some inexpensive managers or index funds or exposures that we can get inexpensively and around those we tend to add managers that we want them to take big bets. We don't want to pay active management fees for a closet indexer. It's easy enough for me in most asset classes to find an index. So some of our managers are quite volatile and you would be very hesitant to own one of them on their own, but in a balanced portfolio they play very nicely with the other asset managers.

Richard Wilson: Your team is a large organization. We also interviewed another top-50 family office for this book, Baker Street Advisors; they mentioned that they only typically work with fund managers of $1 billion or plus, which I see on a very high end. Most family offices I have worked with in the past are looking to allocate to $100 million to $300 million plus managers and then many are open to working with emerging managers, but oftentimes choose the larger one, so where does your team fall on that range?

Bob Benson: It depends a lot on the asset class and the specific manager search that we are looking for. Well, we never want to be more than, actually we don't want to be up to 20 percent of a manager's assets under management. We want to make sure that our clients can get in and out of that fund without triggering substantial losses. So we kind of look at, start with the blank piece of paper and say, "Okay, well how many clients is this going to be an appropriate manager for, and then what would their typical allocation be?" From that, we kind of get a rough estimate, well, this is about how many assets we anticipate going into the fund. And then we say, "Okay. Well, based on that, if we have $100 million, it's going into that, in with a manager that will culminate in the search, how big does that manager have to be because we want to target around 10 percent or so. We will go up to 20 percent before we will sell the fund. But we would prefer to be about 10 percent, 15 percent maybe, the assets under management.

Richard Wilson: Okay, great. Do you use a standard due diligence questionnaire or a custom one while completing a search for a new fund manager?

Bob Benson: We have a fairly standard template that we built in-house. It's five to eight pages long, depending on the asset class, and then we customize that based upon the search. So we typically never remove questions from that DDQ, but at times we will add them. We want to focus as much on the operational side of the manager as we do on the investment in the process. So depending on the type of mechanics that are involved in managing that fund, we could add additional sections that are really specific to that search. But we start with that basic template so that despite our experience in selecting and reviewing managers and monitoring them on an ongoing basis, we are trying to avoid getting caught up in some of the emotional elements that we discussed before in terms of, oh well, I love this presentation, this guy's a fantastic presenter, he knows his stuff inside and out, I have just spent you know a fantastic two-hour discussion with him. I think this is great. We want to be able to fall back and say, "Did you really dot every 'i' and did you really cross every 't'? Is there an issue here, a potential issue, or something in which we have to dive a little deeper?"

Richard Wilson: Where are most of your alternative investments being done?

Bob Benson: Most of our alternative allocations are in hedge funds, both in absolute return as well as directional. Following that, I would say it's probably a tie between private equity and private real estate.

Richard Wilson: Okay, great.

Bob Benson: A lot of our clients really value that liquidity, even if it's only a quarterly redemption cycle for a hedge fund or a fund-of-funds manager. That's much more forgivable in

terms of changes in your spending plans than say a venture capital position.

Richard Wilson: Well, that lays it nicely to my last question. Does your team require managed accounts, and do you like it when you can get a fund manager of any type to offer a managed account solution when you are investing?

Bob Benson: You mean like a unified managed account?

Richard Wilson: Yes. Or, say you went to a hedge fund manager and maybe for investors of $100 million and more, they put together a managed account. I guess it could be called a unified managed account or separate managed account, but not like a broad wirehouse SMA (separately managed account) type account, but more of a fund manager doing it on a one-off basis by request of your firm. Is that something that often comes up in your request?

Bob Benson: It does, typically with a lot of our clients we can get better pricing if we go with separately managed accounts. You also have greater flexibility in terms of realizing taxable gains and losses. So quite often, we will try to get a separately managed account from the manager. In some instances, though, we prefer a mutual fund. It really depends upon the size of the client allocations and the attributes of that and characteristics of that asset class and that manager.

Richard Wilson: That makes sense. I have heard some smaller family offices say that it does cost more money, so for one thing for people to keep in mind, if you are looking at forming your own family office, it's relatively hard to do that, I think, unless you are a very successful multi-family office that has a lot of assets that are going into a fund.

Bob Benson: It is, and with roughly $4 billion under management at Laird Norton Tyee we find we have great access to the managers. They are happy to take a call of a multi-family office that's managing money in the billions of dollars versus a single family office with $50 to a $100 million, and we get a lot of pricing power with that weight as well.

Richard Wilson: Yeah, I can imagine. Do you have anything else that you wanted to really fit in here that I didn't get a chance to ask you about?

Bob Benson: One thing I might highlight is the effort and the resources that I think a lot of the better multi-family offices and even single family offices put towards coming up with the customized asset allocations because the asset allocations decision is extremely important in regards to your ultimate satisfaction with your investment performance. You had mentioned earlier in the conversation about a lot of family offices and multi-family offices are trying to emulate kind of the endowment asset allocation model. In some cases, that is absolutely appropriate, but I would argue that in many cases it's not, and I think you have to be able to customize that asset allocation for each client even if it is essentially just you and your family as a single family office. You have to start, I think, with the blank sheet of paper and decide what the optimal asset allocation would be for you, as opposed to the Harvard Endowment, for example.

Richard Wilson: Right. That kind of goes back to your point you mentioned many times that when it comes to alternatives, hedge funds often get the lion's share because of that liquidity. Your client at some point might need that money for a new business they are starting or for retiring or whatever need maybe, where an endowment, you know, it's pretty predictable about when they are going to need cash, right?

Bob Benson: Exactly.

Richard Wilson: Excellent. Thanks again for your time here over the phone today; I really appreciate it and enjoy what's been talked about. I am sure lots of people enjoyed reading this as well.

Bob Benson: Well, thank you, Richard. I appreciate that.

CONCLUSION

This chapter gave you a look at some of the top multi-family offices in the industry today and a great opportunity to sit down with family office veterans like Charles Grace and Jeff Colin and learn from their deep experience. These family offices manage several billions of dollars for a number of wealthy clients, so it is valuable to see how they are able to meet different clients' needs and deal with the various issues that arise from managing such large family offices. I hope you enjoyed reading these interview transcripts as much as I enjoyed conducting the interviews.

To create this family office book and our *Family Office Monthly Newsletter* we interviewed 36 family office executives. If we included all of those interview transcripts in this book it would reach more than 700 pages in length. To learn more about the insights that we gained through completing these interviews and running our family office association please review our family office newsletter: www.FamilyOfficesGroup.com/Newsletter.

Family Office Mechanics

RES NON VERBA

wilson

CHAPTER 8

Family Office Investments

Rule No. 1: Never lose money. Rule No. 2: Never forget rule No. 1.
> —Warren Buffett (legendary investor and philanthropist)

Chapter Preview: In this chapter, we review what types of investments family offices often use in their portfolios and the reasons behind those interests. The goal here is to explore how portfolios are managed at a high level and what investing models are used. In this chapter, we will also be able to read transcripts of a few interviews we conducted with top family offices and how they invest capital.

The biggest challenge in writing this book is that single and multi-family offices are very private about their operations, clients, and investments. A close second was classifying the different models through which family offices invest their capital. The deeper I dig into the industry, the more I realize that every ultra-wealthy family and family office is unique in its needs of risk management and implementation of capital allocation strategies.

The goal of this chapter is to provide you with a high-level overview of how capital is managed in portfolios at family offices. There are multiple books on portfolio analytics, financial analysis, and risk management already in print so we will not go into detail on those areas within this book.

Many things direct the capital and alter the investments that family offices make. Their portfolios are a reflection of their client interests, biases, marketplace sentiments, cash requirements, time horizons, values, and objectives. One of the benefits of investing through a family office is that they will usually take the time to listen to exactly what you want to get done and why, and help you design a plan to achieve that investment goal. Almost every family office is completely open architecture, meaning they can go out and hire any investment fund manager or help make direct investments in nearly anything within reason and the law.

It is essential to note just how important and dynamic family objectives, values, and time horizons can be, as they each can have a dramatic effect on the investments made. An unexpected divorce, untimely death, a child, or new expensive hobby can all change, to some degree, the cash and financial return requirements of a family. Almost every financial advisor has been told and is required by law to first assess their client's appetite for risk, time horizon for investing, understanding of investments, and so forth. What makes the family office different, however, is its ability to manage everything impacting your financial health across multiple generations, and without restriction on what it can help implement.

My expertise is in bringing institutional quality fund managers to family offices, and through working with family offices and running the Family Offices Group association I have found their investment needs to be unique from high-net-worth individuals, endowments, institutional investment consultants, and other types of investors like funds of funds. Family offices typically are more secretive than other investors; they work off of referrals a lot of the time; they are more long-term oriented than high-net-worth individuals and funds of funds; they need more liquidity than some very large institutions; and they do not want their time wasted, yet at the same time they like to take their time with big decisions.

TRADITIONAL INVESTMENTS

Traditional investment managers would include those who run mutual funds, long-only separate management accounts, ETFs, bond or fixed income funds, or variable annuities. Traditional fund managers often make up the core part of a family office's portfolio when you are discussing core versus satellite capital allocations. The benefit of traditional investment fund managers is their sheer volume in terms of number of funds, liquidity, and relatively low cost basis in some cases. For most family offices, the use of traditional investment managers alone is not enough.

ALTERNATIVE INVESTMENTS

Many family offices prefer alternative investment managers such as hedge funds, managed futures, private equity, and venture capital because of their ability to use multiple types of trading strategies and asset classes to achieve their returns. Many times, alternative investments are looked at as the solution to outperforming the general market.

Alternative investment funds also attract a great percentage of the top talent in finance. If you hold variables equal, the top 10 percent of hedge fund management earners and private equity fund earners outshine mutual fund, bond, and ETF professionals in terms of total compensation. It is thought that many of the brightest minds eventually gravitate toward a hedge fund or private equity structure where the most return can be earned for skill in investment or risk management.

Hedge funds and private equity firms are often used in family office portfolios with the hope of achieving a good risk-adjusted return, or alpha. Hedge funds are more liquid with common lock-up periods or minimum lengths of investment terms of one or two years, while private equity funds are less liquid and typically require much longer investment terms of 3, 5, 7, or even 10 or more years. There are more than 20,000 hedge fund and private equity funds in the world, and their strategies are diverse and dynamic.

There is not enough space in this book to cover hedge fund and private equity strategies in great detail, but it is important to know that both are often included in family office portfolios. To learn more about hedge funds, please see the best-selling book I recently released, required reading for the Certified Hedge Fund Professional (CHP) designation program.

The book, published in 2010 as part of the Wiley Finance Series, is *The Hedge Fund Book: A Training Manual for Professionals and Capital-Raising Executives*. I will also be releasing a book soon in partnership with Wiley and Bloomberg that will detail the major hedge fund strategies in use today.

VENTURE CAPITAL AND ANGEL INVESTOR INVESTMENTS

Venture capital and angel investments are thought to be more risky than private equity investments on a per-investment basis, but they are of great interest to many families who have made their wealth in an industry that attracts consistent venture capital, like technology. Many times, I hear of family offices writing very strong collateral-back clauses into these types of investment agreements, which provides them with some sort of asset in case of a total loss of principal in the business in which they have invested. Venture capital investments can be exciting to make, but the returns are often dramatic in either direction and many family offices have lost money while moving too aggressively into this space without experience in running a venture capital portfolio.

I spoke with one single family office manager on the allure of angel investing and the risks. Jared Hendler of Bajaj Family Office told me, "Everybody gets to be involved; you generally get a seat on the board. If it's a company you really believe in, you might use the product or the service and talk to others about it. And when people see things like Zynga and Facebook and see returns that are off the charts, they say, well, why not put a little bit there. Everybody knows that for every 10, you are lucky to have returns on one; nine will go to zero. But it's fun and potentially very lucrative. So, while venture capital and angel investing can be high risk, many family office investors view this investment area as exciting and fun with a possible huge return on some investments."

INFRASTRUCTURE INVESTMENTS

Infrastructure investments can be defined as those technical structures that support a society such as water supply, roads, electrical grids, and so on. As many governments face further budget challenges, privatizing certain aspects of what traditionally has been a government responsibility is on the rise. Many family offices like the nature of infrastructure investments because of their long-term nature and relatively low risk of principal capital loss. I have noticed that these types of investments are especially interesting to family offices when they have an immediate income component available. These types of investments are expected to increase as government capital fails to meet the capital needs of growing city infrastructures around the world. In the last three months alone I have spoken with several families and sovereign wealth fund groups who are actively searching this space for investment opportunities.

HARD ASSET INVESTMENTS

There are many types of hard asset investments and related investment opportunities. These include investing directly in commodities such as gold or timber, or providing leasing against hard assets with a business plan in place to profit from owning the assets in case of default. These types of investments can be accessed via a fund vehicle or through direct investments.

Many family offices like the sometimes more direct control, at times an inflation hedge, and unique return stream that hard assets can provide. Several of the family offices that I know have built their wealth, in part, through owning commercial real estate. Typically those investments are in the multi-family real estate space with large amounts of capital being put to use in large apartment complexes of typically 60 to 100 units on the small end to thousands of units on the big end. My experience has been that most of these multi-family properties are being purchased in city centers, where renting rates may fluctuate but are unlikely to ever disappear completely. Several ultra-wealthy families that I work with in the United States, China, Singapore, and Canada made all of their wealth in commodities and real estate.

Regardless of the type of investment though, in my conversations with family offices, I noticed one common focus in evaluating investments: You need to understand the investment you are making on a granular level, and all of the risks that are involved. No family office will invest in anything that they do not completely understand, even if the supposed gains from the investment are high.

This point was summed up by Avi Gelboim, a single family office manager based in New York, when I asked him how he constructed his portfolio and considered various investment opportunities:

> *I believe first and foremost in investing in what you can wrap your arms around. We pass on many investments that go on to do quite well, but we pass on them because we aren't able to fully understand all of the risks and everything that goes into them. There are always going to be periods of time or circumstances when investments are going to blow up or at least not work out as well as you would have hoped. What I work towards is at a minimum when an investment goes bad, I want to feel like I understood what the risks were. One of the risks happened to play out in a negative way and so while the investment didn't turn up roses, at least it didn't catch me completely unaware.*

Avi touches on a great point that is important to many family offices I have spoken with: understanding the investment and the risks associated with it.

FAMILY OFFICE INVESTMENT PROCESS

While every family office is unique, most family offices follow a common process that is pictured at the 10,000-foot level. The first step in the process is considering regulations, internal investment policies, family values, and what is practical for the family office to pursue as an investment. The next step, typically, is to create a model or idea portfolio that the investment team will then attempt to build.

Last but not least, the third step would be for the investment analyst or chief investment officer to complete research on those investment opportunities while considering dozens of issues including liquidity needs, peer fund performance, risk management, family politics, income requirements of the

Family Office Investment Decisions

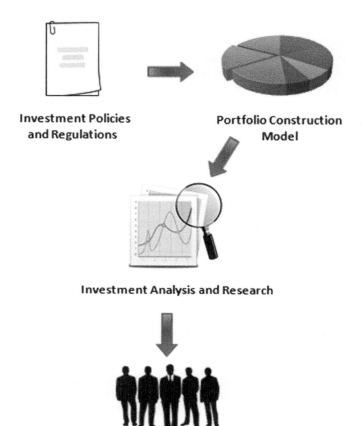

FIGURE 8.1   Family Office Investment Decisions

family, legal risks, the family's investment history, taxation, headline risk, and literally more than 100 other things. Please note: some family offices have no formal investment committee so their approval may not be required before an investment is made.

A whole book could be written, and whole books have, on methods that can be used to construct portfolios. I would instruct those who need more detail on the analytics and risk to seek full references dedicated to these topics, as this obviously a simplified summary of the process.

 See the video "Family Office Capital Deployment Presentation by Richard C. Wilson in Vaduz, Liechtenstein," at www.FamilyOfficesGroup.com/Video20.

I was recently hired to speak in Vaduz, Liechtenstein, at the European Fundraising Summit on the investment priorities of family offices. During my 40-minute speech, "Family Office Capital Deployment," I talked about what family offices want to invest in, what they avoid investing in, what types of funds they prefer allocating capital to, and what trends are affecting family office investments today. I believe this was one of my more concise and clear speeches on the topic, so I hope you enjoy the video, where you can watch the entire presentation for free.

THREE FAMILY OFFICE PORTFOLIO CONSTRUCTION MODELS

 See the video "Family Office Investments." at www.FamilyOfficesGroup.com/Video21.

Three portfolio management and capital deployment models that have emerged through my experience in the industry are the Operating Business Sandbox Model, the Diversified Institutional Model, and the Hybrid Model. I'll cover all of these below.

THE OPERATING BUSINESS SANDBOX MODEL

The first investment model, the Operating Business Sandbox Model, is one only used by single family offices and the smallest of multi-family offices that only serve industry-specific clientele. In this model, the family office is confident in one industry or sector and they invest a majority of the family's assets directly in that area. This could be through reinvesting in one or many operating businesses through which the family grew their original wealth. Many times the investments are made through venture capital, direct investments, angel investor, private equity, factoring, or asset-based lending.

A great example of this model being implemented successfully is found in Kinnear Financial, a Canadian single family office that focuses on commodities. We interviewed Matthew Andrade, director of investment analysis, about how his firm deploys capital.

Richard Wilson:	How do you construct the portfolio at your single family office?
Matthew Andrade:	We don't diversify out of our area of experience. We actually take the opposite approach; we invest in what we know. Jim Kinnear started life as a metals and mining analyst and actually got his CFA at the front end of his career. I have done a fair bit of metals and mining work both and I have worked on the precious metal side. We look for a commodity exposure, preferably with yield by the way of the royalties, that kind of thing. We don't do high tech; we don't do biotech; we don't do real estate. Somebody could say, "I have got the next best McAfee antivirus software," and I would just look at them and say, "Well, I am sure you do, but I have no way to evaluate that." We tend not to do anything outside of the oil and gas or the metals and mining space. The vast majority of my time, I split my day respectively between running the portfolio here, but is common I think with a lot of other family offices, the investment team gets pulled into the operating business, in this case, the royalty business, because of the financial analysis skill sets transfer.
Richard Wilson:	I would imagine even though your sandbox is the oil and gas or metal commodities, you manage it almost like a traditional portfolio in the sense that some of your investments are kind of the equivalent of blue chip commodity investments. Some are very more risky, explorative-type investments, and then some are cash cow, very, very conservative. Is it balanced out like that within that world of commodities or do you guys take a totally different approach, a diversified approach?
Matthew Andrade:	It's kind of a barbell philosophy, where we have a set of yield-bearing investments, not the least of which is the anchor investment in our royalty funds as well as a fairly large position in some yield-bearing oil and gas royalty vehicles as well. On the flip side of that, at the other end of that barbell is the high risk junior oil and gas or precious or base metal mining company.

The thought there is that you could take that from the proverbial 25 cents to $2. There is not a whole lot of middle ground between the two of them.

THE DIVERSIFIED INSTITUTIONAL MODEL

Most family offices that I have worked with and interviewed follow the second model of investing that is a called the Diversified Institutional Model because it is a variation of a diversified institutional or endowment-like model while investing their client's capital. This model tries to take a long-term approach to investing, similar to what an endowment might do while keeping in mind that the family may have some income or cash needs that are not as long term and predictable, as would be the case in an actual endowment portfolio.

Most family offices using this approach use a core/satellite portfolio construction approach. This means that 60 to 90 percent of the investable assets, the core of the portfolio, are placed in traditional investments such as bonds, cash equivalents, stocks, exchange-traded funds, mutual funds, and separately managed accounts that are seen as lower risk and for the most part market-tracking in nature.

 See the video "Satellite Core Investment Model," at www.FamilyOfficesGroup.com/Video22.

The remaining capital in the portfolio is allocated to strategies that are thought to produce alpha, or in others words have more potential to outperform the general market returns found in investments such as equities or bonds. Many times these investments in the smaller satellite portion of the portfolio are made in alternative investments such as private equity, real estate, hedge funds, timber, infrastructure, or commodities like gold. This is an overly simplified description of the model, but many books have dedicated 250 pages to explaining this concept in more detail, so we won't spend more time on the mechanics of constructing these portfolios in this particular book.

THE HYBRID MODEL

The third investment model type combines the Operating Business Sandbox and the Diversified Institutional models. Many times families have an information, research, or experience advantage in a marketplace. To leverage that, they invest 15 to 35 percent of a portfolio within an industry but leave 65 to 85 percent to be diversified over all other types of asset classes and investment types. This allows them, in theory, to go after outsized returns in the space that they enjoy and have had success working, while not putting all of their capital at risk in one area.

To implement this strategy at a multi-family office, clients typically take advantage of the firm's Diversified Institutional Model, combining that with their own managed allocation to their industry, whether that be within the multi-family office or using their own external team or advisors.

In the previous chapter, Multi-Family Offices Interview Transcripts, there were several examples of how modern-day multi-family offices can often implement a Diversified Institutional Model or Hybrid Model for clients. It is interesting to note that the Hybrid Model seems to be the most seldom implemented of the three; typically the patriarch or family office CEO has strong feelings about being in one of the first two models of investing capital.

Many family offices, regardless of their investment model, maintain an investment committee.

FAMILY OFFICE INVESTMENT COMMITTEES

The role of an investment committee is to help make strategic investment decisions, evaluate or select fund managers, discuss portfolio construction and risk management approaches and implementation, and to ensure the long-term preservation of capital and implementation of the investment policy they have been given. Investment committees differ greatly from single to multi-family offices.

Single family offices do not always have formal committees, and are often made up of just three to five professionals, sometimes including one or two external experts or consultants. Many times these committees are less than democratic; votes in the committee are often seen as feedback for the patriarch, but not always followed.

On the other hand, multi-family offices often have investment committees made up of 5 to 12 professionals. Typically, these are internal team members of the family office organization. There are exceptions where a global tax attorney or long-term service provider is allowed to participate in the investment committee, but this is much rarer in a multi-family office setting. In a multi-family office, majority or unanimous votes may be required for certain policy changes or investment decisions to be made, such as selecting a fund manager to allocate capital to.

Regardless of where the investment committee is being constructed, the power of the group's decisions comes from its diversity, objectivity, risk management insights, and real world investment experience.

 See the video "Investment Committees Video," at www.FamilyOfficesGroup.com/Video23.

INVESTMENT COMMITTEE EXAMPLES

In this next section, I would like to share some direct quotes from leading family office executives on how family office investment committees should be or are constructed in the industry.

Chris Allen: Next is a quote from single family office expert Chris Allen. Chris has over 10 years of experience in running a single family office and was interviewed for our *Family Office Monthly Newsletter*.

> *Well, it's all across the board. It's very family specific, but there are some very similar tracks for the families that I've talked with over my career. There is generally one person alive or dead that made the money through some successful business operation or some transaction. Most family offices are a function of a family business that was sold. The family business tended to have a smart accountant, CFO, or treasurer-type that would take care of all the personal needs of the family. The family would split the cost of their personal activity with the business activity because quite often, they were integrally connected.*
>
> *The best family offices that really do make good investment decisions evaluate every single aspect of the opportunity and make a decision that's generally consensus. If you don't build consensus within your investment committee, you're going to end up in a fight down the road.*

Andrew Hector of Candor Financial Management: Some family offices operate successfully with no investment committee at all. For example, Andrew Hector describes below how Candor Financial Management operates in this regard.

> *There is no formal investment committee. We match each client to their objectives, including their financial objectives,*

and their risk profile. They are all different, to differing degrees, but as far as it comes down to investing, each advisor has the obligation and the right to select investments for the client, and they know the clients the best.

That said, most investments are peer reviewed and discussed with the other advisors. We only have three active advisors in the group at the moment and they manage over $600 million under management. We have a very close communicational line between the two advisors here in Perth and the other is in Sydney who we speak with at least once a day. That's how we do it at the moment. As we evolve, the need for a formal investment committee might develop, but there isn't quite that need at the moment.

Bret Magpoing: My experience in the family office industry has been that single family offices are far less likely to have formal investment committees. Bret Magpoing, a 20-year single family office veteran, confirmed this in a recent interview that we conducted with him.

My experience is that single family office investment committees, in the formal sense, are rare. It has been the ad hoc committee many times. I mean, there have been committees that have been in place, in one there was definitely a committee, but it met quarterly or not that often and it was more based around a reporting, of not what we should we be doing, but are we still on a good path here. There was not a lot of advice in terms of strategy on a go-forward basis; it was more almost an audit function, if you will, for that particular family.

In another case, the investment committee met every week and went through the portfolio and individual positions. It was all in-house people; they did not have outside advisors associated with it at all, and it was along the lines of what you indicated, as the Principal having the significant say in things. Ultimately, he wanted to hear people's opinion, but he was going to make the decision and again, that was the situation where his personality was a significant risk taker and that's just the nature of the way that that investment committee came into being.

Marc Lowlicht, Further Lane Asset Management: Some family offices such as Further Lane Asset Management have robust processes instead of using a formal investment committee. Here is an excerpt with Further Lane's president, Marc Lowlicht, on this issue.

> *Instead of an investment committee in a formal sense, we use more of a process that we follow internally. I have, like I said, attorneys and accountants on staff. We will consult on individual clients as need be. They will sit in meetings with clients to provide legal and accounting advice along with my advice. Every once in a while, we will have an attorney sitting with family members that are younger; they will discuss wealth transfer and transfer of the business. Sometimes we will all sit in on a family meeting so everybody is on the same page.*

Rogerio Bastos, FinPlan Family Office: Rogerio, a multi-family office executive from FinPlan in Sao Paulo, Brazil, explains how his team's investment committee operates.

> *We have two different committees; we have one committee for investment approvals, then we have one committee that we use for designing scenarios. The goal is to try and figure out what we imagine is going to be happening in the short-term, medium-term and long-term figures. The first committee is for the approval of the investments. There is a group of us that goes out to visit the managers and does all the due diligence. Once we have done all the interviews with the managers, we write up a memo that is presented to the committee who can decide whether that fund is approved, who can decide on limits on how much money we can invest with that fund or with that strategy, etc.*

Thomas Handler, Handler Thayer LLP: Investment committee and investment process construction is critical to a family office's success, so I asked family office trust and estates expert Thomas Handler to comment on whether a CPA or tax attorney must absolutely be part of a formal investment committee. Here is his response.

> *I think that for those family offices that have sophisticated in-house counsel with a tax background or sophisticated in-house CPA, and if those people are serving on the investment committee, then I think the outside counsel or outside accounting firm is a resource that you go to in special situations. If you get into structured products or synthetics or some sophisticated hedging transaction that's*

got significant tax consequences, you need an independent, outside opinion on those kinds of transactions and/or a fairly sophisticated due diligence run on the people behind this strategy or the product or whatever it is that is involved. I don't think that a person like me necessarily needs to be on the investment committee, but rather as a resource to the investment committee when needed. Those committees would benefit by having some tax person with a good financial background serving on the committee, though, whether that be a lawyer or an accountant.

Paul Tramontano, Constellation Wealth Advisors: To wrap up this section on investment committees, here is a quote from Paul Tramontano, co-chief executive officer of Constellation Wealth Advisors, a top-50 family office.

The key to any successful investment committee is open dialogue and the ability to have constructive debate over the important issues. We have a very thorough process in place that I think is a little bit different from other firms. On a weekly basis, our team monitors every investment decision made by every long-only manager in which we have invested our clients' funds. Before our weekly meeting, our entire investment committee reviews a list of our outside managers showing their year to date return statistics and a log of every trade executed during the preceding week. Often, we will have a brief description of the reasoning for each trade as well. This information is useful for a number of reasons. First and foremost, it allows us to stay very close to what is happening in each of the portfolios, and to understand why managers are making adjustments. It also enables us to monitor our managers for style drift to make sure they are doing what we have hired them to do. As an example, we would not want our developed international managers to venture into the emerging markets as a way to increase return unless we were aware of the style change. Finally, it provides a foundation upon which we can determine the way the portfolios are moving or analyze the way we have money allocated within those portfolios.

In addition, our chief investment officer compiles a weekly research piece that includes recent articles, buy and sell side research, periodicals, financial data, and any other pertinent information the investment committee can utilize for discussion. In concert with our investment performance data, this piece helps to educate our employees on current Fed policy, to shape our investment thesis and to react to the current investment climate. Both the investment information and weekly research piece are distributed in advance of the meeting to allow our committee members ample time to review and digest the information. As a result, when we begin our investment committee meetings on Wednesdays, we are able to frame the discussion from a big picture standpoint on the way we want to allocate capital.

One interesting output of the recent market activity is many managers before the 2008 meltdown used to tell us that they did not put a macro overlay on the way that they looked at investments. In essence, they were hired to buy growth or they were hired to buy value. The hedge funds would tell you they were hired to be long short equity and that is what they were going to do. Flash forward, and post-2008, I think the thought process has changed and most investors do have a macro overlay on all of their portfolios. We have always had that in place and we think that is perhaps a little part of why we have been successful in protecting capital in very bad markets, while still participating when the market gets better.

STRATEGIC VERSUS TACTICAL ASSET ALLOCATION

To understand family office investments, it is important to understand the difference between strategic and tactical asset allocation.

Strategic asset allocation is the carefully planned out placement of assets in types of asset classes and investment areas, knowing that each has different risk profiles, growth prospects, and long-term track records of performance.

Tactical asset allocation is the dynamic movement of investments between geographical regions, asset classes, or vehicles to take advantage of current events, market environments, economic trends, or political environments. Strategic asset allocation is a top-down approach of optimizing the placement of investments. Tactical asset allocation is the adjustment of investments to make timely overweighting of investments in areas that are thought to perform well and underweighting those areas that are appearing weak.

We recently interviewed Peter Schuppli of Cottonfield Family Office AG of Zurich, Switzerland. We asked Peter, a member of the Family Offices

Group, to briefly describe his investment process and tactical versus strategic allocation adjustments. He replied:

> *We have a very sophisticated investment process. We work with a quantitative model, which gives us certain indications about the market, the expectations of the market. We have an investment process with strategic and tactical asset allocation on a quarterly, monthly, weekly, daily basis. So we are pretty close to the market because it's not only about investment, it's also about currency management, cash management, operational risk management. So all these issues are being taken care of within the investment management process.*

Excerpt from Interview with Graham Harrison of Asset Risk Consultants

The following is a short excerpt from an interview we recently completed with Graham Harrison of Asset Risk Consultants in Guernsey that is directly related to tactical versus strategic asset management decision making at family offices.

Graham Harrison: In our view, for most single family offices or certainly for most families who don't have a group of investment professionals who are actually running their money for them day to day, what they need to do is essentially set a strategic framework for their money to be run and then let the professionals get on with it. Then you measure and monitor the professionals against a grade target and parameters.

The second thing that's strategic, asset allocation is terribly important and we rather—I mean, it's somewhat different I think, divide the world of investment returns into three different parts and we talk to them how they want to divide their risk allocation if you'd like, their risk budget between those three different parts, from the three parts.

Richard Wilson: Sure, that makes sense.

Graham Harrison: Once you've determined your strategic asset allocation, our next step with clients is what makes us different I think from the North American model of consulting. This has to do with the way we think the value chain of returns works. All the academic evidence supports the concept that your choice of what proportions to put in equity than bonds and hedge funds and property and cash and that sort of thing will be one the greater determinants of return.

The second most important determinant is if you are tactically allocating between those different asset classes. The third most important would be which company, for example, you're choosing in North America in the equities space. Now, in the North American consulting model, generally, the consultants would make the tactical asset allocation decisions. They may say, "We think emerging markets are really interesting; we think that therefore you should allocate X percent to the emerging markets and we're going to find you the best emerging market manager."

Then they do that for all the asset classes, but effectively the consultant is controlling the asset allocation at a tactical level rather than nearly at the strategic level. What that means is that when emerging markets are in trouble or there is a feeling that the certain asset class is overpriced, it is very cumbersome. For those allocations to be changed often would actually require the investment committee of the family to be called together; then there would be a debate, time would pass, and very often the opportunity to add value by a tactical shift is gone, just because of implementation time.

What happens is that under that consulting model, the tactical asset allocation piece almost disappears. The approach we've taken is to talk to clients about allocation of risk budget to discretionary by their client managers, who are able to make not just the decision as to what to buy in a particular asset class but the proportions that they allocate to those asset classes within an overall volatility or risk budget.

Richard Wilson: Right.

Graham Harrison: This in a sense is, you could say, giving a lot more power to the managers who are appointed. And to our mind it is you get the benefit of not having any one person's tactical view imposed on the whole portfolio because you have a series of managers. Typically we work out and find three or four managers who have very different investment philosophies and ways of thinking, but it might begin in very similar risk budgets.

	We would then get them to go and run portfolios really with the aim of maximizing the return for unit risk taking.
Richard Wilson:	So, it is a lot different than the approach taken by most consulting firms, like you were saying, where the process can take so long to make adjustments that any gain from just being 100 percent strategic is mostly lost. Sometimes it could even be a negative result of trying to be tactical by being too slow at doing so, right?
Graham Harrison:	Right. And what happened is that mostly the investment consulting model for private clients is filtered down from pension fund and institutional investment approaches; what works for an institution doesn't necessarily work for private clients. Our view is that there are very good discretionary managers out there and one is much better off appointing a series of discretionary managers and letting them do the very best they can for a client rather than the consultant trying to pick the best in any one particular area.

Our client base tends to come to us and speak with us because they believe this is true. They would rather have one strategic asset allocation obviously, but then two or three people playing the tactical asset allocation game rather than one person playing the tactical asset allocation game, particularly when the process of playing that is going to be delayed because of the corporate governance processes family offices have.

We were thankful to have the chance to interview Graham because I know that many family offices rely on their team's expertise in managing their fund manager and investment portfolio risks. Another important aspect of family office investing is their use of institutional investment consultants, which I'll cover next.

INSTITUTIONAL CONSULTING FIRMS AND FAMILY OFFICE INVESTING

Institutional investment consulting firms are consulting groups that typically offer no investment funds or products, and focus completely on advising institutional investors and at times, family offices on how to construct their portfolios, manage risk, and select fund. I have spoken with hundreds of institutional investment consulting firms in my normal course of work, and they are a great source of insight on fund manager selection, macro-investment views, and avoiding potential investment pitfalls. Since many family offices use these institutional investment consultants for help in their investing, I thought it would appropriate to interview a top-50 CEO in the area. I did just that by connecting with David Thomas from Equitas Capital Advisors, LLC.

FAMILY OFFICE INTERVIEW WITH DAVID THOMAS, CEO OF EQUITAS CAPITAL ADVISORS, LLC

I had the opportunity to recently interview David Thomas of Equitas Capital Advisors. He shares some of the best practices and insights he has gained while managing over $3 billion in assets under advisement within his institutional consulting firm. I asked David to start out the interview by sharing a bit about his firm's history.

David Thomas: My history goes back to 1982, so I have been doing this for quite a while. Equitas, we started in 2002, but it's just a continuation of the work that I did running consulting divisions for Wall Street firms. We got into these family offices through referrals. We were referred to some family offices that needed particular work. Some of them were generational changes. Some were looking to diversify out of their family business. For example, it may be real estate or oil and gas and they wanted to have financial assets, which is what we do. As a diversifier, they will bring us in, we work through our business model as that of an outside chief investment officer so we either fulfill that role in the fiduciary of that role or we will support an in-house staff in that role to help the family offices meet their goals and objectives as investors.

Richard Wilson: That's interesting. Can you explain one or two unique things about acting as an outside chief investment officer (CIO) versus other investment consultants providing similar services? However, they don't really brand themselves or position themselves as an outside CIO that I know of, at least not very commonly. Are there one or two value-adding things that you guys provide that maybe some other firms don't that makes that difference?

David Thomas: I think it's the way we go about that type of a business model. First of all, it is independence because we don't have a solution or a product to shoehorn investors into. Our trademark business model, our trademark logo is engineering financial solutions, and that's what we do. We don't really care what the solution is; we just care to bring to the table something that fits the criteria of a particular investor. And we have investors, some of them are 80 percent bonds, some of them have no bonds and that's okay, that's what the account calls for. So I think the way we approach it is just as a problem solver for the family offices, that's one of our differentiators.

Richard Wilson: I would imagine that some family offices that might have many people on staff might still use you as a CIO as part of their team. I would also guess that some other people might be ultra-high-net-worth individuals and they might manage a lot of things themselves, but then also use you as a CIO, is that correct?

David Thomas: Yes, some have full staffs that we were brought in to supplement. Some have all their staff in the family business and they would bring us in as the diversifier.

Richard Wilson: I know many family offices have investment committees that have 3 to 5 or even 8 to 12 members. Oftentimes if you are brought in as the external CIO does that affect that? Sometimes if they don't have any investment expertise, I would guess that maybe they wouldn't even have an investment committee, or do you help them form one and participate in one?

David Thomas: Sometimes the investment committee really consists of just the family members. Sometimes they will bring in additional outside members, other service providers, accountants, attorneys to kind of round it out or they will just have other people's opinion on how much diversification they want in a board of directors. A lot of times, the patriarch has all of those anyway. We bring our service to the table in order to find out the collective temperament of the investor or the investment committee and then we build solutions along those lines.

Richard Wilson: I know that every family office is different but is there a common allocation that you are seeing among family offices?

David Thomas: I don't see any golden thread throughout the asset allocation. I don't see any one model that works for everybody. I think it's pretty darn diversified, quite frankly. The golden threads that I see are such things as confidentiality. Family offices like control; they like things relatively low key, and they like a certain temperament to the way they go about things. We have some investors that are embracing alternatives in a large way, some are not. Some like real estate, some don't. Some don't like the bond market at all, some have a majority of their assets there. A lot of the views of a family office you have to take into account because the solution you build is a solution for their particular set of needs.

Richard Wilson: Do you often see a costly fund manager selection or investment mistake that you could share with us that help family offices reading this interview transcript?

David Thomas: The first one that comes to mind is not truly diversifying the investment portfolio. Thinking back to a long time ago, I worked with a group we got to diversify the City of New Orleans pension plan. They had all fixed income and they wanted to diversify into the equity market, which we did for them. As we looked at the styles in the different ways to invest money inequity, they decided they like the large cap value style. We suggested to them, "Okay, we need to be diversified though and we really need to be covering more grounds than that," they thought about that and came back and said, "You're right, so we would like to have six large cap value equity managers."

There is so much overlap; this can happen in mutual funds, it can happen in a lot of areas, so you really have to watch the correlation to see if you are really helping yourselves or not. We are doing a lot of work right now for checking correlation to rising interest rate markets and do we have the right protection in the portfolio for that. I would say some of the errors come in the portfolio engineering process. Sometimes the offices just want to do what they know and if they don't know something they don't do it.

Richard Wilson: By overlap, you mean having, for example, Intel included in all four of those large cap or six of those large cap funds? You are not really diversifying too much at all, right?

David Thomas: It happens a lot more than you know, and now you are not diversified at all.

Richard Wilson: Right. When it comes to alternative managers, do you see managed accounts as something that is really critical to further growth in the industry and the family offices are requesting managed accounts more and more? Is that happening on a case-by-case basis only for very large allocations of say 100 million or more? What's your experience there?

David Thomas: I do see managed accounts as a growing part of that business. I do see it being larger pools of money and I think there are some critical mass issues that may come into play for an alternative manager set up separate account. There is some administration and some work to be done for balancing the administration if you are going to do multiple separate accounts, which traditionally they haven't had there. If you are just into one commingled fund then everybody is in one fund; it's much simpler for the managers and every investor gets the exact same return, exact same diversification, every trade goes in.

Other things I have been seeing, especially in '08, which was particularly tough for the alternatives, that particular bear market. Unlike the bear markets of 2000, 2001, 2002, the alternatives just sailed through that bear market; they did very, very well. They were hurt in the last half of '08 and I have seen a lot of alternatives coming out now where the alternative managers take things out of their document such as the ability to side pocket asset. You know, I am seeing even distressed debt managers writing that out because that was such a problem in 2008 and it continues to be a problem that lingers out there as the liquidity gets worked out. Taking that off the table is good for the industry and good for investors.

Richard Wilson: How important is it for families to have their priorities, values, objectives, and mission statements all down on paper?

David Thomas: I think it's important. I think it helps in the longevity of the family office and the longevity of relationships with all the service providers. If the family can reduce it down to paper exactly what they want to do and how they want to do it, it is just like when you write a business model for a company; your in-house investments are a business, so treat it like a business and have all that written down.

I think it's helpful, particularly when you get to the bumps on the road, where emotions start to come into play and you know there will be some Nervous Nellie members of the family and there will be some aggressive members of the family. You don't have to let your emotions take over when you get to a stress point or some bump on the road. You just go back and read the script and see "what do we do when we have a certain bear market or change in the stock market or interest rates?" You just go back and read the script and do what it says to do and it keeps people on point, on target and without kind of getting distracted into areas that can really become detrimental to the long-term success of the family office.

Richard Wilson: Right. It's interesting as this whole 36-interview series with family offices and my seven-plus years of experience and working with family offices and more with hedge fund managers as well, I have never once heard someone saying to manage your investment portfolio as a business. It's somewhat obvious, I guess; if you have a formal family office formed that that should be treated as a business because it has operations and it has employees, etc. I think many ultra-high-net-worth individuals who may have inherited wealth or sold the business might not yet be thinking of their investments like a business at all.

How do you narrow down and select alternative fund managers?

David Thomas: At Equitas, we just look for the best-of-breed in each category. I would say that the trends that I am seeing are away from the older consulting model when you would go in and do all the search process, the qualitative and quantitative work, and then you would get down to a shortlist and the family would interview the shortlist. That beauty pageant, if you will, type of model; a lot of families don't have time for that anymore and they want us to do it. They want it to be done, but they would like to see who is selected in each area, just to lessen the demand of their time.

Richard Wilson: In my experience, it's been that family offices typically don't want to take the business risk of working with an emerging manager. When you talk about best-of-breed, it probably eliminates those managers with under a hundred million of assets because best-of-breed likely has some institutional-quality trading operations, backup recovery systems, and a very high pedigree team. Is that a correct assumption, that family offices want managers

	with at least a 100 million under management, or is there another number that more often comes up, like 350 million in AUM?
David Thomas:	Yeah it's at least 100 million, though it could be 300. We do some with 500 million. I would probably use 250 million as the mark. The family offices, they just don't want things to go wrong. They would rather have more security than they would have extra return that might come from an up-and-comer. They will leave that on the table, just to have more of an established company.
Richard Wilson:	I guess that capacity in the certain strategy you are looking that would be a factor in that asset level, I believe $500 million. Some family offices might be worried that by the time they grow with the manager, they are going to be kept out in terms of size. At 350 million, however, if they are only growing to a billion or 1.5 billion, then that probably comes into play and how much and when they are looking for capacity, right?
David Thomas:	Yes, it is different, depending on the asset class. If you are talking about bonds, I don't think there is an upper cap; I haven't seen an upper cap. Bill Gross, with hundreds of billions of dollars, tends to move around pretty actively and does a very good job. On the other side of the equation, small cap domestic equity managers have a problem. You know, when you get up over a couple of billion dollars, you just lose some of the liquidity that you need. With alternatives, I think size is the enemy of returns with alternative money managers. Sometimes I will see a particular niche manager that's starting off with $100 million that family offices will want to invest there just to know that at some point, especially if the manager puts up good numbers, the money is going to flow in and then they are going to close. There have been a few exceptional times where I have seen that availability for smaller managers and alternatives.
Richard Wilson:	When you talked about best-of-breed, I think there are some trends in the industry where board members would like to see. An independent governance board formed for the alternative investment fund. A real estate fund, for example, might have six or seven people on it, and they look out for the best interest of the investor instead of being on the business side of making that fund as much

	money as possible. Is that something that you see as nice to have but just isn't a reality in today's fund management industry or is it something you guys are starting to see demanded by family offices and boards?
David Thomas:	Now are you talking about a separate board of directors for the alternative money manager or you are just talking about a separate group inside the family office?
Richard Wilson:	The separate one by the money managers. If that $500 million hedge fund makes a macro fund, they may have formed an outside independent board that would oversee their expenses, what they are spending money on, how they are spending money, making sure that investors are treated fairly, etc.
David Thomas:	A lot of the alternative managers have a board of directors like that. I haven't seen that mandated in the search process, but I think in the alternative industry where we see managers moving from basically a cottage industry into a main stream institutional tool, I think that will be more and more of what we will see over time.
Richard Wilson:	Related to our talk about managed accounts earlier, are there one or two other ways that firms, like yourself in your client's family offices, are requesting more transparency on funds like hedge fund managers? Are there certain requests in terms of having more transparency into their business operations or into their trading activity than in the past? How has that taken form if so?
David Thomas:	I think transparency gets higher and higher every year and I am glad to see that. We have always been big on transparency. We have been, for 10 years, going in and getting the 13F filings from even the alternative managers so we know everything they own on the long side. There is no payment to the administrators inside the alternative management firms because you get the information straight from the SEC. We don't have that on the short side yet, but they will give you at least industry breakdown or some company breakdown in writing. Then when you sit down with them in meetings, they will usually go through their short names in a conversation, although they will not put it in writing.
Richard Wilson:	Okay.
David Thomas:	They are still kind of protective of their short book, and rightly so. There are a lot of reasons it makes it harder

	for them to do their research, if company management knows they are betting against them.
Richard Wilson:	I think that's good to know because I think that managers are often asking how they can be more transparent and try to gauge how important that is to investors such as family offices. Do you see any big trends? You have been working in the industry so long; are there some macro trends that are really starting to take hold or any new trends you have identified?
David Thomas:	Yes, I would say from the investment side, the macro trends are even larger and probably the biggest one is globalization. We are seeing that with the businesses. We are seeing that within the investment profiles and the asset allocation policies that are coming up and we are big proponents of that. International investing, for example; 30 years ago the U.S. was approximately 70 percent of the world capitalization of the market. Now the U.S. is around 30 percent and the world markets are much, much larger. The United States has grown, but fallen behind the growth of the rest of the world. The emerging markets are going to emerge, and they will emerge. I don't think there is anything that will stop them, barring a global depression or World War III.
Richard Wilson:	Right.
David Thomas:	We see a lot of movement into the emerging market countries, both on the equity side and on the fixed income side. Ten years ago, the emerging markets were the junk bond credits of the world; it was like 1 percent investment grade. Now over 50 percent of the country's sovereign debt is investment grade and these are the creditors; in a lot of ways their balance sheets are stronger than the industrialized West, which has all the problems with deficit spending, deficit trade, mortgage problems, real estate problems, over-spending problems, and emerging markets don't. I think that's a trend that will be around for a long time, probably until the emerging market start to get fat, which we are a long way away from that. I think globalization of those investment portfolios is a trend; the alternatives have been a trend. We are big followers of the NACUBO (National Association of College and University Business Officers) research which we think is probably the closest group to having it right when you talk

about asset allocation and diversification. I am not saying they have it completely right, but they are the closest to having it right. A lot of the reasons for that is the people who sit on those boards are these family office members and they are early adopters moving into those areas. We think that makes a lot of sense. The traditional domestic stock and bond portfolios that used to be the core of most of the portfolios, right now for a lot of large universities is just a small minority piece of the portfolio. They are diversifying outside of those assets in a large way.

It has helped them evolve substantially for the last 20 years and outperform almost every year except for '08, when nothing helped. When you have a stressed period like 2008, fundamental investment logic gets thrown out the window and investors run back into the dollar and back into Treasury bonds with a 2 percent yield and T-bills with a negative yield. We have moved through that; I think we will do fine. I think the macros for the investment side are attractive and I believe will even get stronger. As far as the business mix, family offices are starting to run like a business again. The multi-family offices, that's just another business model. They are basically "taking in laundry" and pulling together family offices they want to pool. That's a business model. We tend to do that for our investors without having them necessarily pool their investments with anybody. They like the exclusivity of having their own private account and being able to do their own thing without the pooling process where possible. Where we bring in the pool it's just the knowledge of a lot of different types of investors who know what people are doing, what people are adopting successfully or what people are avoiding successfully. Both sides of that are very important. The knowledge gets pooled. The investments can remain separate.

Richard Wilson: It's a huge advantage that you have in your insights because it's a groupthink in the positive sense; all these best of ideas are being filtered through you and your organization. That collective knowledge your organization has is literally worth billions of dollars and the difference of long-term returns of your client investments having all that extra knowledge and foresight and opinions to be able to consider more perspectives before making the decision. It's almost like you have an investment committee of hundreds of very well-experienced successful investment professionals because you are hearing all these ideas and investment considerations all the time, right?

David Thomas: Absolutely. I mean, we do business with lot of different types of investors, corporations, insurance companies, hospitals, oil companies, in addition to the family offices, universities, endowments and foundations, and you can take a page out of the playbook from another group if it works for you. We work with a local corporation here that has big cash flows, $50 million a month of cash flow. They thought it was kind of an inefficient asset because they weren't getting any return on the cash and they wanted some way to increase that, so we took a page out of the playbook of Harvard University on their foundation. They run negative cash and they manage to a negative 5 percent cash position. To this corporation we said instead of having $50 million of cash every month which you pay down over the course of that month, why don't you start each month with par at zero and set up a revolving credit line that you will run down to $50 million in revolving credit that you borrow against. Then every month, when the money comes in you go back to zero. With LIBOR being so low that you keep the $50 million earning interest in a bond portfolio they had a positive arbitrage over their cost of borrowing. They thought that was terrific and it was. I mean it was a smart idea. It wasn't our idea. We just recognized it, adapted it, and brought it in, coming from a university endowment into a corporation.

Richard Wilson: That's an excellent example. I think a whole book, and there probably is a book written on this, but a whole book can be written just on cash management best practices for family offices. I have been told by multiple people how important that is and one person even said his pretty high-end salary at a family office can be paid for just by his management of the cash, just the extra ROI with the average family office can pay his whole salary if they have 50 million or 100 million or more. There are so many things you can do to optimize that and increase the real interest rate that you are getting versus the inflation.

That was really interesting and such a great example that you provided—exactly what I was trying to get out so that you can take best practices from a different economic environment or a different type of institution like an endowment firm and then use that within the family office. Whereas, if you only work with somebody who has 30 years of experience, but doesn't have access to all that group knowledge, then it's less likely that you are going to keep that in mind or always be hearing these new ideas that are very innovative or just a new way to manage risk or preserve capital.

David Thomas: Just being creative and engineering financial solutions. We had a family office that wanted to increase their float on the checks they wrote. They found out that the slowest mail service in the United States is Dauphin, Alabama. This is way back in the '80s when the interest rates were much higher. So they kept all of their money in a bank in Dauphin, Alabama, earning very high interest rates and when they wrote their checks, it added a couple of more days of float and they thought that was terrific. They had nothing to do with Alabama; they don't even live in Alabama, but they were writing their checks from there to increase float. There are a lot of ways you can creatively engineer financial solutions; you just have to look around and take a page out of any playbook that makes sense.

Richard Wilson: That was a pretty creative solution I haven't heard of before. Each one of those small differences makes a huge difference overall. It's like the very large corporations, which have three or four people on the staff just to hedge currency risk. I mean, it's the same type of things; the tiniest advantage in terms of the percentage point, the basis point, or could be a huge advantage in terms of extra money held in their account.

David Thomas: Now if you bring that more up-to-date, because rates are so low, you can basically do money market funds in local currency sovereign debt internationally. It will have very low duration, but a higher yield. You also participate as the dollar falls. We are the camp where the dollar is being diluted and will fall against some of the more emerging countries whose currency is actually getting stronger. So you can still have liquidity and make a higher interest rate, but can participate by having money outside the

	dollar. This is a creative cash management system for today.
Richard Wilson:	Right. Yeah, it was interesting how Brazil has been paying off their debt, while America's debt seems to only go up. People have traditionally thought of Brazil as relatively high in political risk, ten years ago at least, and now they are becoming more and more healthy, like you were talking about earlier when you said emerging markets such as Brazil are really growing strongly right now.
	I think that about wraps things up though. Thank you for your time today to complete this interview, David.
David Thomas:	Thanks Richard. I appreciate the call.

CONCLUSION

In this chapter, we looked at how family offices invest their capital. Through interviews and research, we looked at many of the different investments that family offices make, from real estate to hedge funds, and the portfolio construction models used by family offices. Furthermore, we heard from family office CIOs and executives on how they invest their clients' money and how they go about making key investing decisions. While the process for investing capital varies by each family office, sound due diligence, constant risk management, and careful analysis were at the heart of all these family office executives' investing processes.

CHAPTER 9

Fund Manager Selection and Deal Flow

By leadership, I mean the general's qualities of wisdom, sincerity, humanity, courage, and strictness...
        —Sun Tzu (ancient Chinese military strategist and author of *The Art of War*)

Chapter Preview: In this chapter, we will explore the fund manager selection process and preferences of family offices. We will explore the types of funds that family offices look at, what characteristics are sought out in investment funds, how to complete systematic character analyses using the 6 Cs Model and a few trends that affect the family office due diligence process and capital allocation in this area.

The ability of family offices to research, identify, and monitor investment fund managers is at the core of how a family office delivers value to its client(s). Many times, the type of financial results that an ultra-affluent client expects can be achieved only through the use of various fund managers who have diverse strategies that ensure that the money is preserved and grown in several methodologies and asset classes.

The goal of this chapter is to provide you with a high-level overview of how fund managers are analyzed and chosen by family offices for an investment. As explained in the previous chapter, we will not be going into great detail here on portfolio analytics or specific ratios to look for. Each family office is unique, and these analytical methods are covered in other well-written books on those subjects.

That being said, one selection of the wrong fund manager can be very costly. Choosing the wrong fund manager could result in principal loss, unnecessary lock up of capital, low tax efficiency for an investment strategy, a bad reputation, regulatory action, or even civil and criminal liability. Family offices have a fiduciary duty to complete due diligence on fund managers and select them with care. The consequences, positive or negative, are great; that is partially why family office expertise is so critical.

THE SIX-STEP FUND MANAGER SELECTION PROCESS

The typical family office fund manager selection process, as seen in Figure 9.1, can be broken down into six macrosteps; there are sometimes substeps to these at larger institutions. This is not a recommended process to follow but rather a collective view of what the industry is employing around the world at the 10,000-foot level.

The Six Steps of Fund Manager Selection

1. The first step is typically to review what is called the "one-pager" or tear sheet of a fund manager. This is typically a very brief, one- or -two-page PDF document that contains the fund's investment performance, team, investment process, disclosures, and complete contact details. It is meant to explain the investment strategy to the investor and present a 10,000-foot view of what the fund offers. Typically these are reviewed for a short amount of time, just 5 to 10 minutes, by investors who know very quickly whether the rest of this process should be followed for the specific fund manager being reviewed.

2. The second step in the process takes place when the investor has some interest in the investment thesis or team of the fund and would like more details; they are sent a PowerPoint presentation, sometimes referred to as a "deck" or "pitch book," on the fund manager. This PowerPoint is typically 15 to 80 pages long and reviews the fund's team, unique edge

One-Pager PDF | PowerPoint | Phone Call Review | Due Diligence Questionnaire Completed | On-Site Visit | CIO or Investment Committee Analysis

FIGURE 9.1 Fund Manager Selection Process

in the marketplace, investment process, risk management procedures, operations, service providers, investment examples, and plans.

3. If the PowerPoint is well received, most investors will want to move to the third step, setting up a phone call to discuss the materials of the presentation. These calls typically last for 25 to 80 minutes and usually consist of a fund manager partner walking the investor through each page of the presentation, stopping for questions, and fielding additional questions at the end of the phone call. Analysts, investment committee members, or the chief investment officer of a family office may start asking tough questions about style drift, the effect of a key executive leaving the team, or how, why, and for how long they may have "gone to cash" in the last recession. It is during these phone calls that investors get a feel for where the strengths and weaknesses of a fund manager are and where more research and data will be needed.

4. Step four involves the review of a due diligence questionnaire, or DDQ, as they are often called. These DDQs consist of 30 to 180 questions and can often be more than 100 pages long once completed by the fund manager. The point of the DDQ is to dig into the granular details of the fund's operations, legal structure, compensation structure, portfolio of investments, future plans for growth, and so forth. This, combined with the one-pager, PowerPoint, and phone call, is the bulk of what many analysts and investment committees use to review fund managers in a relatively comprehensive manner. Sometimes step four is required before step three, and that is important to note. Most of the other steps will not change order, but they can in some situations.

5. The fifth step that most family offices complete while selecting a fund manager is conducting an on-site visit. Sometimes, due to geographical distance, the fund manager will come to the offices of the family office, but this is an exception and not the rule since it is more valuable to see the real office of the fund. A lot can be learned by seeing how a team works together, trades, selects investments, and treats each other day by day. Almost all of the family offices I have spoken to and worked with require a face-to-face meeting, but some will rely on a third-party investment consultant or compliance team to do this for them.

6. Typically, the final step in the selection of a fund manager is further research, analysis, and deliberation by the analyst, investment team, chief investment officer or investment committee, or all of the above. In some cases, a unanimous agreement is required before investing in a fund manager, in some cases only the chief investment officer has the authority to select a fund manager for an allocation, and every family office has slightly different processes for what is needed before a new fund manager is selected.

Family offices can often put a lot of capital to work within a fund manager and they like to get comfortable with their reactions to the marketplace, their team, and their reputation in the industry before investing too quickly. Sometimes this process can be completed in a few as two to four months, but most fund manager selections occur over 6 to 12 months.

 See the video "Warning Signs," at
www.FamilyOfficesGroup.com/Video24.

I recorded a video in Monaco on the top 11 signs that a fund manager is not investing in their own business. This is a short video that will help you steer you clear of those funds that are not taking a long-term approach to running their business.

MANAGED ACCOUNT TRENDS

A managed account is an independent financial account setup where the money remains completely under the fiscal control of the investor, yet the fund manager can direct trades in the account for as long as they have been appointed the right to do so. For example, a family office may place $20 million in a separate account so that a small cap fund manager can have the trades he places for his core fund portfolio of $300 million also reflected in that separate account, in effect mirroring his trades. Typically this means the investor gets superior transparency, as they can see exactly what the fund manager is investing in. Also, if the market starts to go south or the manager underperforms, the investor could cut them off and liquidate the trades almost immediately.

There is a lot of talk at conferences and in publications about the importance and growth of management accounts. In the long-only fund management space, investments being made in separately managed accounts and unified managed account structures have been rising steadily. Many industry professionals expected more hedge fund managers to implement or be asked to offer managed accounts by their investors, but to date this has not happened.

Some investors placing investments of $25 million, $50 million, or $100 million-plus can require a managed account to be set up for them but there are costs, compliance considerations, and time investments involved in providing this type of an account to an investor. Typically only larger investors or those fund managers with little negotiation leverage are placing capital through this form of investment on a common basis.

FUND MANAGER PREFERENCES

In any area of investing, there are now fund managers offering numerous types of products as shown in Table 9.1. These types of funds include mutual funds, ETFs, hedge funds, private equity funds, funds of funds, and real estate investment trusts. Regardless of the type of fund being examined, there are some common things that every family office I have worked with is looking for.

Everyone in the fund management industry talks about how the team behind the fund is most important, but what does that mean? In such a results and performance driven industry, how can you break down judging a team or an individual into components that can be looked at separately and on some level objectively quantified?

GLOBAL FUND MANAGER DUE DILIGENCE

Every family office I have spoken to would like to meet a fund manager at least one time face-to-face so that they can get a feel for what type of person they are dealing with. In most cases, that meeting is preferred at the fund manager's office to make sure that things look and feel professional and hopefully institutional. Family offices want to know that they are more than a confident voice over the phone and a slick PowerPoint presentation.

One challenge in running a family office is completing thorough due diligence on global investment fund managers. Many times, family offices are stretched thin, so until they reach $1 billion to $2 billion in assets, flying to Singapore, Dubai, and Toronto to do an on-site visit with a potential fund manager that may or may not receive capital is not very practical.

I asked Edward Stavetski of SRC Family Office Consultants to explain how he deals with this problem when consulting with family offices on manager selection. He said:

> *We try to see managers whenever we can; we try to visit them at least once a year so you know that there is a back office, you know that there are people there and that there is something there. A lot of times, that's not practical, and you try to do the best you can, realizing that your risk level is up a notch and you are monitoring them probably a little more closely, and where they are a little more than you might otherwise do.*

A few family offices that are based in the United States and Europe simply don't look at global fund managers as a rule and they will only make

TABLE 9.1 Fund Manager's Point of Interest

Point of Interest	Family Office Preferences
Dollar Amount of Assets under Management	When it comes to the size of the fund, manager preferences of family offices will change depending on fund type. For a microcap or small cap fund, the universe is a bit smaller than a global macro or diversified private equity firm. As a general rule for hedge funds and most long-only managers, having $100 million-plus will be enough in assets that 85–90 percent of family offices will at least not deny a meeting with the fund due to being too small. Many family offices will say at conferences and in surveys that they will consider managers of any size, but in my experience those are only managers that have very long-term relationships or family ties already in place. Most family offices look for $100 million-plus fund managers and some require much more in assets before being considered.
Preferred Percentage of Total Assets under Management of a Fund Manager	Most family offices do not want to be more than 5–10 percent of a fund's total assets. Exceptions are made for exceptional opportunities though and I have seen some family offices make up 20 percent of a fund in the past.
Reporting	Consistent and accurate reporting of taxes, returns, positions, and risk is something highly valued by investors, yet not always delivered by fund managers. Many times, even a $1 billion fund manager will be slow to produce a report or send in one late, or they may turn in reports with mistakes and errors in it. Quality reporting is not something many family office investors screen for specifically upfront, but it is sometimes one of two or three factors that lead to a family office replacing one fund manager with another.
Team Experience	Family offices prefer experienced teams with deep expertise directly tied to their investment process, asset class, and investment thesis. Hopefully the team has worked together for some time in managing similar types of portfolios. Many family offices look for consistency in the team to ensure that the track record being reviewed is the true long-term track record of the current fund management executives in place. Family offices want to work with world class teams with deep benches of talent and publicly recognized expertise. While looking at teams, family offices want to find a superior level of integrity and character.

Point of Interest	Family Office Preferences
Team Size	Team size is important. How stable can an investment fund really be if there are just two or three people on the team? Unless there are plans and signs of growth toward adding a few more people soon, some family offices will see that type of fund manager as a startup that has some embedded extra business risk. Most family offices would like to see teams of at least six to eight professionals or more, depending on the investment strategy and assets under management. To be specific, most family offices would like to see teams of 15 to 20 or more professionals behind an investment fund. This does have to be balanced with the investment preferences of the family office though; some family offices only invest in $1 billion managers, while many look for $100 million-plus funds that are under $800 million, so that can greatly change the expected team size of an investment fund.
Compensation Structure	The family office will most likely dig into how team members are compensated. Most will like to see that long-term incentives are in place, such as multiyear profit sharing, vested profit sharing, or bonuses that accumulate over time, or equity partnership offers to senior team members who are critical to the long-term success of the fund. The method is less important than the existence of some tools to keep the team in place long-term; not having these in place can contribute to a family office deciding not to invest in a fund manager.
Investment Style Consistency	Family offices like to see that the investment processes and risk management procedures are carried out like clockwork at funds. They do not want a manager blindly following a strategy that is outdated and want to know that the existing track record is due to a refined approach and not a reckless trend or rumor following coincidence. Analysts will hunt for evidence as to exactly how consistent or nonconsistent a fund's investment and risk management processes are. When a manager does not follow the investment parameters or process they themselves have set forth or claimed to follow, this is often referred to as "style drift," and is again something that often leads to a family office deciding not to invest in a fund manager.

(*continued*)

TABLE 9.1 (*Continued*)

Point of Interest	Family Office Preferences
Investment Process	Family offices have more sophistication than high-net-worth individuals for making various types of fund manager investments, but they do not often have the deep analyst teams that large institutional investors, like pension funds, often have. This means that a fund manager's investment process must be clear enough that a family office analyst or chief investment officer that may not look at fund managers full time can still understand how the investment process works. If the family office does not understand a fund manager's investment thesis, edge in the marketplace, and connection between the team and their own internal research and portfolio construction methods, they may move on and not even complete a full due diligence review on the investment fund manager.
Current Investors	Family offices often select their service providers, business partners, and fund managers based on referrals. They prefer to invest in fund managers that already have received capital from several other peer-level family offices.
Crystal Clear Advantage	This final fund manager preference point is one of the most important. Family office analysts and chief investment officers often look at 20 to 100 fund manager PowerPoints and one-pagers every week. They need to be able to quickly determine exactly what the fund manager's unique advantage in the marketplace is, and how their operations, investment process, and team support that in every way possible. If this is not immediately apparent, the fund manager's marketing materials are often immediately put aside.

exceptions for exceptional fund managers who really cannot be replaced domestically. Another approach, which is more popular with larger family offices, is to hire an institutional consulting firm or risk management consulting group that helps evaluate fund managers and conduct the actual on-site visits themselves. As family offices grow in size, they typically hire more internal analysts and due diligence professionals so that these on-site visits can be completed by midlevel career professionals when intensive travel is required. This is more expensive, but makes for a more cohesive due diligence process.

FAMILY OFFICE PARTNERSHIPS WITH FUND MANAGERS

Family offices work with fund managers in many ways in addition to making direct investments. Family offices like to take advantage of the fact that they have a lot of capital to invest. They like to get exclusive access to deals, preferred terms, discounted management fees, or ownership stakes in some of their investments. The family offices' competitive advantage many times is the amount of capital that they control, so they use this to gain an edge in the marketplace.

I recently conducted an eight-hour training workshop in Boston on the fundamentals of how family offices operate and partner with fund managers. During this workshop we covered the following examples through which family offices work creatively with fund managers:

- Partnering with a seed capital platform of some type or providing seed capital directly to fund managers who have a great team and investment process but need some operating capital or an anchor investor to get their business model off the ground. Sometimes family offices will get preferred terms or ownership stakes in the fund company in return for providing this seed capital. (For more information on seeding, please see www.HedgeFundSeeding.com.)
- Lifting out teams from hedge funds or private equity funds to form a personal, fully owned fund management operation internally.
- Partnering with an existing fund or creating their own asset based lending portfolio that can replicate the returns of an investment fund by demanding strong hard-asset collateral for all loans and taking over those pieces of real estate if the loan goes into default.

Many family offices see their ability to gain ownership interest in fund managers as a solid line of business to produce outsized returns, almost as if they are acting as an angel investor in fund managers. While many family offices receive too much deal flow from small-sized fund managers, those in the seeding or fund management angel investor business want to maximize the number of small funds they analyze each year to ensure that they invest in only the very best.

Family offices are creative with their capital. They are not looking at mutual funds and ETFs as their only investments or even restricting themselves to hedge funds and private equity. At the end of the day, family offices are savvy, capitalist business professionals who want to preserve their capital, but also leverage it to lock in singles and doubles for long periods of time with measured downside risk.

MANAGING DEAL FLOW OVERLOAD

Many family offices are overwhelmed by the number of one-pagers, pitch books, and e-mails they get daily from fund managers, investment bankers, and service providers who want a chance to earn the business or capital of the family office. This has resulted in family offices taking several steps to deal with these daily inquiries including:

- Taking all contact details of team members off their public web sites.
- Setting up a separate e-mail inbox for inquiries that may or may not be reviewed by anyone but a secretary or intern.
- Working on mostly a referral basis or relying on service providers, institutional investment consultants, other family offices, and best ideas coming from placement agents and/or third-party marketers.
- Hiring an analyst or gatekeeper to do nothing but sort through materials and pass only the most relevant information of the top 10 percent to an analyst or executive for further review.
- Only worrying about identifying best-of-breed fund managers when it is requested and needed by a client. At that point, a full-fledged search is conducted, much like an institutional investment consultant would conduct a search for a very specific type of fund manager for an institutional client. This relieves the family office of the job of constantly sorting through incoming marketing materials.

There are some family offices, typically smaller ones, who have launched in just the past three years that take every phone call and respond to every e-mail, but they quickly get overwhelmed. Our firm is not a well-known family office, yet we still are approached by more than 1,000 fund managers a year and since starting our business four years ago, we have received 325,000 e-mails. You can imagine the e-mail volume a top-50 family office or Forbes 500–related individual must get every year.

The result of this deal flow overload is that those with relationships and referrals get through while most others do not. Most of those professionals who start and lead investment funds are excellent at portfolio management, trading, or risk management, but are not great at raising capital or even communicating a message clearly via a conference call. Unfortunately, sometimes those with more time on their hands or more well-connected capital raisers on their team get noticed more than those with solid track records and teams, yet very little capital-raising experience.

Most of the funds that contact family offices never receive any capital from them; they are not a fit for the requirements and investment preferences of this specific type of investor. The inefficiency of this process in both directions is why there is a demand for institutional consultants, due diligence services, and teams like ours that work with both parties daily.

OBJECTIVE CHARACTER ANALYSIS

This chapter starts with a quote from Sun Tzu: "By leadership, I mean the general's qualities of wisdom, sincerity, humanity, courage, and strictness...." I believe that fund managers are oftentimes judged on their level of character and integrity in a much more simplistic way than Sun Tzu analyzed leaders thousands of years ago. As to the importance of developing character, John D. Rockefeller, the famous American oil industrialist and arguably the richest person who ever lived, was quoted as saying: "The most important thing for a man is to establish a reputation and character."

In a book titled *Educating the Character* (Bantam, 1992) by Thomas Lickona, character is defined as doing the right thing despite outside pressure to the contrary. Cassie Barlow, Mark Jordan, and William Hendrix published a research paper, "Character Assessment: An Examination of Leadership Levels" in the *Journal of Business and Psychology* that discusses the topic of character assessments and related research that has been conducted over the past 50 years. The following is a short quote from that paper:

> *The root of the word "character" is the Greek word for engraving. Applied to humans, it refers to the enduring marks left by life that sets one apart from others. Typically, enduring marks are set early in life by our religious beliefs, parental influences, and a child's early interactions. Character is also marked throughout our lives as we partake in great divides in our nation's history or solve moral dilemmas throughout our lives.*

The science of psychology provides a road map for how to evaluate integrity and character, but most analysts and family office executives take a soft, "trust your gut" approach that is not objective or consistent. In the future, I believe this skill and process will be recognized as an important part of the due diligence process.

THE 6 CS OF CHARACTER ANALYSIS

Figure 9.2 is a diagram I created to explain what to look for in analyzing fund managers and evaluating their character. No, this will not predict their investment returns or guarantee avoidance of working with a fraud, but it is a step up from blindly trusting your gut or that of your new analyst while deciding whether to work with someone or invest in a team.

I will now walk you through the 6 Cs of Character Analysis to explain why each is an important component to consider while evaluating someone you may invest in or partner with.

1. **Committed:** The most important thing to remember is that someone who has invested in their self, their team, and their fund management business is planning to stay around and stay in business for a long time to come. If someone has not taken the time to properly prepare their marketing materials, prepare for a meeting, or document their investment process or risk management procedures, how serious can they really be about their business?

   Humans naturally are short-term biased; we reach out for the quick reward, the fast success. When shortcuts are available, many of us like to take them, and sometimes this is done without regard for promises to investors or even industry regulations. What you want to look for in fund managers is a long-term bias in everything they do. Look for

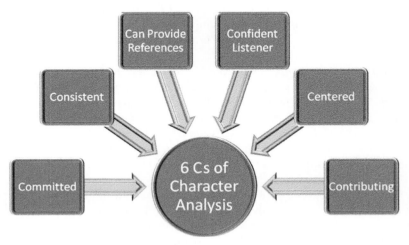

FIGURE 9.2   6 Cs of Character Analysis

signs that the fund manager is committed to working with family offices, committed to running their fund, and committed to being a thought leader or at least on top of developments within his or her asset class and industry.

My mentor and friend Brian Tracy always says that the degree of one's character can be measured by the degree of expediency in which they employ, that those with lowest levels of integrity will always look for what is quick and easy without any regard for the consequences while those with the highest degree of integrity will always do what is right, even if it costs them time or money to do so.

Ask yourself, "Has this person or team gone the extra mile to ensure the long-term success of their venture and possibly established themselves as a thought leader in their space?" You could also ask yourself, "Are they doing the bare minimum with few long-term commitments to the industry or working with your family office?"

2. **Consistent:** The cousin of Commitment is Consistency. Numerous scientific studies confirm that the majority of what we do is out of habit and on a subconscious level. This is where the saying, "How we do one thing is how we do everything." It is true. Time and time again in my interviews with family office managers, they noted how important consistency was in a fund manager. It's crucial that a fund manager has a strategy and a process that is consistent and will not deviate greatly from one quarter to another. Of course, it's impossible to know absolutely how a manager will act in the future, but by speaking with other investors and interviewing the manager several times, you can get a better sense of whether he is consistent.

   From many small and medium-size family offices, I often hear that it is costly and time consuming to meet with a fund manager enough times to complete a thorough evaluation. Typically, I find that it takes three to seven face-to-face meetings to get to know someone well enough to make an initial judgment of character, and it will help if you meet them in diverse environments and locations such as at their offices, over coffee, or at a cocktail reception. It is easy to "pull off" or fake friendliness or interest for one or two meetings, but much harder to do over time. Get to know a manager over several months to see how consistent or inconsistent they are.

3. **Can Provide References:** References are a great way to speed up character analysis. As long as you can trust the source of the reference, you may be able to talk to another family office and leverage their knowledge about some of the very issues we have discussed above. One challenge in consistently taking the time to objectively evaluate the character of

fund managers is the fact that family offices are typically flooded with requests for capital. This is a basic point, but one that can be overlooked or skipped when in a hurry to evaluate a fund manager without feeling like you are asking for too much. Asking for references should never be too much; references are frequently requested by employers before making a hiring decision, and why should you be any less diligent? If someone is angered by the thought of providing references, then that discussion, more than the result, may be educational.

4. **Confident Listener:** In my experience, there are two types of good listeners: Those who are new to an industry or area so they can't help but just listen because they don't know what to say, and those who are very well experienced, confident, and constantly attentive to the needs of investors.

   Most high-character professionals are confident in their knowledge and abilities because they do things that build their own knowledge and business daily, and their time horizon is extra long. They have invested in themselves for so many years, and they are so centered on where they are headed that it is only a matter of hard work and time before they reach their goals. Those who are confident, but not overconfident, are more likely to be better listeners than those who are not, but the opposite can be true if someone is overconfident in their abilities and accomplishments.

   It is critical for many reasons to meet in person while evaluating one's character and one should evaluate confidence under pressure. One of the reasons is to get a sense for how the individual or entire team deals with adversity. When the market is down or when assets are lost, do they still answer their phones? Do they consistently respond to client requests and fulfill commitments, even when it may be easier to not do so? Stressful moments unfortunately can bring out flaws large or small, and it is better to have a sense for how that may play out or affect the service you will receive before you place money with a fund manager.

   Here is a quote from our interview with Charles Grace, who has over 50 years of experience in running multi-family offices and selecting fund managers: "The thing that's most valuable is whether they can listen and communicate."

   All family office investors want to be listened to, and do not want their time wasted. It does not matter whether a fund manager has $200 million or $20 billion in assets under management, if they are bad at listening and responding to the requests of a family office, they will often be shut out of the capital allocation process.

5. **Centered:** Looking for people who are centered means finding individuals who have naturally surrounded themselves with clues of integrity.

Those with a high degree of character have made long-term consistent commitments to their life priorities.

We are the sum of our environment. Harvard professor and researcher William James has argued that the company we hold is more powerful than our education, experience, or practical knowledge and abilities in determining our success or failure in life.

The schools we attend, the friends we keep, the quality of professionals on our team, the conferences we attend, the news we consume, the books we read, the movies we watch, and our family life completely shape our habits, biases, desires, and ethical framework through which we make decisions in life. While assessing someone's character, take all of these factors into consideration. Is the fund manager at the blackjack table, family dinner table, or leading an industry thought panel table at a conference?

There are a few details of someone's personal life that alone could turn off a family office investor, but most details are just additional facts to pay attention to and take notes on while learning more about someone. Recently I conducted an hour-long expert audio interview with a due diligence expert who told me that part of his routine due diligence process now is to check everyone's LinkedIn, Facebook, and Twitter profiles to see what type of a person they are. Naturally most of us already consider these factors, but I believe one's environment is more powerful than most of us appreciate.

6. **Contributing:** The final thing to look for while analyzing the character of a fund manager is whether they create value first. Do they give back to the industry by writing, speaking, leading an organization, teaching, or providing you with market insight or introductions to valuable professionals? Do they listen first and try to be helpful before trying to sell you their fund and raise capital from you? The less pushy a salesperson someone is and the more genuinely helpful someone is, the more likely it is that they are committed to growing a long-term relationship with you, instead of making a quick sale. Look for multiple pieces of evidence that the individual is contributing and not just selling. By making a contribution to their industry, that manager is investing time and energy in those around him. This speaks volumes about the character of that individual and how well he will serve his clients.

By using the 6 Cs of Character Analysis, you should be able to more systematically evaluate teams and individuals who manage investment funds. Over time, a slight improvement in your selection of fund managers could make the difference between thriving and barely surviving.

FAMILY OFFICE INTERVIEW WITH EVAN COOPERMAN OF ARTEMIS WEALTH ADVISORS

Below is a transcript from an interview we conducted with Evan Cooperman of Artemis Wealth Advisors, a multi-family office based in Canada. He has over eight years of experience working in family offices and has experience looking at investment managers and being an allocator of capital in the industry.

Richard Wilson: Do you have a couple of questions you can share with family offices that might be looking to hire a consultant and are not really sure how to tell who is credible and who is going to be a valuable consultant to work with or not? Are there two or three questions they should be asking these consultants to make sure that they are legitimate and they are going to add a lot of value to their specific family office?

Evan Cooperman: The most important topic to ask about will be compensation, since it drives behavior; you want to figure out how the consultant is compensated and make sure they have no conflicts of interest. That will be a big one. I mean, you would expect that consultants should have no conflict, but you never know; stranger things have happened. Families could speak to other family offices or to endowments and foundations to find out who their consultants are and, I guess they can also even just check; a lot of these things might be in the public record. To me the most important thing is always going to be that you ensure alignment of interest and making sure there is no conflict.

Richard Wilson: That's helpful. With the family office that you are working at now, how are you managing the split between investment securities, like individual securities and mutual funds and ETFs, versus hard assets and real estate versus fund managers like private equity, REITs, or hedge fund managers?

Evan Cooperman: As a rule, philosophically, for all families, we would encourage them to have a fairly healthy allocation in the alternative space. It depends on how you define alternatives, but certainly in hedge funds and private equity and real estate, in hard assets, all of that stuff we like.

On the long-only side, it's harder for long-only managers to add a lot of alpha, to add a lot of excess risk-adjusted return over a sustained period of time. There, we would be more likely to either find somebody who can help manage the beta by taking ETFs or have our portfolio managers manage the beta for clients, but it really depends; it's very client-specific. As a rule, I would say not much in the mutual fund space, other than if there were some legacy positions that we have inherited when clients come on board.

Richard Wilson: For each individual family that joins your multi-family office or for the current family served, does each individual family have a separate investment policy, missions, values, and objectives for their family wealth being managed? Is that something where, at the multi-family office level, you guys have something like that set up and people who are congruent within those policies join the multi-family office, or how does that work?

Evan Cooperman: Every family has their own; it's very situation-specific. In terms of the investment policy statement and the asset allocation, some people will love alternatives, some people will be scared of them and not want them. We do have what we would feel is the ideal asset allocation, but you can't always force things because you still have the "sleep at night" factor. Sometimes, even if it makes sense to own an asset but the client will lose sleep at night over it, then they shouldn't be in it.

Richard Wilson: Right. How important do you think it is for hedge fund managers to be offering managed accounts?

Evan Cooperman: In my experience it hasn't been hugely important. You can't expect any established manager to run, in the hedge fund space, a separately managed account for you at a nominal amount. So, if the family offices are looking to write checks for a million dollars or $2 million, I don't think they should expect that they can get a separately managed account. I have seen some managers who do it for a million, but in those instances they are for sure going to be smaller managers who are still actively raising assets. In the post-Madoff world, people were talking about separately managed accounts more,

	but it is not common for smaller amounts. It certainly hasn't been a deal-breaker for any of the families that I have worked with in the past.
Richard Wilson:	Right. One family office I just interviewed based in Luxembourg was saying that at about $20 million or $25 million, it becomes a bit more reasonable to request a managed account, but it depends how large the fund manager itself is; if it is a million dollar fund, that makes a big difference in that negotiation, right?
Evan Cooperman:	Right, absolutely. And as with anything, it might fit the negotiation and it doesn't hurt to ask the question. There certainly are benefits to having a separately managed account because, number one, you get to save some of the transaction cost. Because it's not in a fund format, you avoid the cost of an auditor and administrator. The fact that the assets are held in your name in a custodial account somewhere certainly helps as well.
Richard Wilson:	Okay. Related to the same stream of thought, what other demands does your multi-family office put on fund managers of all types in terms of transparency or governance? Are people expected or rewarded for having governance boards that look out for the best interest of the investor that are independent from the fund or is that again something that only 1 percent of funds are realistically doing in any truly independent way? Is there really not too much governance or extra transparency best practices that are really becoming popular there?
Evan Cooperman:	I guess we can divide the two, right? So you have got your transparency and the governance. The transparency is a tricky one. I mean, what we were able to do in some instances, but not in all was to negotiate with the manager where they would provide us with more transparency than usual as the multi-family office. What they would say is "Look, you can't tell your clients what the book looks like, but we will give you, on a monthly basis or a quarterly basis, a chance to just see a little bit more because we will sign you up for nondisclosure and we trust you." But that's a tricky one; I mean the transparency is tricky, unfortunately, in the hedge fund space.

In terms of governance, you can't really expect it if you are allocating money to a manager with $100 million or $200 million; at the end of the day they are trying to build a business and there is a certain amount of mindshare that goes to certain things, so they are probably not going to have heavy-duty third-party independent oversight in the startup phase.

However, if you are dealing with a multi-billion dollar shop, then you would expect more, obviously, on the governance side and it is very important. We are always looking for alignment of interest and making sure that you understand all of the terms in the offering documents and make sure that you understand whether those terms are aligned with you or not. In Canada, I will just give you an example: I don't know how this still exists, I have only seen it in Canada, but you used to see a lot of fund managers who have a high-water mark with an annual reset. Everywhere else in the world you have a high-water mark and it's perpetual. If you go under your high-water mark, you are not going to receive incentive fees until you get above the high-water mark, right? That makes sense. In Canada, if after a year they are under their high-water mark, some funds reset it, and for me that's a non-starter. There is a whole alignment of interest thing right there.

But that's just an example and there are certain things as well on the due diligence side that become very important, like your administrator, like the prime broker, auditor and so you end up having to do due diligence on those as well because you do have your name brand that you know of or it's not, and in the case that it's not, you better be sure that you are doing due diligence and making sure they are real. And even if it's in the case of somebody that you do know, if they turn out to you and say, "Our auditor is KPMG" and you ask them for a contact name in KPMG, one of the tricks that we like to do is you don't call that guy directly, you call the switchboard at KPMG and you say does so and so work here and if they say yes then you ask to be transferred because it would be very easy for somebody who wanted to be a perpetrator of fraud just to say look, here is my auditor, it's KPMG and then they

	give their friend's name and phone number, they answer the phone and say yes, I work at KPMG and I audit the fund. So things like that, just little things that you can do that will help protect you which I find surprisingly not enough investors do those things.
Richard Wilson:	Sure, yeah and that was pretty interesting, especially the one-year reset. I could see somebody defending themselves with a three- or five-year reset saying we will go out of business if we go five years and have no chance of getting a performance fee, but one year, that does seem kind of ridiculous. I have never seen that here in the United States or down in Brazil, but that's interesting.
Evan Cooperman:	I know. There are a few well-known funds with a modified high-water mark, but not a lot of them do yet. With a modified high-water mark they say that if we draw down and we are below our high-water mark, we will get half the incentive fee until we get back to the high-water mark, but then again we will continue to get half the incentive fee until we recoup—don't quote me on this because I can't remember the exact number—but it might be 50 percent of the loss. So I guess the idea is we don't want our employees and traders to be too worried about being below the high-water mark because it can negatively affect behavior. We don't want to worry about staffing issues and keeping people motivated, so we will continue to collect 10 percent instead of 20 percent. But then once we get above the high-water mark we will still continue collecting 10 percent until such time as we recouped another 50 percent of the loss, whatever the drawdown was. So that was interesting. So I have seen that as a variant.
Richard Wilson:	Right, makes for a less volatile business model for sure.
Evan Cooperman:	Right. So that was an interesting one; I mean, that was one of the few where I could maybe say, that made sense.
Richard Wilson:	Right. I have seen a really interesting one and I think that if someone appointed me and put me in charge of a hedge fund right now that had a decent size of assets, this is what I would do. What they did is they set it up so that their performance fee was still earned and calculated over an annual period, but what they would

do is pay out that performance fee over a three-year period afterwards and if they fell below and they went to negative performance they would then not be paid that fee. So in other words to collect the performance fee, they had to have continued positive performance. I mean, otherwise, you might take a big risk, take home a big payday and then they have to shut down the fund the next quarter.

Evan Cooperman: Brilliant, I like that. So almost it's an escrow and gets called back if they have losses.

Richard Wilson: Yeah. I think that would be popular with investors in this type of environment, where if things look like they are going alright for four months and then everyone gets afraid about another recession coming or about debt loads and governments all over the world and stuff like that, things can get pretty volatile pretty quickly.

Evan Cooperman: That's great. No, I like that one. The more alignment they can get the better. I mean it's cliché, but it totally makes sense.

Richard Wilson: Okay. Can you explain a bit for family offices which are operating just as one- and two-man shops and they want to form an investment committee to improve their decision-making process and also just improve kind of the robust nature of their family office operations and make them a bit more institutional, like how should an investment committee be formed or operate? Do you have any best practices or tips you can provide there?

Evan Cooperman: It's an interesting question. So certainly, I think the investment committee helps because it formalizes the discipline. What you find is that these family offices, they get started and then the Principals park themselves in the office and now they want to allocate some capital and then their buddy at the golf club tells them about this deal and then somebody tells them about this deal and word gets out that they are allocating capital. They start to put money to work and then they take a step back all of a sudden and they say "Hold on a second, I have got 60 percent allocated to real estate. I never really intended that, and all of a sudden I'm in all this illiquid stuff." And then they start to try and figure out more of a discipline. I think it's always good to start with the end in mind and really sit down and draw out a plan; to the extent that you can use your investment committee to help in formalizing that process, it would be really helpful. I don't know if in your question you are saying how do you actually populate the investment committee, I don't know, I mean that's a challenging one. What kind of people would you want to have on it? But certainly a lot of the value that I added in my past life was just forcing clients to go through the discipline, to write the investment policy statement and make sure that it fits for them. Then we weren't really an investment committee, but we treated it like one. So a client would come and, in some cases monthly, and sit down and say "Here's our ideas and here is our target asset allocation with specified ranges of allowable variance and here is our existing allocation" because they are coming with some sort of legacy portfolio that they have and here is what we need to do to move from target to actual. It doesn't happen overnight; it doesn't happen quickly. Then every month you sit down and you say "Okay, here is where we want to be and here is where we actually are and here is what we need to do to get us closer to our target and our goal" and things change. It's interesting how when you are forced to sit down every month and devote mind share to it and really think about what moves you need to make next, you start to get to know your portfolio and start to get a better feel for it and the families learn a lot about themselves in that process as well. So, whether it's a formal investment committee or something informal that they are doing with consultants, I think that there is definite value added in that process.

Richard Wilson: Right. One thing I have found is that within both alternative investment funds and family offices, the best run firms have very well-defined and evolved processes that are followed every day and on ever investment. The value may come from a highly experienced team, but the firms which make it to the top 5 percent of the industry and stay there have documented processes and procedures that are followed by everyone on the team.

Evan Cooperman:	I'm listening to you talk about it and the way you frame it and it makes sense. If you are evaluating a hedge fund manager, or any manager for that matter, you are going to try and figure out what is their secret sauce. What is it about their gray matter and their process and everything else that would give you some sort of feeling about whether there is going to be sustainability of their outperformance? Part of that will be driven by their having some sort of clearly defined process that they follow that allows them to pick the security that they are picking. So when you take that same approach to families they are going to go through a lifecycle too, right? Because they set up the family office and then of course they are going to get pitched by everybody under the sun and start to build their asset allocation. Then after that, once they have allocated the money, they are going to start to deal with the other issues around kids and family education and all of that needs to be in the process, right? What are you going to do with all the planning side of things as well? You need to treat it like a business.
Richard Wilson:	True. I believe most people who start a family office or alternative investment fund have never run a small business before. Most get in that position due to their expertise in portfolio management, wealth management, or trading. The investing landscape is so global and diverse it can be hard for small- to medium-sized family offices to actually travel to visit each fund manager that they are considering to invest in, right?
Evan Cooperman:	If you want to do proper due diligence, you need to go and visit, so it becomes difficult. Top managers are located all over the world. You do need to do real due diligence; you do need to look these managers in the eyes and check out their operations and see what's going on there.

There is one thing, I don't know if it will come up at some point in the questions, but this is an intangible. It's hard to quantify and it's hard to nail down. One of the big things in the alternative space that you need to figure out when you are doing due diligence, which is not the check-the-box thing, is to see what your gut tells you about the integrity of these people. You can

invest with somebody who is a shark who makes a lot
of money and that could be very good, but when things
go south; will they have the strength of character to see
things through?

That becomes relevant when you go to something
like 2008, where you have a manager who is down 50
percent, 60 percent, 70 percent and he's sitting there and
he is saying "I am so far below my high-water mark, I
am never going to make it back; I'm just going to close
up shop, take a year off and then I'll come back and do
it again." I have dealt with managers who were down
significantly through the last crisis. There is a lot to be
said for the guy who was down 65 percent and said "I
am going to retrench and I am going to find my way out
of it. I have got confidence in this portfolio." He had
to let staff go and he had to do a lot more by himself
and he fought his way back. He was in credit and so
credit came back quite strongly and he made it back,
and then got above his high-water mark. He actually
loved us because he said that we were one of the first
allocations that he got during the depths of the crisis.
We were the first incentive fees that he collected because
his high-water mark was low on those new dollars.

Long story short, I really don't know the answer. I
don't know how you put your finger on it; when you
meet somebody and you try and figure out whether this
is the kind of person who will have that strength of character who says I am going to fight it out and I am going to do what's right for investors. I think it's something that you should try and figure out how and that's
for family offices, whether you can figure out a process
that's repeatable and do due diligence on that kind of
trait, probably not. I think it's a huge intangible that's
very important.

Richard Wilson: I think it's a great point. I have heard somebody say
that same thing that does full-time background checks
on fund managers and there is some subjective element
to it of whether these people just seem like the types of
people who are putting in the extra effort to invest in
their business and relationships and long-term things.
Most of the time that signifies a somewhat honest person versus someone who is just out there to ride a wave

	of some sort of asset bubble that's coming up and then get out of the game really quick.
Evan Cooperman:	Right. Then you can tell if they are too slick and they have got all the right answers. Some of it you just get with experience and being around long enough, but I guess you want them to be very responsive. The other thing that always turned me off was some managers you are kind of "lucky" to get your allocations to; the arrogance and the hubris can be an issue as well and that's something that you know. There have been times when we did not invest with managers who have done exceptionally well because we felt that we wouldn't be able to get the response and to me the responsiveness is important. We don't hound managers every month, but if we have a question or a concern we want to know that they are going to respond. We have dealt with multibillion dollar managers who are still very responsive, even if it's a disproportionately small allocation for the questions that we are asking.
Richard Wilson:	That brings up a good point. I think you are basically getting to the fact that family offices should have an open line of communication with the investment managers they have brought on and investment managers who are reading or listening to this should pay attention to the fact that the allocation to them could rise or dip based on their investor relations efforts, right?
Evan Cooperman:	Absolutely. They may not be having direct dialog with the portfolio managers at these firms, but then they better have a good dialog with the IR people who are very familiar with the portfolio and give substantive answers to the questions that you have.
Richard Wilson:	Sure. I know of a royal-family-connected family office that is trying to raise capital for their hedge fund, and they are doing so globally. If they had someone from their team travel to Canada to meet with you in person could that replace an on-site visit at their offices?
Evan Cooperman:	Well, I guess there are two ways you can head. One way is it could be a family office that just doesn't have the resources to do on-site visits, but they invest anyway. Sometimes the manager comes in and gives a great pitch and they have a great pedigree and the family likes what they hear and they are prepared to miss that step

in the due diligence process. Or it's coming to them through a third party marketer or a consultant or somebody else that they are relying on, some other third party who has done the due diligence. At the end of the day, the funny thing is investing should be a rational decision, but it's not always. It's emotional and part of the emotional thing is "I like you guys, you sound like you have a good story and you make me feel warm and fuzzy and I trust you. I will take a flyer." Then they may just write a smaller check. So I don't think it's necessarily etched in stone that to make an allocation you have to fly to the manager's office in Hong Kong and see how they execute a trade. It really just depends on the family and what their tolerance for pain would be. However, at the end of the day nothing will replace an on-site visit and meeting the key people involved.

Richard Wilson: Right. That reminds me of something from some of the full-day training workshops I have done on family offices in the fund management industry. I talk about how there is a study that shows that with the average purchase, the relationship you have with the person who is selling you something is twice as important as the objective facts about the purchase. That study wasn't done on how family offices invest in fund managers, obviously, but I think it's interesting that it plays that big of a role. I think people often discount, that in our industry, it may account for 30 percent of an investment decision, or more.

Do you think that the long-term relationship and meeting face-to-face with family offices is something that more fund managers should be doing and family offices like you would appreciate having more of a multi-year relationship with these managers instead of just hearing from them over the phone and over e-mail a lot of the time and not really getting to know them as peers in the industry, etc.? Is that important, that relationship versus the objective information?

Evan Cooperman: Look, I think it's hugely important in the beginning. I mean if you want to get through any sort of sales cycle as a fund manager, it's massively important in the beginning. I don't think I would invest with anybody without meeting them; it would be highly unlikely or unusual. I have dealt with third party marketers who have brought me ideas in the past where they are based in Vancouver or New York or London and they may come with a manager on a road show. I might meet the manager once and then that's enough to kind of spark some sort of interest. But there is that nuanced step in creating the dialog with the family. At some point, somebody has to contact the family and in that Principal's head, it needs to be not just another pitch. There needs to be something that tweaks them that is intriguing that will allow the fund manager to come in to tell the story. If you figure out the secret sauce for that, because I think it will be different in every case, you will be doing okay.

Richard Wilson: Okay. You have done a lot of consulting work for family offices; do you think that family offices are pretty well served by using the standard industry cookie-cutter Due Diligence Questionnaire (DDQ) or just taking DDQs from fund managers, or do you think that if a family office has a specific set of investment policies and risk procedures that they should really come up with their own very customized DDQ? You have been in that consulting world so many times with family offices; what do you think the right approach is?

Evan Cooperman: Right. I will be honest with you. I mean it's not the most glamorous answer, but an industry-standard DDQ works pretty well. I guess it depends on how large the family office is. If it's a multi-billion dollar family office and they have got a highly institutionalized process with very specific investment criteria, then they can start to define and customize their own. But otherwise, the standard DDQs are probably okay. I have always tried to avoid, when I do due diligence, relying too heavily on checking the box. I think you need to have a checklist and there are certain things you just need to cover.

You need to know whether they have an independent third party administrator and whether who they say the administrator is, is exactly the administrator. You need to confirm those kinds of things, right. There are certain things that are checking the box, but there are other ones that are just more like we talked about; the gut checking and trying to figure out whether they

	are honorable people and just looking in their eyes and seeing what kind of vibe you get which you can't do through a DDQ. That's why you need to meet with them. I think that the standard DDQ is probably sufficient for most families, unless they are really large.
Richard Wilson:	Okay. One thing we are digging into for this interview series is investment preferences or criteria of family offices, can you talk to that point?
Evan Cooperman:	No problem. The short answer is 20 percent guaranteed with no downside. I'm being facetious, but really, capital preservation with some sort of reasonable rate of return is pretty much universal among family offices.
Richard Wilson:	Yeah, I have been asking family offices in earlier interviews where they rank capital preservation in their list of priorities for an investment and I just stopped asking because they all said the same thing, that it's number one.
Evan Cooperman:	Well that's true, but if volatility is super low and everybody is doing well and their buddy at the golf course says he is making 20 percent and they are only making 8 percent, then they may feel like capital preservation is not as important of an issue. But you're right; currently capital preservation is the priority.
Richard Wilson:	I see. Well, that wraps up my questions for today. Thank you for your time, I appreciate it.
Evan Cooperman:	No problem, Richard, thank you.

CONCLUSION

While family offices provide their clients with a range of services, performing due diligence on investment opportunities and selecting talented fund managers are among the most important qualities for a family office manager. As you have learned in this chapter, family offices employ a careful, multistep process to select a fund manager and weigh a variety of factors when evaluating the fund. In the end however, a family office may make a decision based on certain intangibles outlined in the section on character analysis. Family offices are trusted with millions, even billions, of dollars by their clients and they take that responsibility seriously when evaluating and ultimately selecting a fund manager for their clients' money.

CHAPTER 10

The Future of the Family Office Industry

Look back over the past, with its changing empires that rose and fell, and you can foresee the future, too.
    —Marcus Aurelius (Roman emperor from A.D. 161 to 180)

Chapter Preview: The goal of this book is to provide a granular view of how family offices are operating, investing, and evolving as a business model. In this chapter, we will shift that focus to where the industry is headed. This chapter is based on my own experience in working with family offices around the world as well as on some quotes directly from top family offices on how they are preparing for the family office industry of the near future.

The family office industry is changing rapidly as governments change taxation and investment regulations. These changes have been occurring more rapidly than at any other time in the past 40 years. At the same time, the combination of wealth generation and the awareness of the family office model provides a fertile ground for at least a decade of further growth in the space.

THERE IS NO FAMILY OFFICE INDUSTRY

Ironically from within our large family office association, I recently heard someone say that there is no such thing as a family office "industry." I categorically disagree with that statement. Furthermore, I believe that as the industry matures, we will naturally see more catering toward this segment, including further risk tools, investment solutions, software platforms, training programs, conferences, and media attention. This is the most obvious of predictions because it is happening right now, but I wanted to point it out for those of you who are relatively new to the family office space.

To help further the family office industry as a distinct area we developed the Qualified Family Office (QFO) program, which recognizes those family office wealth management firms as being unique from general wealth management firms. The QFO is a standard qualification that helps family office firms distinguish themselves from private banks and wealth management firms in the marketplace that do not operate as family offices, and it gives prospective clients a better idea of who has created a dedicated solution for the ultra-wealthy. For more information visit www.FamilyOfficesGroup .com/QFO.

Before I comment on some of the upcoming changes in the family office space, I thought you may find it interesting to review the comments of five family office executives on what they think the future of the industry looks like:

■ **Greg Kushner**, president of Lido Advisors:

> *I do think that we are going to continue to see additional family offices being established, and I do think the trend of moving more towards the multi-family office will certainly also continue.*
>
> *I do truly think that the family office is going to grow because there is a really needed service to high-net-worth families and it's a way to keep the families together. How many horror stories have you heard about when grandpa died then all the kids don't talk to each other and there is war and problems, and those are always going to continue. Money does awful things to people sometimes. I do think that for the more intelligent, more enlightened family office or family, the family office is a way to hopefully keep the families together and through use of philanthropy and common goals of the family office, I do think that's the way that the families have a better chance at least to keep together. I think the family office industry is certainly going to grow; it's certainly growing at the moment and I don't see that letting off anytime soon.*

▪ **Angelo Robles** of the Family Office Association:

> *Single family offices are absolutely on the increase. Let alone domestically here in the U.S., but unquestionably around the world, in Asia, in Latin America, in other parts of the world, in Australia and even in Europe, let alone again here in America.*

▪ **Brian Hughes,** managing director of strategic relationships at the Threshold Group:

> *I think there are certainly some trends. I think most of us are in agreement that there will continue to be more consolidation. I think that figuring out ways to grow will be a driver of what the industry looks like in three to five years because frankly, growing organically is a challenge for most firms and they grow at the rate they want to grow just organically and have a pretty honed process to be able to do that. I think acquisitions and mergers are more likely to continue to happen. I think those firms that are smaller firms, let's say under $3 billion, that are struggling to survive are going to get gobbled up. I think that you might see potentially some joint ventures between firms.*
>
> *You might also see joint ventures between different disciplines in wealth management—a tax firm partnering with a wealth management firm or a law firm partnering with a wealth management firm or investment advisor firm. We certainly have some of those out there already. Some of them have been doing it for a long time, very few of them are doing it successfully, but I do think that that's a trend that you will start to see more of as firms try to figure out alternative ways to grow in businesses. Areas of expertise are going to be needed by most of these firms. In other words, understanding what people call the soft issues or human capital issues, including understanding family philanthropy, and understanding how education happens within a family about their wealth.*
>
> *There are trends that are influencing and driving that type of advice and firms that are able to credibly provide that advice, I think will continue to expand and grow and the firms that just want to focus on investments, they will have their place because frankly, some families are only looking for one particular type of solution because they have got the other stuff figured out.*

Those firms that do that and do that well and are consistent and can demonstrate that, they have low turnover and they can retain key people and they can show that they are growing. I think those are the firms that will survive.

■ **John Gryzmala,** a New York–based Single Family Office Executive:

Maybe my answer is prejudiced because I have been in the single family office space for so long, but I feel that is the trend of the future. I think multi-family offices are okay. They clearly serve a purpose. I just know with my family, the mantra was—when I want an answer, I want an answer now. My boss would quite often give me a project and an hour or two later call me and say, "Are you done yet?" because that's how the patriarchs think quite often.

I think that's a little bit of a shortcoming with the multi-family office. I don't know if they might have a relationship manager, and I am sure they give excellent service. I know with my family, it would not be acceptable. He wanted that hands-on person that was there for him basically 24/7 to deal with whatever is on the plate. I mean, I could give you many examples. He rented an apartment out in Beverley Hills a number of years ago. He called me up and said, "Can I get a car tomorrow?" Well, "Can I get a car?" is his polite way of saying, "I want a car tomorrow."

A great big family office organization doesn't need to be set up. It could be done in a very lean and mean fashion with relatively low overhead. For many years, I worked out of the family's home. And for many years, I also rented a separate office, of course which added a little bit to the overhead. But I don't think the single family office should scare away a family because in effect, everyone that has a job you can justify as a single family office. If somebody pays the bills, chances are they have a cleaning lady; chances are they have a babysitter for their kids, maybe not a full-time nanny. Someone is managing all of those affairs.

■ **Lukas Doerig** of Marcuard Family Office:

I think there is a growing demand for family office services, but it will probably take some more time. On the other hand, it is interesting that in Switzerland just in the recent past, there have been many single family offices also set up because Switzer-land is quite liked for its advantages; it is a growing trend. Also, more people realize, and unfortunately only after having lived through certain crises, you want to have an independent provider who is really able to provide you this advice without any conflicts of interest, because if not, just over the long run, problems will come up.

SHIFTING INVESTMENT CRITERIA

Family offices are, for the most part, getting most sophisticated. While some family offices operate on an outsourced solution delivery model, which I think can be more hit or miss based on who is selected, most family offices are reinvesting profits heavily in talent and technology. This is translating into many family offices having a very strong board of advisors, and even stronger fund manager due diligence processes. I believe this will result in more liquid, better risk-adjusted returns for family office clients over the long-haul and again help secure the family office industry as a growing niche within the wealth management space. As family offices mature and grow in asset size, many will require larger fund managers so that their business/operational risk exposure is mitigated in making those investments.

FAMILY OFFICE JOB GROWTH

Finding talent for family office teams will continue to be a challenge as the industry expands faster than the pool of experienced family office executives. To help with this challenge, the Family Offices Group is committed to helping post family office industry jobs on www.FamilyOfficesGroup.com. This may eventually be a "paid" service, but if you have purchased this book and would like to post a position that your family office would like to fill, we can at least post that first job on our job listings area for free to thank you for reading our book. To see current job listings, please visit www.FamilyOfficesGroup.com/Jobs.

If you need a job posted, please e-mail me directly at Team@FamilyOffices.com to get that done.

FAMILY OFFICE TRAINING

I discovered a few years ago that there was no comprehensive training platform for single and multi-family offices. The only options were to send your team to training on very niche subjects like financial analysis, hedge funds, or risk management. To help "provide value first" in that area, our team has placed more than 200 video modules and 50 expert audio interviews within a single family office training program that your team can gain access to. The video and audio content covers many areas, including family office best practices, financial modeling, private equity, hedge funds, financial analysis, family office marketing, investment banking, and more. This training platform is called the Qualified Family Office Professional (QFOP) program. Learn more about gaining access by visiting www.FamilyOfficesGroup.com/Training.

NEW GLOBAL HOT SPOTS

In most developed nations, the wealthy are accumulating assets more rapidly than the middle class. At the same time, many emerging economies are thriving with annual growth rates of 4 to 10 percent. Others, according to Economy Watch, are growing at an even faster rate. Ghana's economy is growing at a blistering 20.15 percent. It's a $23.4 billion economy.

The *CIA World Factbook* 2012 (Skyhorse, 2011) notes that many experts believe that by 2015 China's upper class will be larger than America's middle class, especially with an estimated GDP growth rate of 10.3 percent. Growth in countries like China, Brazil, India, and Russia will ensure that the family office format of wealth management services continues to grow in popularity over the next five to seven years.

I believe that as the world buys into family offices more and more, additional family office hot spots will be created. These new spots could be the South Pacific, Middle East, and South America, among other smaller regional areas in need of more business-friendly governments who understand the private and complex needs of family offices. A healthy percentage of new ultra-high-net-worth families are coming out of places that are not always thought of first when it comes to wealth management, including Indonesia, South Africa, Argentina, Brazil, Nigeria, and Turkey.

 See the video "Japan Family Office," at www.FamilyOfficesGroup.com/Video25.

 See the video "Singapore Family Office," at www.FamilyOfficesGroup.com/Video26.

 See the video "Family Offices in the Cayman Islands," at www.FamilyOfficesGroup.com/Video27.

I recently recorded several videos in Tokyo, Singapore, and the Cayman Islands while speaking at conferences in those locations.

FOUR GLOBAL DRIVERS OF FAMILY OFFICE INDUSTRY GROWTH

Through working with family offices for almost 10 years and after interviewing 36 family offices for this book project, I have developed an understanding for exactly why this industry is thriving. The family office space is an exciting place to be. I don't understand how, but some try to argue that there is no familly office "industry," as discussed earlier. I disagree and find that these professionals often don't work directly in the industry. There are now multiple family office associations, family office consultants, family office capital raisers, family office conferences, and best practices and services only found at family office wealth-management firms. The industry not only exists, but it also is becoming stronger every year around the globe.

In writing this book we had the chance to connect with Shane Giles of Opus Private, a multi-family office based in Guernsey. We asked him about the trend of the family office industry growing in size, and this is what he had to say:

> *I think part of the reason is that the top people who are in family offices right now, had previously got to the top of the ladder in terms of aspirations at a big financial institution and had experienced fundamental conflicts or restrictions in the way they could operate. This is what happened with me. I felt that I could not get the best results for the clients because I was not allowed to use external asset managers and I had to work with my employer's own banking facilities, or preferences as regards lawyers or any other third parties.*
>
> *So by being completely independent and not being restricted to using a single service provider, I have given myself a flexible and completely impartial platform upon which to manage our client's affairs. There has certainly been a distinct trend in recent years as more leading individuals have left the very big institutions, and comfortable livelihoods, to establish their own platform thus enabling them to work freely. This ultimately results in getting what's best for the client as opposed to getting what's best for the institution.*

Following are the four global drivers of growth in the family office industry:

1. **Rise of the Ultra-Wealthy:** The daily rise in the total number of ultra-high-net-worth professionals around the world is growing the demand for family office services. Wealth has been created daily in every country since the beginning of time, but today, business owners in economies

such as Singapore, Indonesia, South Africa, the Czech Republic, Argentina, and India are thriving as never before, and wealth is being created at a faster rate than ever before. More Ferraris are sold in China every year now than anywhere else on earth. What all of this means is that there are more people than ever who need the portfolio management, taxation, charitable giving, and cash-management services that family offices can offer under one roof. It is also important to note that even if the number of ultra-wealthy individuals were not growing, the media are talking about the family office industry more every year, so the percentage of wealthy people aware of family office services is on the rise.

2. **Wealth Management Firms Upgrading:** The second driver of wealth that I have identified is that wealth management firms want to serve the clients better and naturally collect more fees. In order to achieve these two goals, they are trying to provide more holistic financial wealth management solutions and many are raising their fees and the minimum assets a client must have before they will accept them as a client. While many wealth management firms may require $500,000 or $1 million to become a client, many wealth-management firms are now requiring at least $10 million and calling themselves family offices. This can cause frustration by some more traditional family offices that helped form the industry, as it can cause some confusion of what a family office really is or is not. Regardless of which side of that argument you support, there is no denying that some of these converted wealth management firms upgrading to family offices are going to succeed, and that is a source of growth in the number of family offices and the assets they help manage.

3. **Multi-Family Offices Lowering Minimums:** Another source of growth in the space is found on the other end of the spectrum in traditionally very closed-door multi-family offices. Many multi-family offices require $30 million to $100 million to join their firm, but due to the combination of economic volatility and perhaps rising costs many have lowered their new client minimums to just $10 million to $20 million. From their perspective, if they already have the infrastructure in place to serve their clients, well, accepting a few more clients at $20 million each will help them leverage that further and in turn further reinvest those profits into improving their family office offering.

4. **Banking and Trust Executives Taking Off Handcuffs:** I probably won't make many large investment banking or trust company friends with this growth driver description. In my experience, I have found that most banks and trust companies of large size have internal cash management products, fund managers, long-only fund solutions, and services that provide limited options to clients that are somewhat self-serving. For

example, at most family offices, the family office charges the client per-haps 1 percent for managing their assets every year and makes no additional or less money based on what fund manager or cash management approach the client makes. Any additional or saved costs that occur in the portfolio are ported through directly to and from the ultra-high-net-worth client's balance. At a bank or a trust, however, the relationship manager may earn commissions, or a division may earn more of a profit if more clients select fund manager A over fund manager B due to agreements in place. This has led to frustration on the part of both the relationship manager and client. Many times, it only takes one or two large ultra-high-net-worth clients who have had enough of that model before they become an anchor client for a new multi-family office offering by that trust or private bank relationship manager. In other words, many times ultra-high-net-worth individuals will tell someone that they want to work with them but they don't want their hands tied any longer, and they will help them set up a family office solution for them and others like them.

Another source of growth is the conversion of single family offices to multi-family office operations. While I see this as an interesting trend, I don't believe it greatly increases the number of family offices or the assets they manage, so it is more of a trend than a driver of total industry growth.

This is a topic I have thought about a lot as I try to further position myself as a resource to this thriving industry. I spoke at a Family Office Summit in Sao Paulo, Brazil, early in 2012 on this exact topic. A 27-minute video of my speech is available online.

 See the video "Family Office Summit Sao Paulo, Brazil Speech on the Four Drivers of Family Office Industry Growth," at www.FamilyOfficesGroup.com/Video28.

CONCLUSION

The family office industry is thriving globally. There will always be new ultra-wealthy individuals being created, and as regulations, global business, and taxation evolve and become more intertwined, the return on investment for paying family office fees will rise. Regardless of the mainstream media's focus on a pending debt crisis, currency wars, or political instability in certain regions of the world, I am bullish on this industry over the medium- to long-term horizon.

Conclusion

The best way to predict the future is to create it.
—Peter Drucker (writer and management consultant)

The family office industry is a dynamic environment that is evolving and thriving as a wealth management model and financial solution for the ultra-affluent. Please remember to go back through the book to access all of the video modules, audio MP3 interviews, and PDF templates you may not have had time to take advantage of before.

Thank you for taking the time out of your busy life to read this entire book. I believe that the more knowledge and genuine help that you give away, the more opportunities will unexpectedly come your way over time. It is amazing how much valuable knowledge can fit into a book that costs under $60, yet most professionals read very few books per year.

I personally have invested over 300 hours in recording videos, conducting phone interviews, and writing the text of this book in a way that I hope most will find practical and actionable, whether you are a family office or looking to hire or work with a family office in some form. If you would like to join the Family Offices Group, our 40,000-member family office association, you may do so at www.FamilyOfficesGroup.com.

Also, it would be of great help to me if you could leave a review of it for me. To write up your short, two-minute review, please visit www.FamilyOfficeBookReview.com. Once you leave a review, e-mail me for a special gift that I will send to you in the mail; I know reviews take time, and I value your feedback and participation.

 See the video "Thank You Message," at www.FamilyOfficesGroup.com/Video29.

The appendix includes a list of free multimedia resources, top family office web site resources, and enterprise-wide training solutions for family offices. Also at the end of this book is information on how you can take advantage of the Family Offices Group.

Above all else, I hope that by reading this book you have gained two to three practical ideas or insights that you can take action on right now. Best of luck in your family office–related business.

Your friend in the family office industry.

[signature]

RICHARD C. WILSON
Family Offices Group

P.S. Feel free to ask me questions about the book's content or what we do. E-mail me at Richard@FamilyOfficesGroup.com, and I will get back to you as soon as possible.

Family Office Newsletter

We offer a concise monthly newsletter on the family office industry.
Recently, our team conducted a survey of several thousand members of our family office association and found that a monthly family office newsletter was something almost everyone wanted access to. Our family office, ultra-wealthy contacts, and members in our association have a strong desire to stay abreast of new trends and resources in the family office industry and constantly be improving their family office to better serve their clients. To meet this need, we have developed our popular newsletter, *Family Office Monthly*.

This newsletter provides insights into the evolving world of family offices, providing a concise look at one aspect of the industry each month.

In addition to using our team's knowledge of family offices and our large industry association, we recently recorded phone interviews of 36 audio experts with family office veterans. Many of these experts are CEOs and chief investment officers of multi-billion-dollar single family offices and top-30 multi-family offices.

This monthly newsletter series allows you to access the direct advice of our team as well as these industry veterans that we interviewed who have more than 756 years of combined experience.

There is no other resource like this in our industry. We guarantee that you will get high return on your investment by reading this publication each month. This newsletter looks at exactly how family offices are operating, investing, growing their businesses, and serving their clients right now. If you were wondering how you could now take your family office knowledge to the next level, this is the immediate solution for you.

Sign Up for the Newsletter: If you are interested in receiving this monthly print newsletter, please e-mail us at Newsletter@FamilyOfficesGroup.com or call us at (212) 729-5067 to learn more.

Newsletter URL: www.FamilyOfficesGroup.com /Newsletter

About the Author

RICHARD C. WILSON: FAMILY OFFICE FOCUSED

Richard C. Wilson provides institutional best-of-breed fund manager ideas to family offices. Richard wrote the most popular book on hedge funds, which has been read by more than 100,000 people. He runs several associations including the 40,000-member Family Offices Group and a pair of alternative investment associations, the Hedge Fund Group and Private Equity Investment Group with over 200,000 members in total. He is a leading global speaker on family offices and has spoken at and chaired more than 50 industry conferences and summits in Zurich, Monaco, Singapore, New York, Liechtenstein, Brussels, Sao Paulo, Tokyo, and the Cayman Islands. In 2011 alone Richard traveled more than 160,000 miles and these travels have led to sharing stages with prime ministers, dinner with a prince, and a wedding ceremony for a royal family in Europe.

Richard has worked with and interviewed many of the top family offices and ultra-wealthy families in the world. He continues to serve them through providing a newsletter, *Family Office Monthly*, which provides concise monthly insights to UHNW individuals and family offices; the *Qualified Family Office Professional* (QFOP) program, which is one of the industry's first training and certificate programs dedicated exclusively to training family office employees, executives, and business partners; and *Richard Wilson Capital Partners,* laser focused on helping family offices and the ultra-wealthy increase their access to best-of-breed alternative investment fund managers.

Richard has been on numerous radios shows in the United States, Europe, and Canada, has been named one of America's Premier Experts, and recently has appeared on the *Brian Tracy Show,* which is shown on

ABC, NBC, and Fox affiliate channels around the United States. Richard has written several books, including a best-selling book in 2011 on hedge funds called *The Hedge Fund Book: A Training Manual for Capital Raising Executives and Professionals* (John Wiley & Sons, 2010). It has sold several thousand copies in hardcover format and has been rated the number one investing book on the Kindle platform.

Richard's educational background includes earning a bachelor's in Business from Oregon State University and an MBA from the University of Portland. He has also completed extended master's-level coursework on the Psychology of Influence through the ALM program at Harvard University, studying under Dr. Richard Wolman and analyzing the research of Dr. Robert Cialdini.

If you have not already, we encourage you to join the Family Offices Group association for free and learn more about us by visiting www.Family OfficesGroup.com. To learn more about our monthly *Family Office Monthly* newsletter, please visit www.FamilyOfficesGroup.com/Newsletter.

THE FAMILY OFFICES GROUP & RICHARD WILSON CAPITAL PARTNERS LOGO

The logo to the left is a modern graphical representation of the Wilson family crest dating back to the 1700s. The Wilson family has generations of capital-raising backgrounds and has raised over $1 billion. The Wilson name has long stood for ethical practices, long-term focus, and work ethic and that is in line with the Latin words inscribed on the family crest—"Res Non Verba," which means "Actions not Words." Many of the capital-raising practices including operating models, strategies of listening, and processes of relationship development have been cultivated over the past 40 years through fundraising and capital-raising expert Thomas D. Wilson and now embedded in the operations of Richard Wilson Capital Partners.

To learn more about Richard Wilson Capital Partners, LLC, please visit www.RichardWilsonCapital.com or e-mail Richard directly at Richard@RichardWilsonCapital.com.

RICHARD WILSON CAPITAL PARTNERS, LLC

Richard Wilson Capital is laser focused on connecting family offices to best-of-breed fund managers.

We leverage our family office expertise and knowledge to make sure that everything we do is custom-built and structured for family offices.

We apply our Proprietary Family Office Filter and 6 Cs Model to sort through the 20,000 fund managers in the industry.

We provide a stable of best-of-breed fund managers of institutional quality to our family office relationships. We represent only managers that, based on our research and experience, will be of interest exclusively to family office investors.

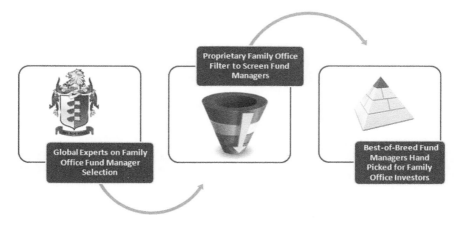

We meet with and talk to ultra-wealthy clients, single family offices, and multi-family offices every day about their investment preferences, fund manager selection process, and needs not being met. We constantly listen to the needs of family offices and think only of how we can bring world class fund managers and investments to their attention every year. To learn more about our platform, team, and how we could work with your family office or fund please e-mail or visit:

Richard@RichardWilsonCapital.com

www.RichardWilsonCapital.com

Qualified Family Office Training

RES NON VERBA

wilson

The Family Offices Group offers an in-depth training and certification program for family offices and professionals who work in the industry at www.FamilyOfficesGroup.com/Training. This program is called the Qualified Family Office Professional (QFOP) program.

The family office industry is a knowledge business, and those with training and experience in the space are worth $250,000 to $1 million-plus a year because of their knowledge and real-world experience. As in many areas of our knowledge-based economy, practical, functional know-how is an asset that can be consistently built or that can grow stale and decay.

You can't speed up the experience of those on your team, but you can speed up their learning curve on critical and functional areas of family office knowledge. The fact is, the more consistently and aggressively you grow your team's knowledge assets, the better you can serve your family office clients.

Some of you already know that our team runs several financial and management training programs on hedge funds, private equity, investment banking, financial analysis, and several other areas. In total, these programs have attracted well over 3,000 participants from more than 30 countries around the globe. By creating these programs, we have produced over 1,250 video modules and more than 250 expert audio interviews. The result is a massive wealth of multimedia content that is directly relevant to the training of family office employees.

Time after time, during my conversations with family offices, the need for more central industry training comes up. This is why we created the **Qualified Family Office Professional (QFOP)** training and certificate program for anyone looking to learn more about family offices. This platform provides family office professionals with a comprehensive training program to further improve your knowledge in areas important to family offices.

Modules of our family office training program cover:

- Family office management, business development, and leadership
- Hedge funds, private equity, and venture capital
- Family offices, trusts, and wealth management
- Financial analysis, financial modeling, and investment banking

The Qualified Family Office Professional program is a comprehensive training platform for family office teams that can be used to help bring new members on board, provide continuing education to existing team members, or to help someone experienced take on new responsibilities more effectively. Access to continuing education has been shown to reduce employee turnover and improve the effectiveness of those same employees. As the family office industry expands, we see a growing need for a comprehensive industry training solution that boosts employee efficiency and ultimately helps your family office better serve its clients.

To learn more or enroll in the Qualified Family Office Professional training program, please visit www.FamilyOfficesGroup.com/Training, call (212) 729-5067, or e-mail us at Training@FamilyOfficesGroup.com.

Free Monthly Newsletter: A complimentary subscription to our newsletter, *Family Office Monthly* (see Appendix), is included for all family offices that enroll in the Qualified Family Office Professional training program.

Qualified Family Office Program: If you run a family office and are interested in having your organization recognized for its dedication to the family office industry and ultra-wealthy clients, you may want to have your firm complete our Qualified Family Office (QFO) program. This is offered to recognize family offices that have a dedicated team serving ultra-wealthy clients. To learn more or provide feedback on this process, please visit www.FamilyOfficesGroup.com/QFO or e-mail us at QFO@FamilyOffices Group.com.

Index

Printed and bound by CPI Group (UK) Ltd, Croydon, CR0 4YY

05/03/2023